James Dean Revealed!

James Dean

INTRODUCTION BY DAVID DALTON

Revealed!

James Dean's sexsational lurid afterlife from the scandal and movie magazines of the fifties

---

FROM THE COLLECTIONS OF
ALAN BETROCK AND
JERRY FAGNANI

A Delta Book
Published by
Dell Publishing
a division of
Bantam Doubleday Dell Publishing Group, Inc.
666 Fifth Avenue
New York, New York 10103

Library of Congress Cataloging in Publication Data

James Dean revealed / [edited by] David Dalton.
p. cm.
Articles previously published in various periodicals.
ISBN 0-385-30309-2 (pbk.)
1. Dean, James, 1931–1955. 2. Motion picture actors and actresses—United States—Biography. I. Dalton, David.
PN2287.D33J37 1991
791.43'028'092—dc20
[B] 90-13992
CIP

Book and cover design by David Dalton and Kip Shaw

Printed in the United States of America
Published simultaneously in Canada

April 1991
10 9 8 7 6 5 4 3 2 1
KPP

CONTENTS

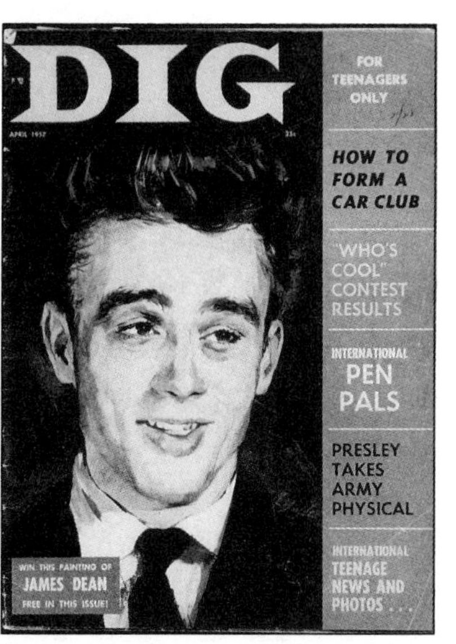
DIG
FOR TEENAGERS ONLY
HOW TO FORM A CAR CLUB
"WHO'S COOL" CONTEST RESULTS
INTERNATIONAL PEN PALS
PRESLEY TAKES ARMY PHYSICAL
INTERNATIONAL TEENAGE NEWS AND PHOTOS . . .
WIN THIS PAINTING OF
JAMES DEAN
FREE IN THIS ISSUE!

TRUE

STRANGE

INCREDIBLE · WEIRD · AND FACTUAL

THE MYSTERIOUS POWER OF STALIN

FAKE GHOST HUNTERS

KING OF THE DEVIL WORSHIPPERS

INTRODUCTION

BY DAVID DALTON

A SAD HEART IN THE SUPERMARKET

Like vegetation gods, the late summer deaths of pop mythology's holy trinity—Marilyn, Elvis, and James Dean—are celebrated annually on August 6, August 16, and September 30 respectively. The question as to whether they are, in fact, deceased is a matter that becomes increasingly problematic each year.

I see from the tabloids in my supermarket that Elvis has been sighted again. A priest confirms it was he. The dead, as you might have expected, spend most of their time in coffee shops.

Indeed, Elvis's life beyond the grave has been far more active in the ten years since his death than it was in the decade before.

Generally, such quasispiritualistic materializations are dismissible as naive effusions of disturbed individuals. But Elvis in *The New Yorker*! A long article from a correspondent in Arkansas details a search for The King in various roadside joints—apparently he's still hungry.

This bimonthly resurrection of dead stars is a fairly recent phenomenon and dates, as it turns out, to the death of Elvis's twin from the Pop Book of the Dead, James Dean, with whom he was often paired and compared in fifties movie and scandal magazines.

Dean still makes appearances, too—in March 1990 along with the World War II bomber found on the moon. But he turns up now with less frequency than he did in the late fifties. Perhaps his time is running out.

In the fifties Jimmy dictated a number of autobiographical sketches from the other side: a book, *Here Is the Real Story of My Life;* an entire one-shot magazine *Jimmy Dean Returns!* ("Read His Own Words from the Beyond"); and several articles, including "James Dean Speaks from the Grave!" (included here).

These days, when Jimmy returns, he seems wearier, more distracted, and altogether more metaphysical than he was in his heyday of more frequent posthumous visitations (the hereafter has that effect on some people). In *Rebels United,* author Joel Brean (a pseudonym) describes a conversation with James Dean (the true self).

OPPOSITE: Cult into occult. Jimmy makes the cover of the supernatural exploitation magazine, True Strange. For story, see page 138. BELOW: This 1956 one-shot purported to be Jimmy's autobiography as told to Judith Collins "from the beyond."

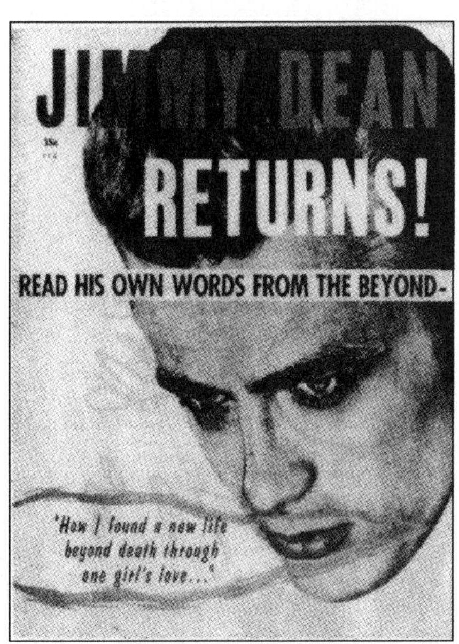

JIMMY DEAN
RETURNS!
READ HIS OWN WORDS FROM THE BEYOND-
"How I found a new life beyond death through one girl's love..."

The ongoing quest for The King in Jim Palmer's comic strip, "Lil' E," from the rock 'n' roll magazine, Memphis Star.
REPRODUCED BY PERMISSION.

The scene—a taxi somewhere on Interstate 465, Indiana, April 8, 1973.

JOEL: Where did you start today?

JIM: Friendship.

JOEL: Where's that?

JIM: In the World of the True Selves.

JOEL: I don't understand.

JIM: Don't you believe in the hereafter?

JOEL: Yes, of course. But how could you return to Earth?

JIM: It isn't easy. I'll explain later. May I smoke? . . . Is this your car? It's nice and clean.

Later, during one of those awkward lulls that occur in cab rides, Jimmy reads Joel's mind.

JIM: It must be a record—going 2,000 miles by taxi to see Elvis. [How could he know?] ESP in its telegraphic application.

JOEL: But how could you know of Elvis Presley? He didn't make his recording until January 1956.

JIM: You forget that Elvis made his first appearance on the Louisiana Hayride on March 3, 1955. I was very much an earthling then.

JOEL: It's too bad that you didn't get to hear him through the late fifties.

JIM: I did—through vibrational transference.

JOEL: What?

JIM: Joely, I never learned how to explain electricity. May I rest a few minutes?

TWILIGHT OF THE GODS

The 1940s are generally considered the golden age of movie magazines. Movie stars were the gods and goddesses of Hollywood, America's mythology. Up until the midfifties, movies were paramount in the hierarchy of celebrity. And it was in the movie magazines that fans followed the exemplary lives of the stars. Here, mere mortals could glimpse the gods and goddesses at play, albeit, very contrived play. Somebody is cooking dinner, sailing the sea, painting sunsets, romping with his pet. And the gods said: "Let's play house!"

Stars did all the things other people did: They had barbecues, went shopping, puttered around their gardens, and indulged in their main off-the-set activity—redecorating. Of course, all this took place with a clarity that mere mortals did not possess. Stars might say of themselves, as Gogol's wife said in Tommaso Landolfi's story: "It is true that I, too, pee, but for entirely different reasons."

These displays of mundaneness were intended to demonstrate, among other things, that the stars were mortal like the rest of us. But, to the fan, they were merely *simulating* normal behavior, since stars, as the word suggests, are magically in synch with the movement of the heavens. Originally, somewhere in the Fertile Crescent between the Tigris and Euphrates rivers, around 5,000 B.C., priests ritually traced out the movements of the stars and planets. This is the source of both the celebrity mania and the real estate industry, since everything they touch or live next door to becomes charismatically charged and appreciates in value.

WEN DIE GÖTTER LIEBEN

Die Wahrheit über James Dean, über sein kurzes, verheißungsvolles Leben und seinen tragischen Tod

Donald Rodgers, einer der besten Freunde, die Jimmy hatte, schrieb diese Serie exklusiv für STAR-Revue

Im Actors' Studio, Amerikas berühmtester Schauspielschule, nahm James Dean Unterricht, obwohl er bereits in Fernsehsendungen und auf New Yorker Bühnen große Erfolge zu verzeichnen hatte. In André Gides Stück „The Immoraliste" sah ihn Elia Kazan, einer der besten Filmregisseure der Welt, und verpflichtete ihn vom Actors' Studio fort für seinen Film „Jenseits von Eden". James Dean spielte in diesem erschütternden Kain-und-Abel-Epos den Kain, den verlorenen Sohn Caleb. Die Arbeit an diesem Film war für Kazan sehr schwer, weil Jimmy starrköpfig an seiner eigenwilligen Auffassung der Rolle festhielt. Plötzlich aber änderte sich Jimmys Haltung, er wurde weicher, umgänglicher, eher bereit, den durchdachten Anweisungen des erfahrenen Regisseurs zu folgen — denn Jimmy hatte sich verliebt, so verliebt wie nie in seinem Leben zuvor. Pier Angeli, die in einem benachbarten Atelier drehte, wurde die große Liebe seines Lebens — und die größte Enttäuschung, die er niemals überwand. Als Pier Angeli ihn verlassen und — sehr überraschend — den italienischen Sänger Vic Damone geheiratet hatte, stürzte sich Jimmy von einem Abenteuer in das andere. Doch in Wirklichkeit blieb er immer einsam und sehnte sich nach Liebe und Verständnis.

8. FOLGE

„James Deans erster Film „Jenseits von Eden" wurde von der Uraufführung an ein außergewöhnlicher Erfolg. Kritiker und Publikum waren sich einig, daß Elia Kazan einen einmaligen Schauspieler entdeckt hatte, der berufen war, inmitten all der Mittelmäßigkeit von Hollywood zu zeigen, was Kunst im Film vermag. Die Filmgesellschaft Warner Bros., die „East of Eden" gedreht hatte, nahm James Dean noch vor der Premiere in einen Sechs-Jahres-Vertrag. In dieser Zeit sollte Jimmy neun Filme drehen. Mehrere Stoffe lagen bereit. Man hatte sie bisher nicht verfilmt, weil Warner Bros. vergeblich nach dem Hauptdarsteller gesucht hatten. In den nächsten zwölf Monaten drehte James

sagte gar nichts. Nach einer Weile kam er in meinem viel zu großen Bademantel ins Zimmer, hockte sich schweigend in einen Sessel und rauchte. Schließlich meinte er: „Es war zu scheußlich. Ich mußte es erst richtig abwaschen." Er deutete noch an, daß er zu einem intimen „Fest" eingeladen gewesen sei. Aber es habe ihn so angekelt, daß er weggerannt sei. Mehr sagte er nicht darüber, und ich fragte ihn nicht.

Wir diskutierten bis zum Morgen. Obwohl Jimmy mit keinem Wort Pier Angeli erwähnte, obwohl er überhaupt nicht über seine eigene seelische Situation sprach, wurde mir doch klar, wie einsam er sich fühlte. Gewiß, er hatte zahlreiche Freundinnen und

Dean and Natalie Wood in the German magazine STAR-Revue. *The title reads "When the Gods Fall in Love."*

Jerry Fagnani, who bought many of these magazines during the fifties, expresses the reaction of the typical fan: "I was spoon-fed by the studios, and I swallowed it whole. All this stuff about him speaking from beyond the grave or possibly disfigured, living in New Mexico. I thought it was fascinating. To the fan, it all seemed remotely possible. We really wanted to believe it."

IN WHAT WAY IS CONNIE STEVENS LIKE A BACH CANTATA? READ ON

In the same way that most people would be hard-put to distinguish between a crocodile and an alligator, you might not see a great deal of difference in style between an article entitled "James Dean, Genius or Jerk?" and one called "Was James Dean a Psycho?" But you would be mistaken. They are as distinct as night and day. The first comes from a movie magazine, the other from that lurid and short-lived phenomenon, the scandal magazine.

Although neither had a great hold on reality, they skewed their subjects in very different ways. Movie magazines had been around since movies began. They were an extension of the dream factory and perpetuated its hallucinated vision of life. Everything was done with the cooperation of the studio's publicity department. "The Secret Life of the Charlie Chaplins," for instance, seems promising but turns out to be an "at home" story. As teen idols begin to dominate the scene in the fifties, the movie magazines' natural tendency to sappiness becomes positively giddy.

OPPOSITE: *The February 1956 cover of scandal magazine,* Whisper, *featuring one of the most notorious Dean rumors. The story is on page 133.*
BELOW: *Full page ad for Robert Altman's documentary,* The James Dean Story.

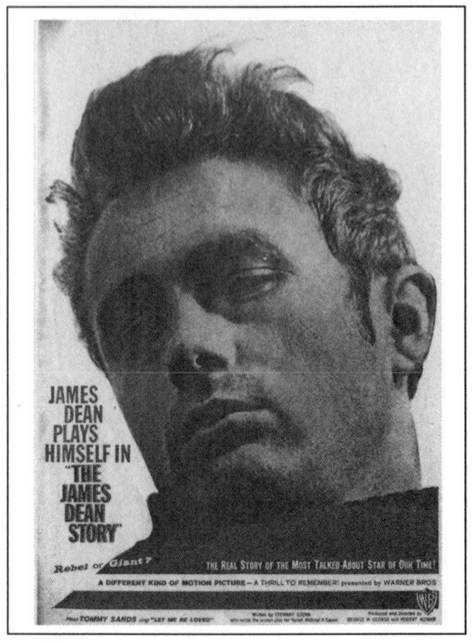

The earnestness and effort that is exerted on the flimsiest of concerns is always a source of astonishment in reading these articles from the fifties.

The themes are extremely limited: romance (who's dating whom), "at homes," the new movie, career crises (real or imaginary), personal crises (who's breaking up with whom), the Proust questionnaire (what's-your-favorite-color type of thing), interviews and profiles (including statistics).

The tone and thought sequences of these articles are meant to mimic the scrambled, soft-focus workings of a pubescent girl's brain. Encephalographic transcriptions: her concerns, her questions, her enthusiasms. Then again, perhaps this is the only way you *can* write about this stuff.

Take this opener from "Why Johnny Doesn't Go for Sandra (and Vice-Versa)." "Sandra Dee pushed her foot down on the accelerator. Her T-Bird glided smoothly down the winding road leading to Universal International studios. It was eleven forty-five. In fifteen min-

ROCKY MARCIANO'S SECRET SHAME

WHISPER

PDC

Feb. 25c

OPEN LETTER TO BETTY GARRETT

TV'S BIGGEST GHOST —THE OLD PAYOLA

GEORGE RAFT: THE $10,000 PATSY

ADULTERY: AMERICA'S FASTEST GROWING CRIME

HOW TO HAVE A NEW CAR EVERY YEAR

IN THE PIT: EARTHA KITT

CORNELIUS VANDERBILT'S REFORM SCHOOL WIFE

utes she had a date with John Saxon." Whoever is writing this sure knew a lot about Sandra Dee. All those details! They had to have been there.

The fan magazines presented themselves as intermediaries between the stars and the objects of their devotion. Like go-betweens, they were dispensers of secrets and never-before-revealed facts — usually of an entirely unexceptional nature: "Why Does Elvis Have to Wiggle?" or the unintentionally humorous "How Natalie Handles Older Men."

We spend the day with Bob Wagner and his appliances. We follow him around as he makes coffee, hangs a picture, throws a ball to his dog. Every action an epiphany. This is the traditional world of the movie magazines. Airbrushed, scripted. Life in the movies, as seen on television.

Among the many proposed to inherit Dean's mantle, Tony Perkins may have been the silliest.

TONY PERKINS

CALL HIM REBEL!

He's tall and lean, dark and slightly terrific.

His fight against Hollywood will amaze you!

By FLORENCE FLETCHER

■ "They're trying to label me a carbon copy of somebody or other and I don't like it!"

This brief but bitter complaint is Tony Perkins' own "rebel yell," and seeing that it comes from Hollywood's busiest young actor, it sounds a mite ungrateful.

But Tony isn't ungrateful–he's just angry. And that makes him a rebel in any language. He's fighting hard for his individuality, for the right to be himself, and in a town where a young newcomer is at the not-so-tender mercies of publicity writers and columnists, for a while, this is a tough fight.

It started with Marlon Brando and continued with James Dean, this rebellion among Hollywood newcomers against conformity and "sameness" and custom, and so when a new young actor arrives who is "different," who tries to keep his private and public lives separated, he is promptly labeled "rebel." Just let him appear once without his hair combed or in a slightly wrinkled suit or sans tie; let him refuse just once to pose for a magazine layout or to show up at an important premiere–and he's called "another Brando" or "another Dean."

By coincidence or not, this tag has usually been hung on the young actors who

(*Continued on page* 58)

Between-scenes pose on set of Paramount's *The Lonely Man* is typical of Tony. He's 6'1½" tall, will be 25 April 4.

Nothing very serious ever happens in this world. Ask Natalie. "If you're eighteen and a Hollywood actress, it's not exactly like being eighteen. Already you've got the Thunderbird, the pool, the ermine jacket." And when "Our Girl Audrey Has a Problem," you know what it's going to be. All problems revolve around romance, a paradoxical activity, since its goal, marriage, has to be postponed indefinitely. It would automatically take a player out of the game.

Tony goes from gun in Friendly Persuasion (left) to romance with real-life date Norma Moore in Para.'s Fear Strikes Out (below).
Most dramatic part to date is role of Jim Piersall, ballplayer who had mental breakdown, fought way back to big league greatness. Next on busy schedule is Tin Star for Para.

However odd or unlikely the candidate—Sal Mineo, Marlon Brando, Tony Perkins—every rising star had to conform to the prototype. There is something eerie about the Easter Island interchangeability of the classic dreamboats of the fifties: Tab, Bob, Johnny, Pat. Mr. Smoothies with machine-tooled, water-repellent, Turtle Wax-buffed hides. As if molded out of some biosynthetic polymer miracle flesh. That optimistic American obsession with smoothing things out,

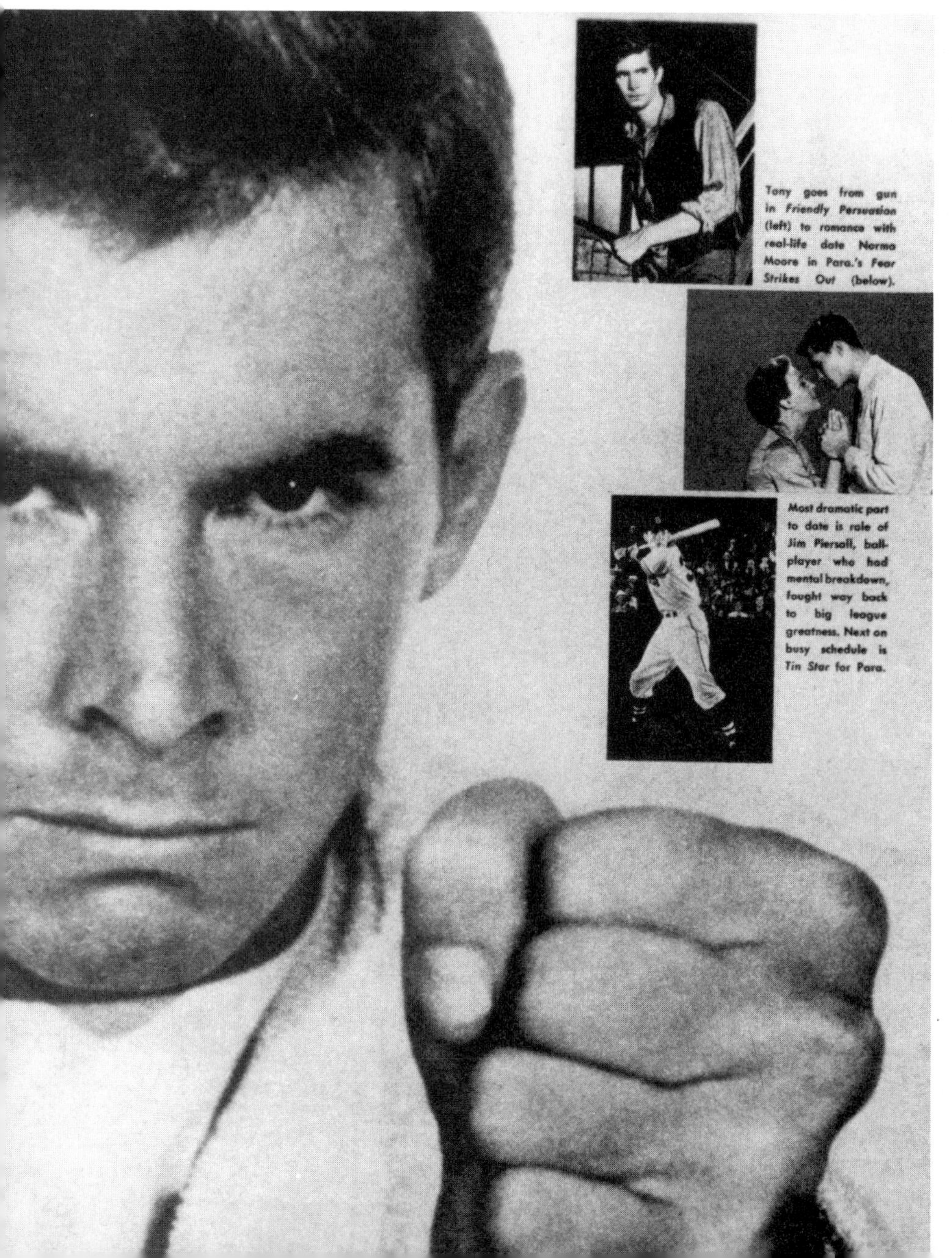

tidying up, homogenizing all of life. These are replicants with extruded personalities, your basic pleasure models. Commodity androids planted by the KGB to melt the brains of American teenagers.

THE AMAZING JAMES DEAN HOAX

Perhaps the most curious aspect of James Dean is the posthumousness of his fame. Like an Egyptian saint, it is James Dean's death rather than his birth that is celebrated annually. Before the 1955 car crash that took his life at age twenty-four, Dean had appeared in a successful Broadway play, a couple of dozen TV melodramas, and starred in a movie, *East of Eden*. He was relatively unknown, therefore, when *Rebel Without a Cause* opened on November 1, a month after his death. But in the two years following his death, a fanatical cult—"The Girls Who Worship the Corpse of James Dean"—began to develop. Just how spontaneous this outpouring was has been questioned ever since. Thus, the James Dean conspiracy theory.

In September 1956, "James Dean: God of a Morbid Cult," appeared in *Exposed* magazine. The over-the-top mode is in gear right from the first line: "James Dean—intense believer in the occult, intense student of reincarnation . . . pursued death as if it were a beautiful woman, a Bridey Murphy who promised to reveal all the intimate secrets of the great beyond."

The article goes on to suggest that "the following questions which were continually on his mind during the last two years of his life" might have been the cause of his death: "Did I, James Dean, once exist in another life?" and "Is my talent really my own, or is it someone else's, perhaps that of some person in a bygone era?"

And then there was the recurring nightmare (twice in two weeks) that "he might have been a famous theatrical producer in another life." Dean thought it was entirely possible that "back in the 1750s . . . [he] was slain accidentally by an actress on the stage of his own theater." Talk about baroque worries!

Dean apparently further aggravated his mental state by studying "Aztec culture, expressionistic literature, age regression, and dozens of occult works on philosophy."

From here the piece moves briskly to a description of the cult and its belief. Cult members are easily recognizable by the following: "red jackets, they drink milk right from the bottle, eat only licorice candy and use the expression, 'Well, then, there, now.'"

It then listed the principal rumors surrounding his death: (1) Dean had committed suicide by driving his car deliberately into the path of the other car; (2) he was not dead but was so badly hurt, so terribly disfigured in the smashup, that it was kinder to the public to announce him dead; (3) the love of Maila Nurmi (Vampira) had turned to hate when Dean forsook her for Pier Angeli (etc.), which caused her to place a voodoo curse on him, thus the crash, etc.

The following article in the January issue of *Inside Story*, entitled "The Amazing James Dean Hoax!" accused Warner Bros. of cooking up the various rumors that fueled the cult. "Early this year [it portentously begins] four men gathered in a secret conclave in the plush executive offices of Warners' studio in Hollywood. They were about to launch the most fantastic project ever conceived in a city known for its addiction to the weird and cockeyed." Basically, the theory was as follows: Warner Bros. became alarmed that James Dean's violent death might cast a morbid pall over the fate of his two unreleased movies, as had happened, for instance, in the case of Carole Lombard. "People just don't like to see a picture which has a dead man for a star."

This record offer from a movie magazine is one of many pieces of Deanabilia for sale after his death.

Then one day the Warner Bros. publicity department received a letter from a distraught fan. This letter, the Ur letter, contains the Kabbalistic words: "Jimmy lives!" And those devious fellows up at Warner Bros. in sharkskin suits and in the midst of a dilemma pounced on this information with unsavory relish. They would make James Dean's untimely death—just think about it!—the theme of their campaign. They would reincarnate him!

Now this produced a hybrid as unstoppable as kudzu, an obsession with sex and death being a genetic component of the seething teenage brain.

But conspiracy theories are well known to be contagious. What if the conspiracy theory itself turned out to be a conspiracy? It did, after all, originate in a scandal magazine. This led to the obvious speculation that "Early this year, four men gathered in a secret conclave at *Inside Story* magazine, etc."

After James Dean's death, a new sensibility entered this marzipan kingdom. Suddenly the fan magazines were forced to deal with the morbid and bizarre subjects that had previously been the domain of the scandal magazines.

New magazines were (briefly) created to exploit this. One of the oddest was *Love and Tragedy*. As the editorial in the first issue explains, "If you wonder why we have linked love and tragedy it is because, strangely, they are close akin in the emotional storms that stir the fabulous people who make our movies. In these pages you will read of the hidden heartaches of the stars and the crushing calamities that have befallen them. For our cover we have chosen

jimmy dean's last miles

This is the photo record of that tragic day; this is the path Jimmy took to death.

This is Grapevine where Jimmy got a speeding ticket 2 hours before his crash Sept. 30, '55.

In this little cafe he had his last meal, a sandwich and coke, 33 miles from accident.

Jimmy's last mile, looking west on highway 466; where picture ends, his Porsche crashed.

This is the tragic intersection: a car traveling toward jimmy suddenly turned to the left.

Where these girls stand, Jim's car came to rest virtually demolished after the impact.

From shed at right of this garage came the ambulance that took Jim to hospital.

Here he was pronounced dead; he'd sustained a broken neck, been killed instantly.

From hospital body was taken to Kuehl mortuary in Paso Robles to remain for 3 days.

Then after the inquest this hearse took Jimmy to airport for his final journey home.

James Dean because he personifies the greatest tragedy that has ever befallen Hollywood."

James Dean's death and the ghoulish stories it summoned up provided a link between the movie magazines and the scandal magazines.

Exploitation magazines first slithered on to the shore in the early fifties. Brasher and more ruthless, they presented a brutal alternative — an antiworld of vice and freaks — to the fluff of the movie magazines. Scandal magazines fought back against the bland Ozzie and Harriet images of American life with weapons neither television nor the fan magazines could use: sex, drugs, violence, corruption.

The old restraints had been abandoned. A wonderfully seedy, fascinating underworld of weird stories and strange concepts was revealed: "I Spent 3 Months With 4 Men on a Raft," "They're Passing Dope in Ball Point Pens," "Why Big Bosoms Are a Billion-Dollar Business," "I Dealt Sex on a Gambling Ship."

The scandal magazines boomed in the early and midfifties, led by *Confidential*. They were tougher, more adult, and far more cynical than the fan magazines. But because of lawsuits and oversaturation, most had died out by the late fifties, and those that survived into the next decade were driven out by the cheaper, more sensational tabloids.

LA MÉTHODE
REVUE DE CINÉMA
SPECIAL ACTOR'S-STUDIO

In France they took him seriously. Dean on the cover of a magazine devoted to Method acting.
OPPOSITE: *Tantalizing and spooky account of Dean's last afternoon from a movie magazine.*

It is appropriate that whenever Jimmy, Elvis, or Marilyn *do* put in an appearance these days, it's in the tabloids, which are in some ways the great grandchildren of the scandal magazines that flourished in the two years after the death of James Dean. Overnight, the world's axis had shifted; everything became a little odder. The mysterioso headlines and ludicrous claims of fifties scandal magazines—"James Dean's Black Madonna," "Proof in His Own Handwriting: James Dean Knew He Had a Date with Death," "Ghost Riders of Polonio Pass"—now seem hilarious, even ghoulish in a camp horror-movie sort of way. But to the fans who bought these magazines in the late fifties, this stuff was not funny. They read them just as Renaissance readers had read the actual travels of Marco Polo and the totally fabulous adventure of Sir John Mandeville—without distinguishing much between the two.

Jerry Fagnani: "Fans who read movie magazines in the forties belonged to a simpler, less troubled time. By the fifties, Rockwell America was on its way out; the people sitting on the porch were fading away. In the forties, the writers on these magazines, when they dealt with emotionally charged subjects, were simply reporting a lost love affair, the death of a loved one, without any poetic

This still from *East of Eden* shows Jimmy leaping from the top of one boxcar to another. It is inscribed: "Try and catch me. You think I have to come down from up here don't you. I hate all earthlings. Love Jimmy."

component to the writing. A typical layout in *Photoplay* was the star's 'at home,' likes and dislikes, a review, gossip columns and a nice color cover, often something drawn. My mom was a reader, and the information just caught on with me. The movies were to me the world. Current events. They taught you about everything. The Van Johnsons were there, the Ty Powers were there, the Tab Hunters were there. But when Dean died, a macabre element entered into this make-believe kingdom, a cloud passing over fantasyland, a sense of menace that was fascinating and morbid."

Like an Asiatic mystery cult, the way fans responded to his death ushered in an era of freakishness. An actor dies in a car crash and suddenly . . . altars! Suicide pacts! Supernatural appearances! Fantastic obsessions! Rumors run rampant! His coffin in Indiana lies empty! He's not really dead but badly disfigured and living in New Mexico! These girls are serious.

"Jimmy with the Beautiful Mouth: Our names are Lillie and Francine. We both work in a San Francisco department store. Each week, we are putting aside in a joint bank account $25 for you. We have $650 saved up for when you come back.

"As soon as we have $1,000, we intend to leave home and set up a place for you and us. We will not be jealous of each other at all, for you are the man of our dreams. We promise that if you share us equally, we will never give you any trouble. We don't expect marriage either, for you can't marry both of us. If we have babies, these babies will be the family's babies. We don't care what people will say at all. We just love you and dream about you."

The people who engineered this had no idea it would go on for four years, never mind four decades. Indeed, it has now cross-fertilized into other personalities. Elvis, the Morrison cult, etc. It all came from Dean.

A COMIC BOOK BIOGRAPHY

This comic book biography of James Dean appeared in 1956 as a one-shot magazine called *Elvis and Jimmy*. The front half of the magazine promises some spectacular Virtual Reality sensations—"You are going to feel the ideas and memories and sensations that pass through Elvis's mind as he is singing"—but it is a typical compilation of biographical snippets, quotes, and portentously phrased conjecture about The King.

The second half of the magazine is the cartoon biography reproduced here in full, portentously titled, "The Triumph and Tragedy of Jimmy Dean." It presents itself as a voyeuristic mental movie: "No photographer was there to film these intimate moments of Jimmy's life. But here you will see them, in all their drama." The story leans heavily toward romance (the publisher is, after all, The Girl Friend–The Boy Friend Corporation), but the most interesting element is its almost border ballad fatality, an ominous folktale about doom and compulsion.

In the first frame we hear that "perhaps because of some mystic foreknowledge of her son's future artistic successes, his mother gave him the second name of Byron, after the great poet." Gloomy moods ("perhaps premonitory of what was to come so soon") overwhelm him, often in settings as emblematic as a medieval book of hours (a weeping willow on an island). These moods, as has already been established, are connected to fate and thus can (briefly) be exorcised only by the "magic presence" of love. When that fails, the demon, here taking the form of the irresistible "lure of speed," springs into action. The Porsche Spyder itself has become possessed and "with a roar, the mighty compact engine bloomed into life." The headlights of the oncoming car loom over Jimmy like a monster from hell.

The concluding panel shows an impassive profile-conscious Jimmy rising hieratically above the crash; the landscape's sordid reality is accompanied by a spiritualistic prayer.

Told in shallow tableaux by Lou Cameron, the drawings are almost noirish in their use of shadow and silhouettes. Cameron did a number of these stories for the same publisher, and they all have this dark, brooding mood to them. Much of the characterization is stereotyped and the articulation wooden, but the scene in the coffee shop (frame 10), and the women in Jimmy's life materializing out of cigarette smoke (frame 52) are wonderful evocations, as is frame 64, which shows a sultry girl on the phone, saying: "Jimmy, it's the studio calling again! They want you there right away!" To which an exhausted Jimmy replies, "I'm so tired, so tired . . . I want to get away somewhere, somewhere far away. . . ." (Two odd notes: Jimmy appears to buy the same car twice and the negative take on *Rebel Without a Cause*.)

"Goodbye, Jimmy. You've gone to a rendezvous you always sensed was not far away. But those who die young are always beautiful in the memory of those who loved them; and in that way, perhaps, they are blessed."

1
On February 8, 1931, the baby boy who was to become famous as Jimmy Dean was born. Perhaps because of some mystic foreknowledge of her son's future artistic success, his mother gave him the second name of Byron, after the great poet.

2
Seldom have mother and child been closer than these two. The day when a schoolmate came running to tell him the terrible news scarred Jimmy's life forever.

3
His grief was unquenchable. He even wished he had the courage to kill himself. He couldn't stand being around other people; instead, the nine-year-old boy would wander off by himself, brooding, pining.

4
Even in high school, back in Indiana, his grief and the loneliness it bred persisted in Jimmy. It gave him the reputation of being a strange one, an outsider. . . .

5
Then one day the wall of loneliness around him was broken by a girl who felt sorry for this boy with the brooding eyes. And Jimmy responded at once, eagerly, to her kind-hearted gesture.

6
Jimmy was a natural in high school dramatics. He played the comic role of a monster in a farce called "Goon With the Wind" but also serious dramatic parts. He might even have dreamed of being another Rhett Butler some day.

7
Rapidly he developed into one of the most popular boys in Fairmount High. And yet, lurking underneath this surface gaiety, there remained the mystic, tragic vein left by his mother's death. . . .

8
After graduation, Jimmy spent many hours debating with himself over what kind of career he should try to make his own. Medicine? The law? The stage? He had enjoyed acting in high school, but did he have any REAL talent?

9
At length he wandered back to California, attended college for a while, but only half-heartedly. He managed to pick up a few bit parts on TV. They were hardly what you would call distinguished roles, and very little acting talent was required. . . . After all, you don't have to be a great actor to have a pie flung in your face.

10

Serving as a pie-target wasn't getting him anywhere. He made his way to New York, determined to attend an acting school. To keep body and soul together he got a job as busboy in a cheap cafeteria. The hours were long, the work dreary. At night he was so tired he could hardly drag one foot after another.

11
Doggedly he "made the rounds" from one agency to another, seeking a break—any kind of part in a play. It always seemed that he got the same answer. Still, he kept on.

12
One day, a break!—a TV part! But when he found out what it was, his face fell. Were these pies going to follow him around all his life?

13
Haunting Broadway and the theatrical district as he did, he saw many famous stage stars leaving the stage doors of the theatres. One was Marlon Brando. Standing on the outskirts of the crowd, Jimmy watched the brilliant young actor sign the autograph books held out to him.

14
But Jimmy's fortunes were reaching the turning point, although he didn't know it. A woman agent's intelligent, perceptive eyes saw the untapped well of talent that lay inside Jimmy, and she devoted all her energy and enthusiasm to putting him over.

15
In his first Broadway play, "See the Jaguar," he didn't have a line to say. But the part did call for many changes of facial expression, and he was often the center of attention on the stage. Others praised him, but while waiting in a Greenwich Village cafe for the early morning reviews, Jimmy told the truth about himself as he saw it.

THEY DON'T LIKE THE PLAY, BUT SEE? --THEY SAY THE ACTING WAS FINE!
I STILL SAY I STANK.

16
The newspaper critics panned "See the Jaguar," but more than one called attention to the boy with the "sensitive, mobile" face named James Dean.

WHAT'S WORRYING YOU, DARLING? I KNOW SOMETHING IS.
IT'S JUST THIS MOOD I GET INTO ONCE IN AWHILE--- I CAN'T EXPLAIN IT.
BEER
NICKS
ΕΛΛΑΣ

17
This favorable mention should have buoyed him up, but unaccountably Jimmy fell into a mood of deep depression. Often during the few short remaining years of his life these moods were to seize on him—perhaps premonitory of what was to come so soon. . . .

YOU'RE WASTING YOUR TIME TRYING TO BE AN ACTOR, JIMMY! YOU'RE A NATURAL, BEATING THAT SKIN!
PLAZA
TOROS

18
He found some kind of release from this shadow-haunted, gloomy spell in bouts of wild emotion—capering through Greenwich Village with a roistering mob of various dubious types; beating savagely on an African drum. . . .

YOU MEAN IT? THEY'VE GIVEN ME THE PART? *HEY!*

19
Immediately on the heels of this episode of blank despair and wild abandon came thrilling news—a major part in "The Immoralist." Jimmy threw himself into the work of studying for it with passionate zeal. He wished to LIVE the character he was to portray, so as to make him a creature of flesh and blood, rather than just a cardboard figure. . . .

20
His hard work and devotion paid rich dividends. The cynical, corrupt Arab youth that Jimmy portrayed in "The Immoralist" seemed literally to live on the stage in front of the audience's eyes. It was an artistic triumph for the boy from Indiana—and the taste of success was very sweet.

21
The play didn't last long—but Jimmy's bandwagon was really beginning to roll. A call came from Hollywood. . . . Jimmy said goodbye to the girl who had given him consolation and love during the bitter months of drudgery and poverty in New York.

22
Arriving in Los Angeles, Jimmy paid a visit to those scenes of early tragedy that he remembered so well—the house where he had lived with his doomed mother, the place where she died, the weeping willow tree in the park where he had sat grieving. . . .

23
The picture he had been called to Hollywood for was "East of Eden," taken from John Steinbeck's novel. Elia Kazan had picked Jimmy out for the part of Cal Trask, and Jimmy looked up to Kazan, knowing his work as a stage director before coming to Hollywood.

24
But, perversely, another of his gloomy moods stormed over him. He was accused of being temperamental and "difficult" on the set. The reason was not so-called "artistic temperament." It was the remembered grief of his boyhood, the consciousness of an endless quest for the love that had been taken from him when his mother died.

25
Knowing that his first picture was to be directed by Elia Kazan was a great thrill for Jimmy. But an even greater thrill, in some ways, awaited him. That was when he met a girl called Pier Angeli—a girl whose charming smile and dark eyes immediately banished from his mind all the other girls he'd ever met. . . .

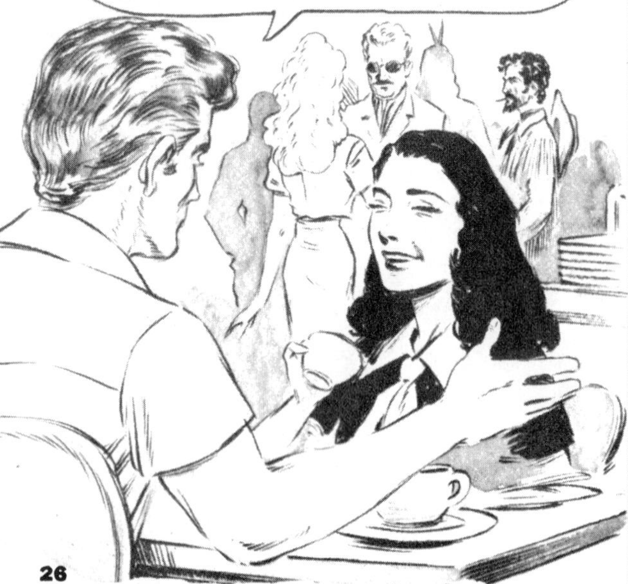

26
They seemed to take to each other at once. Everything Jimmy said found an immediate response . . . if it was a joke or his deepest thoughts about life.

27
He confessed to friends how much Pier had come to mean to him, and how swiftly. Their backgrounds, their family upbringing—totally different—did not seem to offer any barrier to what Jimmy dreamed of as an idyllic romance. . . .

I CAN'T TELL YOU HOW MUCH KNOWING YOU AND LOVING YOU HAS CHANGED EVERYTHING FOR ME-- CHANGED THE WHOLE WORLD!

28
Even the gloomy moods to which he had fallen prey in the past were exorcised by Pier's magic presence. The world was transformed; he felt confident and sure, almost for the first time since his mother had died. . . .

29
But Pier was a girl with her own life to live—her own family and her family's traditions. Though their youth and their intensity cried out to each other, there were difficulties that seemed insuperable—if not to Jimmy, to Pier. . . . One night Jimmy heard the shocking news.

30
Its effect was to plunge him again into a mood of deep despondency and self-pity. He knew he was acting like a child, but he could not help himself. Just as some people will push the aching tooth that hurts them, out of sheer perversity Jimmy stood across the street from the church where Pier and Vic were married and watched the radiant couple. . . .

31
He tried to keep his emotions bottled up. But it was no use—he had to burst out with the gnawing bitterness inside him. Not that he blamed Pier. He blamed instead the evil star whose baneful influence had seemed to follow him ever since the day of his mother's death.

32
But it seemed to make good sense to try to develop some new interest. And for Jimmy, still only a boy in the sense of years, though old beyond his time because of that past tragedy, there was an emotional release in the sheer physical sensation of speed. . . .

33
Hurtling over the broad California highways gave him a feeling of exhilaration, of being someone all-powerful enough to rise above the twists and turns of daily life. Speed soothed and stimulated him at the same time. The girls he took with him were scared, but he would come back from these breakneck drives with glowing eyes and flushed skin and fast-beating pulse. . . .

34
"East of Eden" opened. If Pier had been with him, as his date for the great night, he would have been supremely happy. But as it was, he wished he could be somewhere else—the flashing image he saw of himself on the screen, the audience's applause, seemed a mockery.

35
More and more, speed sang its intoxicating song to his inner ear. . . . He listened to serious, well-meaning advice given to him by friends and studio executives, and received it with an outward show of respect but an inner cynicism.

36 & 37
He found a new friend—not a romantic interest but someone who would listen sympathetically to his doubts and misgivings. Even this was not a true release. The only true release seemed to be the siren, speed. . . .

38
Maybe a visit back to old scenes would help him. In New York, he was surrounded by admiring friends—and people who were frankly envious of his success in "East of Eden". But even an attempted renewal of the love he had known there did not come as the balm he had hoped for.

39
One of the signs of Jimmy's increased importance at the studio was the new dressing room given to him. Much more than just a place to change clothes and put on make-up, it was literally a complete apartment, with living room, bedroom, kitchen and bathroom.

40
"Rebel Without a Cause" sounded like an exciting picture, and for a while Jimmy was enthusiastic about the possibilities his part offered him. But somehow he felt there was something missing at the heart of the movie—something that didn't ring true. . . .

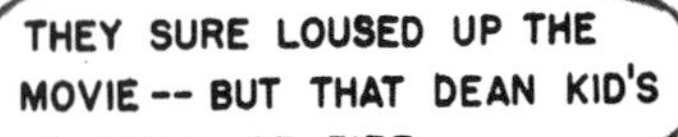

THEY SURE LOUSED UP THE MOVIE -- BUT THAT DEAN KID'S A BALL OF FIRE.
YEAH, THE HOTTEST THING SINCE VALENTINO.... I WONDER IF THIS BOY WILL DIE TRAGICALLY TOO?

41
Many of the studio's executives privately felt the same way after seeing the first screening of "Rebel" in the studio projection room. But although the picture was a jumble of ideas that never quite meshed into an effective whole, Jimmy's part in it was a triumph.

NO, I GUESS IT ISN'T LOVE, NAT-- IT'S JUST A SWELL FRIENDSHIP. AND YOU KNOW SOMETHING? I'M GLAD IT'S THAT WAY....

42
Still his endless search for love and understanding continued. He found genuine, unselfish friendship with Natalie Wood, who liked him for himself—not because he was Jimmy Dean the rising new movie star. But though true friendship is a rare gift to receive, it isn't love. . . .

THAT'S THE SPYDER, MR. DEAN. IT'S A REAL COMPETITION CAR. MAXIMUM SPEED, 140.

GEE!

43
Though he realized it only very dimly himself, one way Jimmy's quest expressed itself was in his craving for more and more speed. His first Porsche wasn't fast enough for him, and so he bought another, the super-powerful Spyder, a racing car.

YES, IT'S A WONDERFUL CAR, JIMMY, BUT SOMEHOW--SOMEHOW SOMETHING ABOUT IT FRIGHTENS ME....

44

45
He found a new friend—and what at first he thought was a new romantic interest—in Ursula Andress. Never did anyone yearn more desperately than Jimmy yearned to fall deeply, passionately in love. Yet an uneasy feeling that that was not his fate always seemed to bar the way. . . .

46 & 47

Speed, speed—more and more speed! Jimmy started going to racing meets in his Spyder, for here he could let the car out to its limit—and no interfering cops to give him a ticket. Often he was cautioned about his driving by professional racing drivers, and Jimmy listened to them respectfully and always promised not to take any chances—but the lure of speed was irresistible.

THESE THINGS AREN'T JUST TOYS, JIM--THEY'RE DANGEROUS MACHINES, DEADLY AS A GUN, UNLESS YOU KNOW HOW TO HANDLE THEM. SURE, YOU CAN LEARN, AND YOU'VE GOT THE MAKINGS OF A REAL GOOD DRIVER--BUT UNTIL YOU'VE HAD SOME MORE EXPERIENCE--NO KIDDING, JIMMY, TAKE IT EASY!
YES, SURE.
31
169 F

48
In lonely hours late at night, pondering over his life, Jimmy reached the conclusion that if he could devote himself to one person, he would find the stability he needed. But who?

49
He reviewed his feelings about all the girls he knew, asking himself what each one meant to him . . .

50

. . . and, in turn, what he meant to them.

51
Only in the case of Pier had there been the immediate sense of recognition that comes with every true romance. Yet somehow he had failed her, or she would not have left him for Vic.

52
So the answer was not here. The endless quest had to continue. If only there were some signposts to guide him on his way! But he knew he must always remain Jimmy Dean, the lonely seeker, surrounded by friends yet never at ease in his heart. . . .

JIMMY, GEORGE STEVENS HAS PICKED YOU FOR THE PART OF JETT RINK IN *GIANT*. IF YOU GIVE THE PART EVERYTHING YOU'VE GOT, I BELIEVE YOU'RE GOING TO BE THE BIGGEST NAME IN HOLLYWOOD. AND THAT MEANS--- WHAT ARE YOU GRINNING LIKE THAT FOR?
"BIGGEST NAME IN HOLLYWOOD---" IT ALL SOUNDS COCKEYED, UNREAL..
53

DO YOU CALL A MILLION BUCKS UNREAL? YES, I MEAN IT; THAT'S THE KIND OF MONEY YOU'LL BE GETTING INTO. AND THAT MEANS YOU'VE GOT TO START TAKING LIFE SERIOUSLY. YOU'VE GOT TO HAVE A BUSINESS MANAGER; YOU'VE GOT TO TAKE OUT A LIFE INSURANCE POLICY---
WHAT DO I WANT WITH A LIFE INSURANCE POLICY?

54
Friends told him that the unknown would-be actor of yesterday was becoming big business, and that like any business he must be managed properly. He had been accustomed to fling money around carelessly; and as for insuring his life—

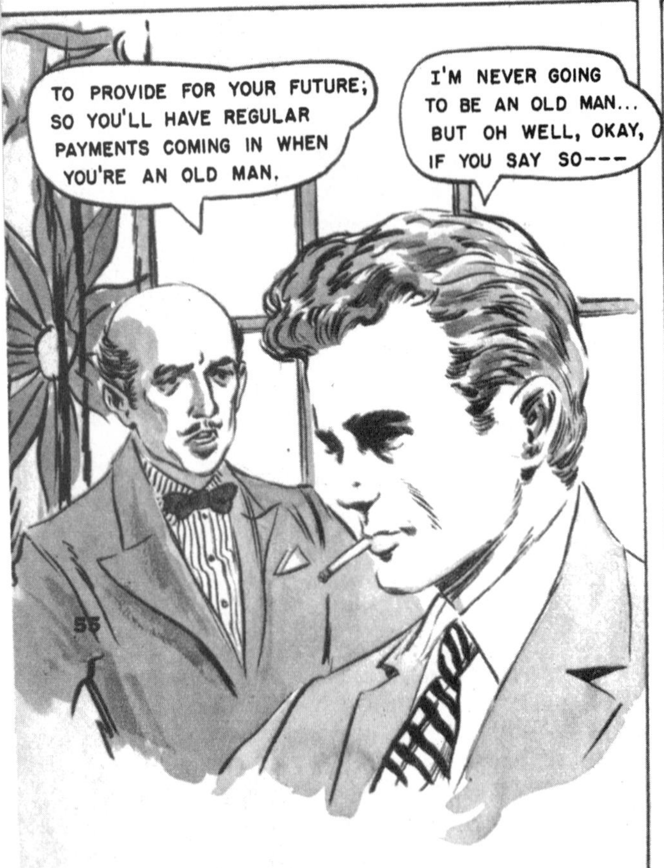

TO PROVIDE FOR YOUR FUTURE; SO YOU'LL HAVE REGULAR PAYMENTS COMING IN WHEN YOU'RE AN OLD MAN.
I'M NEVER GOING TO BE AN OLD MAN... BUT OH WELL, OKAY, IF YOU SAY SO---
55

AS FOR THE BENEFICIARY--- THAT IS, THE PERSON TO WHOM THE MONEY WOULD BE PAID IN THE EVENT OF YOUR DEATH-- WHAT NAME SHOULD I WRITE IN, MR. DEAN?
I DON'T KNOW.... MIGHT AS WELL MAKE IT MY FATHER, I GUESS.

56
But still, he agreed. A business manager was hired to keep watch over Jimmy's income and expenditures, and he took out a life insurance policy that would start paying him back after the age of 40. Jimmy laughed when he heard that. He just couldn't imagine himself being 40 years old.

57
In the meantime, preparations for making "Giant" were going ahead. George Stevens, the director, was a meticulous craftsman who insisted that everything should be just so. He had been told that sometimes Jimmy was an unpredictable quantity—but perhaps Jimmy would be impressed by the big-name star who was appearing with him, Elizabeth Taylor, and that would keep him in line. . . .

ANY MOMENT NOW GEORGE STEVENS IS GOING TO BLOW UP. JUST WHAT IS IT THAT GETS INTO JIMMY, ANYWAY, THAT MAKES HIM ACT LIKE A KID?
IN SOME WAYS, THAT'S ALL HE IS -- A KID. BUT A KID WITH GENIUS . . . .
ET #17
ANT
DIRECTOR

58 & 59

Jimmy was impressed, all right—but his reaction was exactly the opposite of what anyone would have expected. Instead of following Liz around with humbly worshiping eyes and behaving like a good little boy, Jimmy set out to make her laugh. On location in Texas, he cut up and capered all over the place.

I APOLOGIZE, MR. STEVENS . . . I PROMISE I'LL CUT OUT THE FOOLING AROUND FROM NOW ON. SHAKE?

60
Finally, George Stevens read the riot act to Jimmy—and, afterward, counseled him wisely and sympathetically, as a father might have—the father Jimmy had never really known. The man's obvious sincerity impressed Jimmy, and from then on he and Stevens were friends.

WHAT A DIFFERENCE! THAT BOY'S GIVING THE PERFORMANCE OF HIS LIFE.

61
Whereas before no one had exactly known what would happen when Jimmy came onto the set—or even if he'd get there on time—now he was as punctual as clockwork. Even the bored and often cynical technical assistants on the movie could see that Jimmy Dean was pouring his whole heart into his role.

WHY WAS THERE SUCH A BIG CHANGE IN YOU, JIMMY?
WELL, FOR ONE THING I REALIZED I WASN'T GIVING STEVENS A FAIR DEAL. AND FOR ANOTHER--

62
At night, under the deep Texas sky, sitting by a real old-time campfire, Jimmy talked a little about himself—just enough to hint at the presence inside him of that mystic vein left by his mother's death. . . .

--I CAN'T EXPLAIN IT, BUT--SOMETHING SEEMED TO TELL ME THAT THIS WAS GOING TO BE MY LAST BIG CHANCE AS AN ACTOR. . . . AH, I GUESS I'M JUST TIRED.

63
. . . for somehow he was more conscious of this mystic quality now than ever before. . . . But maybe that was just the effect of the brooding purple night, the changing shapes of the leaping campfire flames, the emotion wrung out of him every day by the great performance he was giving in the picture.

64

He came back to Hollywood more tired than he had ever been. One night he rushed from the set without bothering to change, went to a friend's apartment, threw himself down on a couch and slept as if he had been drugged. Even when the studio called, it didn't seem important. It was important only to get away—get away. . . .

65
At last "Giant" was finished and Jimmy had the chance to get out of town. Rolf Weutherich, expert driver and mechanic, agreed to accompany him to a race at Salinas. . . . Jimmy slipped behind the wheel; with a roar, the mighty, compact engine bloomed into life. . . .

GEE, THIS IS GREAT. . . . SOMETIMES I FEEL I'M ONLY REALLY LIVING WHEN I'M BEHIND THE WHEEL OF THE CAR LIKE THIS, DOING EIGHTY OR NINETY OVER THE OPEN ROAD . . . . IT'S A FUNNY THING, BUT I FEEL---

66

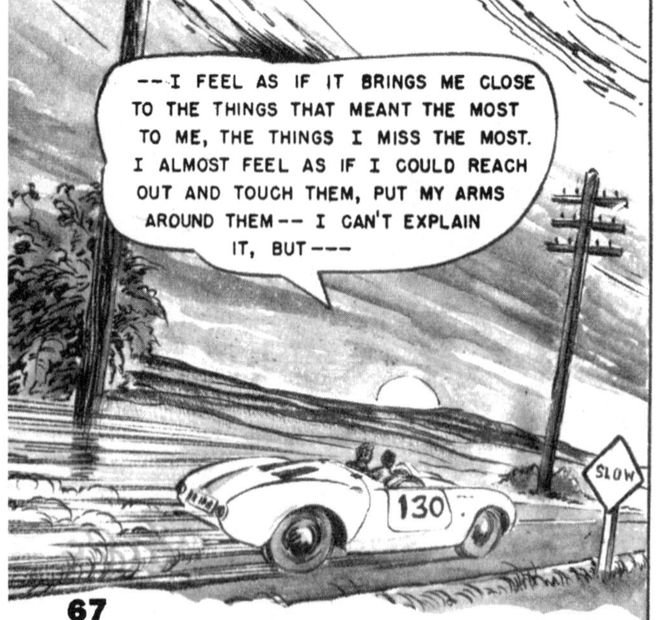

67
The speeding miles of Highway 466 fled under the Spyder's snub snout. The speedometer's dainty finger edged ever higher and higher. The hot glare of the highway faded as the shadows crept up from behind the hills. . . .
YOU HAVE EXACTLY TEN SECONDS TO LIVE, JIMMY.

68
FOUR SECONDS TO LIVE.

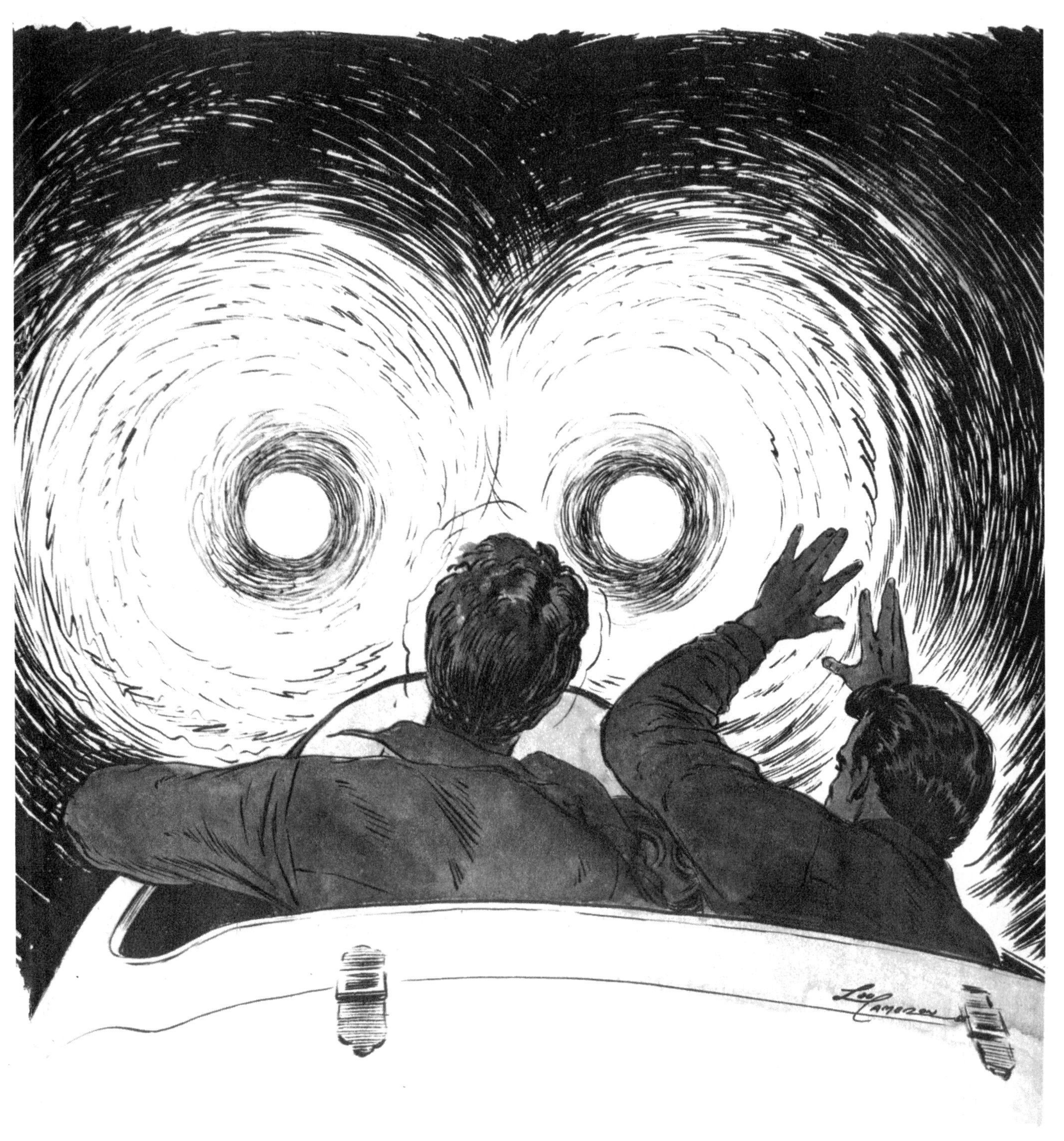

69
NO MORE SECONDS TO LIVE. . . .

70
Goodbye, Jimmy. You've gone to a rendezvous you always sensed was not very far away. . . .

. . . But those who die young are always beautiful in the memory of those who loved them; and in that way, perhaps, they are blessed.

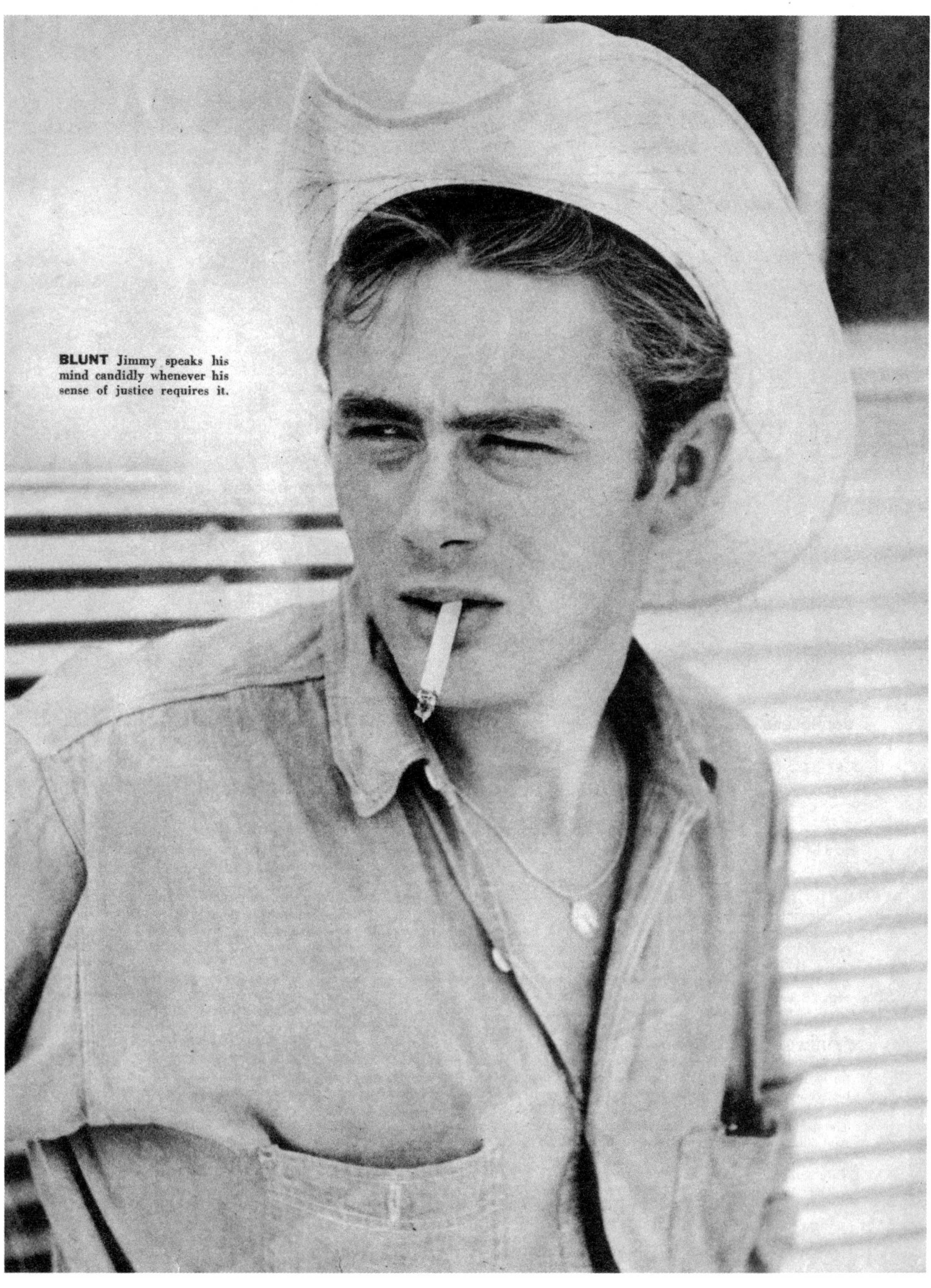

BLUNT Jimmy speaks his mind candidly whenever his sense of justice requires it.

TOUGH GUY OR BIG BLUFF?

BEFORE THE CRASH

James Dean appeared in barely a dozen magazine articles before his death. It's curious therefore to see how he was perceived by the Hollywood assembly line while he was alive. Today, Dean seems of an entirely different order from dreamboat teen stars like Tab Hunter and Robert Wagner, but to the movie magazines, he was just another type who had to be fitted in somewhere. And although Jimmy didn't exactly fit into the clean-scrubbed category, he was not exactly without precedent. Before him there was Brando.

"He's Not Marlon, He's Himself," "Tough Guy or Big Bluff," and "Lone Wolf" all refer to the resemblance between Dean and Brando, and the comparisons are not exactly unfounded since Dean idolized Brando and had adopted the bike, the boots, the bongos, and "last year's wardrobe" from him. Also, the comparison/denial formula was a time-honored way of introducing a new young star—by comparing him or her with a more established one. Eventually Dean himself would be enlisted in this equation (see "The Search for Mr. X" on page 78).

The Procrustean bed of the movie magazines even manages to fit Dean into the dreamboat mold. The conclusion of "The Girls in James Dean's Life" is pure eligible-bachelor boiler plate: "There's no doubt about it—Hollywood's gals are on a Jimmy Dean kick. Where will it all end—at the altar or in frustration—nobody knows."

In "The Dean I've Dated," starlet Lori Nelson—stars only date other stars—prepares the case for the defense: "They've called him a carbon copy of Marlon Brando, a screwball Bohemian, a 'dirty shirt' actor, an egocentric nonconformist and other things even worse. The James Dean I know is none of these," she concludes, "he's dynamic and deliberate, devilish and direct, but he's *not* eccentric." Sorry to hear it.

Dean's responses, however, are not characteristic of movie magazine interviews. These early articles are the only ones in which we hear Dean's own words, and his responses are a strange combination of the Bohemian, provocative, and cool. In answer to the persistent Brando taunts, he drawls, "I'm neither disturbed by the comparison, nor am I flattered." And to a gossip columnist, Dean snorts, "A lone wolf is a four-legged animal who by his own effort burrows in the ground."

In his Warner Bros. bio Jimmy depicted himself thus: "A neurotic person has a necessity to express himself, and my neuroticism manifests itself in acting." Anyone who puts this sort of thing in their press kit is asking for trouble.

> ***"Visitors to the* Rebel Without a Cause *set were horrified when, between takes, James Dean walked over to the garbage can, filled a paper plate from it and then pretended to eat the conglomeration."***

HE'S NOT MARLON

...he's himself

Jimmy says: "I'm neither disturbed by the comparison nor am I flattered."

THE scene: A late afternoon cocktail party in Brentwood.

The discussion: Is Jimmy Dean trying to out-Marlon Marlon?

The case for the prosecution (as presented by one learned, somewhat tipsy young man): "Look at that guy! The dungarees, the bongo drums and the motorcycle, the same sloppy speech, and the slouch—it's Brando all over. Why, he even thinks like Brando."

The case for the defense: (Here we must leave the party-goers and speak to some people who are less prone to follow popular

BY DAVID STEWART

opinion, who don't rattle off generalizations and who, more important, happen to know Jimmy.)

Natalie Wood, the talented young actress who plays Jimmy's sweetheart in Rebel Without A Cause: "Jimmy has a little boy quality about him and a wonderful sensitivity in his acting. He'd be a perfect Romeo." (Editor's note: Can you see Marlon as Romeo?) "I don't know about Marlon, but Jimmy is himself. He does what he likes and means it sincerely. Jimmy's a sports car enthusiast and I'm just waiting for the day when Marlon takes it up, too, so that people will say he's imitating Jimmy."

An actor from the same picture: "Marlon is brute force in contrast to Jimmy's poetic quality. Jimmy's more likeable and I think he has a wider appeal for women. He brings out the mother instinct in them. Brando challenges them on a rough-and-tough, man-woman basis."

A veteran Hollywood reporter: "Brando sifts his interview requests with a fine tooth comb and condescends to grant a few hours to the more important publications. He acts as though he expects someone to uncover a skeleton in his family closet. I wouldn't say Jimmy exactly bends over backwards, but he is acutely aware of the value of publicity and its importance to him. He's planning to catch up on all the interviews he's neglected so far and I hear he's seriously thinking of hiring a press agent."

A production man: "I've seen them both on the set. Marlon comes in, clowns around, has a ball and hops right into a death scene. He makes faces at his leading ladies when they're trying to play a serious bit. Jimmy walks on the set, hardly speaks to anyone, and concentrates completely on the job he has to do. If he *(continued on page 52)*

Jimmy's motorcycle is a symbol of freedom to him and not an emulation of his confrere, Marlon Brando.

Co-star Natalie Wood and Jimmy receive a visit from newcomer Perry Lopez on their Rebel Without A Cause set. Perry's to be seen soon in Warner's Darkest Hour.

worked on the same picture with Marlon, he'd go nuts."

And finally Jimmy himself: "People were telling me I behaved like Brando before I knew who Brando was. I'm neither disturbed by the comparison, nor am I flattered. I have my own personal rebellion and don't have to rely on Brando's."

It would be hard for Jimmy to consciously ape Brando even if he tried. The two have met only a few times and Brando was reported to have commented, "Don't you think you're going a little too far to attract attention?"

At this point, we'd like to get in a few hundred well-chosen words of our own. We've always felt that Brando deliberately turned himself into a legend because he found that what started out as his own personality quirks soon became profitable publicity. Then, when the blue jeans and T-shirt bit outlived its usefulness, he swung around to the homburg routine. He says he refuses to give interviews because his words always end up garbled. That may be true in a few cases, but his beefing about being misquoted always makes the papers. There is also something irresistibly attractive about a man who is inaccessible and unattainable.

Jimmy, on the other hand, really hasn't found himself in Hollywood. He's giving out with the shy routine because he really is shy. He hasn't made many friends yet and he hasn't been able to straighten out his feelings about working in movies. Asked about publicity, he'll say, "Maybe it's necessary, but I just can't see it. Who cares about me?" Or, when asked what he thinks of Hollywood, he will answer, "I prefer New York." Basically, Jimmy considers himself a stage actor, while Brando knows that at this point he can write his own ticket with any studio in town.

Brando has been characterized as rude and thoughtless. People tend to lump Jimmy in the same category because he concentrates so completely when he is working. "He talks to very few people," said a studio executive," because it interrupts his creative mood. I can understand why some people think he's aloof, but I've never seen him actually be rude to anyone." (continued on page 54)

Whether he's rude or thoughtless, Brando has rolled up quite a list of people who wouldn't nominate him as their favorite actor. These same people, however, are very much attracted to Jimmy. Brando gives off the feeling that he just doesn't want to be bothered, while Jimmy picks up sympathy because he scurries away with a nervous, frightened look. We sincerely believe Jimmy is on the road to finding his place in Hollywood and by next year should be completely adjusted.

Perhaps the best summary comes from a top actress who met both Dean and Brando at a gathering. "I thought Jimmy had a very shy charm," she said, "but I couldn't stay around Brando long enough to find out what he had." ★★

Janie Powell took advantage of the big money in Las Vegas while waiting for desired role in Carousel to come through.

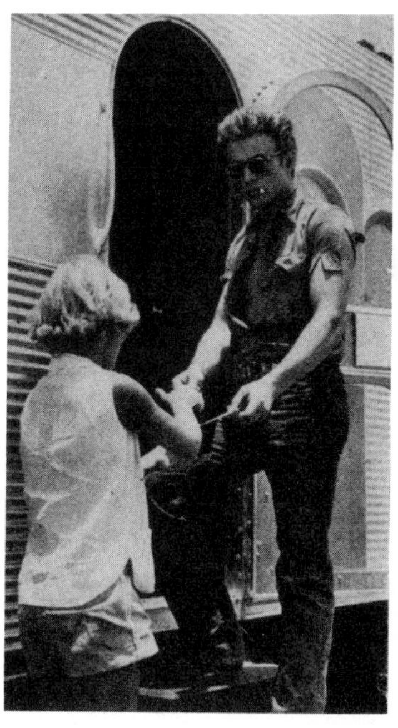

This let's pull no punches report goes a long way toward answering—coolly and dispassionately—a lot of questions about Jimmy Dean, including that oft-repeated query: Is he a . . .

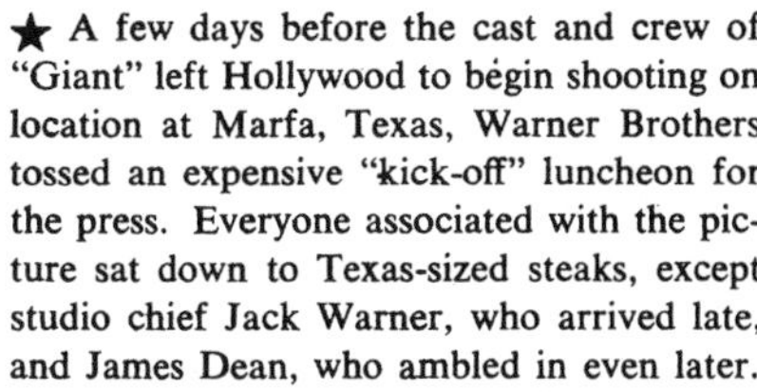

TOUGH GUY OR BIG BLUFF?

★ A few days before the cast and crew of "Giant" left Hollywood to begin shooting on location at Marfa, Texas, Warner Brothers tossed an expensive "kick-off" luncheon for the press. Everyone associated with the picture sat down to Texas-sized steaks, except studio chief Jack Warner, who arrived late, and James Dean, who ambled in even later.

Partly because Jimmy is considered Hollywood's newest important "find," partly because his off-screen behavior has seemed unpredictable—if not incomprehensible—most people focused their attention on him. In short order, this is what they observed:

For such an important occasion, the male guests and crew wore tailored suits. Jimmy arrived wearing a red-flannel shirt and well-worn jeans.

Director George Stevens announced it was high time Jack Warner meet his brilliant young star Dean, and publicly introduced them on the spot. As everyone laughed, Jimmy smiled carelessly, but he was obviously a little embarrassed.

"Haven't you really met Mr. Warner before," someone whispered to Dean as he shifted uneasily in his chair. "Aw, I've seen him around a few times," he replied with a shrug.

Elizabeth Taylor, Rock Hudson, Mercedes McCambridge, Jane Withers, Dennis Hopper and others in the cast each took a bow as producer Henry Ginsberg introduced them to the gathering. Jimmy, instead of turning on a big smile as the others did to acknowledge the applause, squirmed in his seat, fiddled with his big horn-rimmed glasses and stared at the floor.

Soon, one of several photographers covering the event came over to take Dean's picture. As he focused his camera he politely asked Jimmy to remove the horn-rims. When the photographer repeated the request, Jimmy reacted by snapping on his dark lenses.

A guest standing near Jimmy needled him good-humoredly. "It wouldn't have killed you to take off the glasses. Who do you think you are—Clark Gable?"

Jimmy grinned sheepishly. "I don't have any make-up on," he responded. "I was afraid the bags under my eyes would show. Besides," he added, "I haven't shaved yet."

Despite this image of Jimmy which most of the press carried away that day, among those who know him better there is a contradictory theory which is gaining momentum: That basically James Dean is not a tough guy, a big bluff or an eccentric as he is often pictured.

Few except Dean know the truth about this intense 24-year-old actor who is currently an enigma to Hollywood, and he shies strangely away from discussing his personal life. Yet, possibly nearer the truth than even he realizes or will admit lies the fact that because Jimmy finds himself an overnight sensation, his awkward and hard-to-explain behavior is a youthful cover-up for not knowing quite how to handle his sudden stardom.

Discerning students of psychology contend that a re- *(Please turn to page 76)*

JAMES DEAN

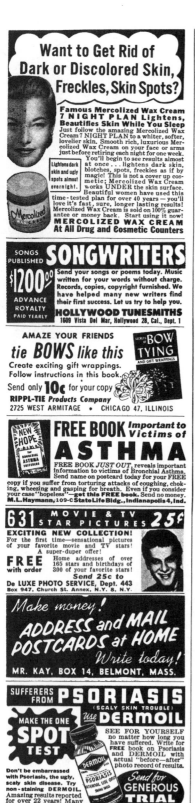

(Continued from page 35)

bellious attitude, such as Jimmy mirrors to the world, often can be a defense mechanism to hide real inner feelings of insecurity or social inadequacy. Dean's behavior since arriving in Hollywood continues to provide enough interesting material to make such a theory interesting.

Critical praise for his very first screen performance in "East of Eden" was enough to establish Dean firmly as a new star of great depth and promise. And with it came a deluge of letters from enthusiastic new-found fans. At the rate Jimmy is answering them, however, his autograph promises to become as rare as Greta Garbo's. Indeed, one 13-year-old girl, set on forming a James Dean Fan Club, has complained that she is still waiting for an answer to her letter telling him of the plan.

Yet, when the spirit moves him, Jimmy can be as charming as a fortune-hunter serenading a wealthy widow. He was articulate and polite when he met Mercedes McCambridge and they fell to discussing their movie roles. When Dean rose to leave, he leaned across the table and said shyly, "It was nice meeting you. I've always admired your work." Then he dug his hands in his jeans and shuffled away.

On another occasion, Liz Taylor turned up at Warner's to discuss her role in "Giant" with the director and stayed to lunch with him in the studio commissary. Jimmy, attired in his customary slacks and leather jacket, wandered by their table and stopped for coffee. He ended up, however, taking Liz on a personally-conducted tour of the lot in his new car. Everyone agreed that for a fellow who pretends to carry a chip on his shoulder, luscious Liz completely disarmed him.

His affability with her was particularly noteworthy to several studio workers who remembered his aloofness on the set. When "Rebel Without a Cause" was shooting in Griffith Park, while other members of the cast gathered in a group to laugh and talk as they ate their box-lunches, Jimmy, silent and moody, carried his lunch some distance away from the circle and ate in sullen solitude.

Much has been said about Dean's personal rebellion against conventional dress and transportation. One story which persists has a lady scribe telling him to his face, "My husband has a shirt like the one you're wearing, but his is clean." Whatever he's trying to prove, Jimmy's still working on it. A few weeks ago, summoned by a famous Hollywood columnist to her home for an interview, Jimmy made a rare compromise by discarding his jeans and leather jacket for a charcoal suit. But with it he wore a black shirt, tie and heavy riding boots, and arrived with his hair tousled. Before he left, he had dropped a cigarette on the rug and shrugged it off with, "Call the cops." His comment afterward was, "I don't care what people say or write about me."

Dean's choice of a motorcycle (he pronounces it motor sickle) instead of a more conventional means of conveyance is a source of great misunderstanding, however. Because Marlon Brando, to whom he has been compared, first startled Hollywood by arriving at the studio and appointments astride one, Jimmy has been accused of imitation. The little-known fact is that Jimmy and motorcycles are old friends, and a natural choice for him, even in Hollywood. He's been riding them since he was 16 and has owned seven. While living in a rural area of Indiana, where he grew up on a farm, Jimmy first started riding them to school of necessity. Later, he recalls, he used to go out for the cows on it.

"It scared them, too," he remembers with a grin.

Jimmy pretends to be aloof to criticism,

Dean hopes to write in future; he feels he's "too youthful and silly" to write now.

yet occasional reference to his "tearing around town" astride his machine invariably causes him to rankle. "I do not *tear around* on it," he declares vehemently, "but intelligently motivate myself through the quagmire and entanglement of your streets." More recently he's been riding with Keenan Wynn on jaunts. "I've lost some hide," he admits, "but you expect to take a fall once a year."

These days, Jimmy's motorcycle is more often parked under his garage apartment above the Sunset Strip and his attention is focused on a new enthusiasm—sports car racing. Arriving in Hollywood, Dean admittedly wasn't fired up the least bit over the fancy swag Hollywood offers.

"I don't need money," he said with youthful confidence. "I've always gotten along. Just so I can buy a few records and eat I'm happy."

It is significant, however, to those who contend that Dean's words and actions are indeed a cover-up, that soon after he banked his first movie earnings, he splurged a reported $4000 for a shiny white foreign-made roadster. Since then he has taken to racing it personally in various week-end hot-rod competitions, while the brass at his studio court ulcers. Once he came in third in a Sunday race at Palm Springs, and his [illegible] have been wider [illegible] Oscar.

Jimmy believes he'll [illegible] And he's the first to admit t[illegible] win at everything he does. In fact, the studio's reticence in ordering him to stop the dangerous sport he attributes directly to the fact that he has been winning. For while it was common knowledge that Warner Bros. is definitely concerned over the hazards Dean risks each time he races his car at break-neck speeds, contrary to printed reports, no studio official has ever ordered him to stop. According to Jimmy, "They sort of shoot around it, but they've never said, 'Don't do it.'

"Everybody likes a winner," he sums it up, "and so far I've been winning."

In Jimmy's passion for racing—and winning—students of psychology can find another possibly significant key to his off-screen behavior. Like mountain climbers, they point out, those who race at dangerous speeds subconsciously feel compelled to keep proving themselves in the eyes of themselves and others.

It was inevitable that anyone as talented and attractive as Jimmy Dean would set feminine hearts aflutter. And plenty of Hollywood's glamour dolls are admittedly eager for him to call them for dates. So far, he's played it as though he couldn't care less. Such disinterest, plus the fact that he's so different from the average Hollywood charm boy, only works to intrigue the girls more.

One girl, to whom he acknowledged an introduction with only a nod, said later: "He certainly appeals to me. I guess it's because I'm the type that likes to take in stray cats and dogs and he sort of reminds me of them."

Another lovely was impressed because throughout lunch he said practically nothing. "Why he's so intense," she related, "that if you ask him 'How are you?' he's stuck for an answer." She sighed. "He's probably very complicated."

Since Jimmy's unrequited romance with Pier Angeli before she became Mrs. Vic Damone, he has taken out so few girls that recently someone accused him of being a lone wolf.

"A lone wolf is a four-legged animal who by his own effort burrows in the ground," was Dean's answer. Was he going to date some of the screen lovelies who have made it clear that they'd like nothing better than to know him better?

"I don't care to take out Hollywood stars," was his answer.

When he turned up at a night club table with Maila Nurmi, the 32-year-old actress who is billed on TV as Vampira, gossips made much of the date. The truth about his "romance" with Vampira Movieland now tells for the first time.

"I have never taken Vampira out," says Jimmy, explaining that he had simply joined a group at her night-club table once.

More recently, Jimmy has been calling Lili Kardell, a pretty young Belgian-born actress. In fact she was the last girl he dated before he left for the Texas location for "Giant." The fact is that so far no girl has claimed Jimmy's interest half so much as his career.

Dean often sprinkles his conversation with slang but when he's discussing his craft his talk becomes lofty. "At the time in youth when all your interests and dreams are coming into focus," he explains it, "you find a craft—acting—to help you untangle your natural resources."

Yet in Jimmy's long-range plans, acting is but a stepping stone.

"My talents lie in directing even more than in acting," he says matter-of-factly. "[illegible] my great fear is [illegible] the seat of my [illegible] too youthful and [illegible] But some day . . ."

Meanwhile, acting promises to occupy Dean for some time to come. His current contract with Warner Bros. calls for nine pictures in six years, with 1956 off for him to return to Broadway where he started. Even though he's risen faster in films than on the stage, Jimmy says he'll never give up Broadway entirely.

"It's a fertile, wonderful, generous city (New York)," he contends, "if you can accept the violence and cadence. There are so many things to do. I go to dancing school, take percussion lessons, acting lessons, attend concerts and operas." In fact, Jimmy's current plan calls for him to return to Broadway, the stage and TV almost as soon as he finishes his role of Jett Rink in "Giant." He can hardly wait.

At this stage, even the prospect of winning an Oscar holds little allure for him. "I'm not interested in an Oscar," he said. "All I'm interested in is learning about the tools of my trade as an actor."

A few months ago Dean's expanding progress as an actor was threatened with interruption. He was called by his draft board for examination and re-classification. According to present schedules, however, Jimmy's actual induction is still two years away.

Even so, many in Hollywood who have already served with the armed forces are gleefully making predictions.

"Dean may have Hollywood buffaloed," says one, "but wait until he encounters his first top sergeant!"

This, it seems, is when more than a few people feel you'll get a final answer to the query, "Is Dean a tough guy, a big bluff or a bright young man not too certain of just how to handle sudden, overwhelming, overnight success?"

Our theory? We don't think he's nearly so tough as some of his actions would seem to indicate. We don't think he's a big bluff, either. We think his unexpected, and sometimes hard-to-take behavior is apt to be just a big cover-up—one that will last until he's a trifle more secure, considerably more settled and probably more mature an actor and citizen. Right or wrong, we're willing to go along on this theory and give Dean the benefit of the doubt—for now.

THE END

■ Several weeks ago Warner Brothers tossed a press party to announce the production start of *Giant,* starring Elizabeth Taylor, Rock Hudson and James Dean.

The shindig was held at the studio, and unlike any of the other principals, Jimmy Dean arrived late. He wore blue jeans and an old red flannel shirt. When the producer introduced him to the audience, Jim refused to rise or smile, or even acknowledge the applause. Moodily he sat in his seat, stared at his boots. When a photographer came close to photograph him, he quickly put on his dark sun glasses.

"Would you be kind enough to remove your glasses, Mr. Dean?" the photographer asked.

Jimmy made out as if he didn't hear.

"Why don't you give the guy a break?" a reporter asked the twenty-four-year-old acting genius from Fairmount, Indiana. "After all, he's got a job to do."

Dean shook his head. "I didn't mean to be rude. It's just that I've got bags under my eyes, and I need a shave."

In another corner of the room, a studio representative, watching the entire scene, muttered under his breath. "That's typical of the guy. I hope the Army drafts him and teaches him a little cooperation."

Jimmy is not particularly well-liked by some of his studio colleagues these days, because he refuses to show up for interviews, declines to be photographed, breaks appointments with reckless abandon and insists upon keeping his private life private.

"Maybe publicity *is* important," he admits. "But I just can't make it, can't get with it. I've been told by a lot of guys the way it works. The newspapers give you a big build-up. Something happens, they tear you down. Who needs it? What counts to the artist is performance not publicity. Guys who don't know me, already they've typed me as an odd ball."

So, too, as a matter of fact, have a lot of Hollywood girls who've met Jimmy at various private parties.

One young actress, who prefers to be nameless, tells about the recent time Dean came to a bongo-drum "kick" with his girl friend Lilli Kardell.

"After we were introduced," she recalls, "I said, just by way of starting a polite conversation, 'You're getting a lot of good publicity these days, all about your wonderful performance in *East Of Eden.*' His answer to that was, 'Most of it is a bunch of ———.' Only he didn't put it that delicately.

"I don't know," this actress continues, "whether he was trying to compensate for his shyness or what. He certainly is not typical of Hollywood actors. He will come into a room and for twenty or thirty minutes he'll say nothing. He won't even open his mouth. Then, mention something about drums or acting or bull fighting, and you can't stop him. He talks on and on with great power and intelligence. He's a strange one, all right."

Lilli Kardell, the nineteen-year-old Swedish actress, once under contract to Universal-International, has dated Dean more than any other girl in movieland. Although she declines to use the word love, she admits she's "gone" on the little guy.

"Jimmy," she explains in her (*Continued on page 75*)

Daredevil Dean is hell on wheels. Racing his Porsche in local meets, he wins handily at 120 mph plus, earns the respect of racing pros but the word around the studio is "that crazy kid is going to kill himself."

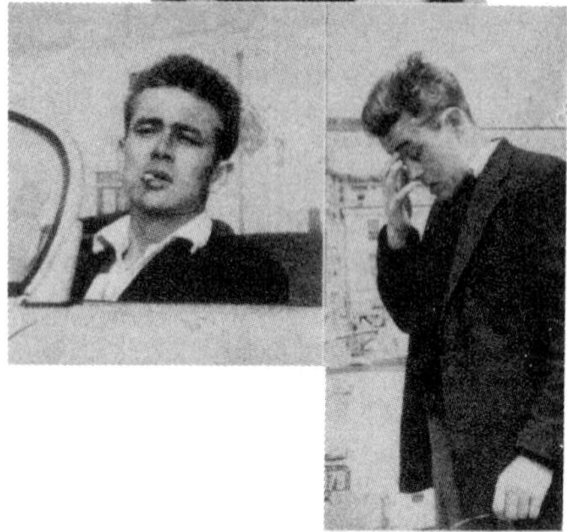

James Byron Dean is a free-wheeling individualist who breaks all the

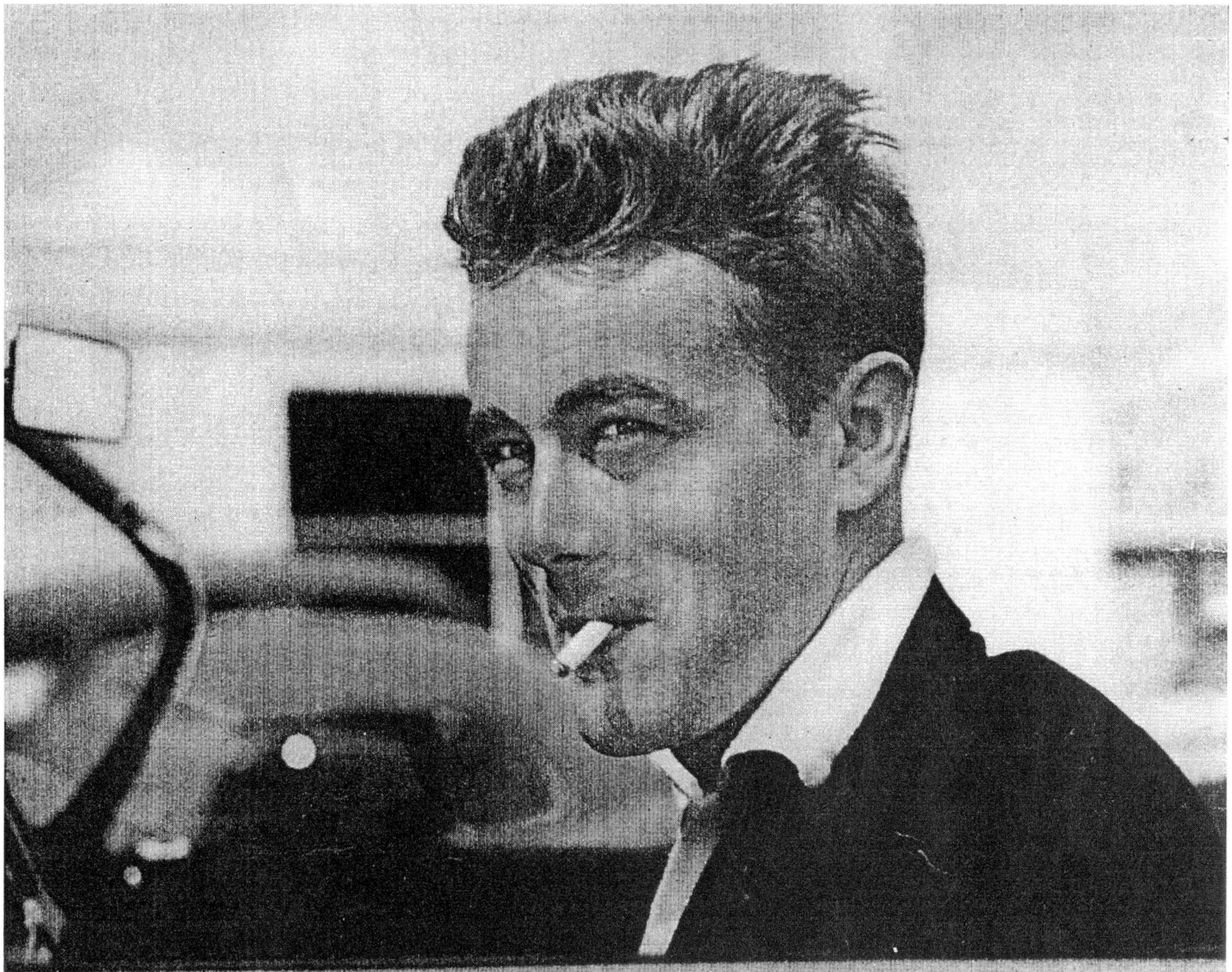

LONE WOLF

ules except one—he travels fastest who travels alone / by Richard Moore

lone wolf

(*Continued from page 28*) Scandinavian accent, "is a nice man. Some of those things he does, it is because he is youthful, and it takes time to handle fame. One must first learn how. But he is really very polite, very kind. They tell me he does not smile enough. Not true. He smiles much. He has a good sense of humor."

In other film quarters, however, the Dean sense of humor is generously described as "slightly perverse."

Jimmy himself, for example, likes to tell how he scared the wits out of a supposedly sophisticated and worldly photographer.

"A couple of months ago," Dean narrates, "this fellow, you know Dennis—well, Dennis went back to Indiana with me. Wanted to shoot me on the farm. Hometown stuff.

"One day we walked into town, and I stopped by Wilbur Hunt's. Wilbur runs a kind of general store in Fairmount. He's also the town mortician, and in the back he's got a selection of caskets. 'Mind if we shoot some stuff in here?' I asked Wilbur.

"He's a wonderful guy. 'Help yourself,' he said. So we went into the back. There were these caskets. I got into one of them and lay down. 'Go ahead,' I said to Dennis. 'Start shooting.' He thought I was kidding, but I always wanted to see how I'd look in a casket. Besides you should've seen the expression on Dennis' face.

"Anyway, he shot the pictures. Great stuff. Sent them into *Life*. Know what? The editors wouldn't publish a single one. Printed some stuff of me around the farm. Country boy—that routine."

Country boy—those two words—offer the key to Jimmy Dean's seemingly strange behavior. He acts awkward and this awkwardness is interpreted as rudeness. Actually, it seems that Jimmy retreats into his shell when he can't handle a new social situation, such as a studio shindig or a top-level interview or a swank Hollywood get-together. He appears sullen and non-cooperative, but largely because he feels out of place and doesn't know what to do. Also, he is by nature fiercely independent and resents doing anything that rubs against his grain.

Let him like something, however, and he goes the whole hog.

Not too long ago he was at a party with Eartha Kitt and a bunch of other talented entertainers. Eartha started to sing. Jimmy sat down on the floor and grabbed a bongo drum. Two friends joined him. Eartha singing and Jimmy on the bongos. You should've dug it. Simply crazy, wild, out of this world.

Later that night they began to use the tape recorders. Jimmy has three or four which he uses all the time. "Great," he says. "Help me in my work. Like this part of Jett Rink I play in *Giant*. I had tape recordings of fellows with Texas accents. The thing to do is not to exaggerate the drawl. Get it just right."

Jimmy and Eartha sang and played the whole night with about ten other Hollywood characters. Dean recorded the festivities, and next day in the sanctity of his one-room garage apartment, played the tape recordings over and over again.

Mr. and Mrs. Winton A. Dean, Jimmy's dad and step-mother, pose with portrait of their son.

He has a great collection of African chants and knows a lot about tribal customs and *mores*. He is also a bull-fighting *afficionado* and one of the crack stock-car racing drivers in the country. This love of racing is currently giving the Warner moguls a fit.

During the filming of *Rebel Without A Cause*, for instance, Jim Dean raced his Porsche in the Palm Springs and Bakersfield Meets. As soon as he was finished with his Saturday scenes, he'd take off for the racing grounds. He was a winner in both races, hitting over 120 mph.

According to a veteran California driver, "This Dean kid is fearless. He drives as if he had some secret agreement with Death to lay off him. He's relatively new to speed-racing out here. Matter of fact we never heard of him until he showed up down at the Springs. We thought maybe he was one of those Hollywood characters looking for kicks or publicity. Hell, no. This kid really knows the business. He's one helluva fine rider. Knows what he's doing every minute."

In addition to his Porsche, Jim recently bought himself a hopped-up British Triumph motorcycle. Frequently he tears into the studio astride his mount to give one executive heart failure. The executive watches Jim zoom down the road, then sadly shakes his head and mutters, "That crazy kid is gonna kill himself."

At this point in his life James Byron Dean is living strictly for himself. He has no one to support, no one to please, no one in the world to cater to except James Byron Dean.

Although his father and step-mother live only eight or ten miles away from his Hollywood hideaway in the hills, he rarely visits them. Just why he isn't there more often is hard to tell.

Winton Dean, Jim's father, has what he thinks might be an adequate explanation for his son's behavior.

"I'll tell you this," he says. "My Jim is a tough boy to understand. At least, he is for me. But maybe that's because I don't understand actors, and he's always wanted to become one.

"Another reason is that we were separated for a long period of time, from when he was nine until he was eighteen. Those are the important, formative years when a boy and his father usually become close friends.

"Jim and I—well, we've never had that closeness. It's nobody's fault, really. Just circumstances. I came out to California in 1936 with Jim and his mother. Came right out here to Santa Monica. Worked in the Veterans Hospital, dental technician. Did the same thing back in Indiana. Back there I worked for the Veterans Hospital in Marion.

"A few years later, Jim's mother came down with cancer. She was only twenty-nine. The doctors told me it was hopeless. I didn't know what to do. How do you tell an eight-year-old boy his mother's going to die? I tried. In my own stumbling way I tried to prepare Jim for it. Tried to tell him about the sorrow that was coming. Many times I tried to tell the boy what was coming. I just couldn't make it.

"Jim's mother passed away before she was thirty. I was broken up. So was the boy. I couldn't look after him and work, too, so I sent him back to Indiana to live with my sister and her husband. They raised Jim on their farm. And what a fine job they did. In high school, you know, he was a standout athlete, specializing in track and basketball. Absolutely tops.

"When Jim came out here," Mr. Dean continues, "to go to Santa Monica College, he stayed with us—I was remarried by then—and we got along just fine. He was always crazy about acting, and I remember saying to him a couple of times, 'Jim, acting is a good hobby but why don't you study something substantial? Why don't you become a lawyer?' But no, it was acting with him all the way.

"Nowadays, he lives in a world we don't understand too well—the actors' world. We don't see too much of him. But he's a good boy, my Jim. A good boy, and I'm very proud of him. Not easy to understand. No, sir. He's not easy to understand. But he's all man, and he'll make his mark. Mind you, my boy will make his mark."

On the basis of only one film, *East Of Eden*, Jimmy Dean has already made his mark. After *Rebel Without A Cause* is released and *Giant* is completed, the studio expects that the boy will become "the hottest actor in the business."

By then, however, Jim may not be in the business. He may be enrolled as a private in the Army of the United States. Only a few weeks ago he was called down to the Los Angeles induction station for his Army physical. Although he's extremely near-sighted and can't see very well without glasses, he is otherwise in good physical condition.

A stint in the service doesn't faze Jim one bit. Other actors bemoan the loss of revenue that military service entails, but Dean has never built his life around money. "Never had much," he says, "and don't need much. If the Army wants me I'm ready."

When that particular remark was relayed to a Hollywood beauty whom Dean had been seeing frequently before he took off for *Giant* location work, she pursed her lips and wrinkled her brow.

"Sure, he's ready to go," she repeated. "Jimmy Dean is ready to go anywhere, any place, any time. He's a free soul. Only," she pouted, "I don't want him to go. With all his crazy ways he's the cutest little guy we've had around Hollywood in a long, long time. A regular little tiger, that one." END

DEAN'S (ON STAGE) DAD

As a personality Jimmy Dean may be a little on the wacky side but as an actor, this young man is respected as one of the most powerful and authentic dramatic talents Hollywood has produced in years.

Jim Backus, who plays Dean's father in Rebel Without A Cause, *recently explained to friends what it meant to act with Jim.*

"In this particular scene," Backus began, "Jim and I were supposed to have a fight on the stairway of the family home. I played his father and he played my son. He's just seen a boy who's been knifed, and his mother wants him to go tell the police. He doesn't want to, and so we fight.

"I've played fight scenes before, but nothing like this. Jim is so carried away. He works himself up into such a pitch of intensity, I thought he was going to kill me. No kiddin'. In one rehearsal he grabbed me by the lapels, half-carried me down the stairs, fought me across the living-room sofa.

"This kid is as strong as a bull. In another rehearsal, he broke off parts of the stair railing, but even though we grappled, he always held onto me so that I wouldn't get hurt."

Although Dean is only 5 feet, 8 inches tall and looks like a studious bookworm, he is all muscle and sinew in addition to being all talent. Great talent at that.

The GIRLS in JAMES DEAN'S Life

Here's Jimmy on the steps of his own house. With his first picture, "East of Eden," the young actor became a top star.

FIRST THERE WAS PIER ANGELI. THEN, MARILYN MORRISON. NOW NATALIE WOOD IS JIMMY'S DATE.

by BILL TUSHER

A SENSITIVE high-strung young Indiana farmboy who walks in an almost perpetual slouch, shuns the limelight like a pestilence, uses a drawled conversation which is a strange mixture of long-haired thinking sugar-coated in jive talk, and who peers curiously at the world through horn-rimmed glasses and dresses like a truck driver on his lunch hour, is becoming the greatest romantic excitement to which Hollywood has thrilled in many years. Jimmy Dean, whose lean, five-foot, not quite ten-inch frame makes him anemic compared with the burly six-foot-four romeos in whom Hollywood specializes, has without any noticeable effort ushered in a new and somewhat-bewildering era in tinseltown's lush history of lady-killers.

The young man who achieved almost instant screen greatness as the lonely, restless boy in "East of Eden" has—to his frequent irritation—found himself compared constantly with those other notable disciples of the dirty-shirt school of acting —Marlon Brando and Montgomery Clift. They do have much in common. All three have lifted mumbling to dramatic eminence. All three have made almost a cult of gadding about in levis.

All three are dedicated actors, and all three are as one in their disposition to hole up between pictures in New York, the better to soak up culture and count up their Hollywood lucre.

But Jimmy Dean parts company from Marlon and Monty in one department—girls!

The lovelife of Brando *(Please turn to page 67)*

James Dean's newest movie is Warner Brothers' "Rebel Without a Cause."

JAMES DEAN

(continued from page 21)

and Clift has been kept pretty well under wraps, and the little that is known about their relationship with the fair sex has been quite ordinary, including even Brando's much publicized engagement to Josanne Mariani-Berenger.

During his first year as a galloping knight on the Hollywood sound stages, Jimmy Dean has been in and out of more romances than you could shake a matchmaker at. He got kicked in the teeth with his ardent courtship of Pier Angeli, but instead of heading despondently for the nearest railroad crossing, he picked himself off the floor, shook the disappointment out of his system, and became one of the most sought after bachelors in fableville's younger set.

It almost would take a statistician to keep up with his amours. His circle of girl friends thus far includes two divorcees — west coast television's dark haired, sinuous Vampira, and Johnnie Ray's former wife, Marilyn Morrison; wholesome and wise Lori Nelson; the more worldly and garrulous Terry Moore; Louise de Carlo, a pretty girl who adorns the chorus of the movie version of "Guys and Dolls"; Lili Kardell, a wide-eyed Swedish lovely with roller-coaster curves, and just-turned-eighteen Natalie Wood, who combined work with pleasure by being on the receiving end of Jimmy's affections as his co-star in "Rebel Without a Cause."

Even Pier Angeli, who spurned Jimmy for Vic Damone, was—and still is—in his cheering section. As Pier pointed out while she and Jimmy were going together, and as she repeated since her marriage to Vic, her admiration for Jimmy simply never spilled into love. But she thought, as do her bevy of successors, that he was quite a guy.

All of this would indicate that Jimmy is heralding a new style of male sex appeal. He is not a muscle-flexing hunk of beefcake. It is not his chest expansion, but his brain power, his personality, his lost-soul mannerisms and his deeply philosophical approach to life that have made him so attractive to a tantalizing assortment of lovely young women. His shy, uneasy ways—a welcome contrast to the strutting peacocks they are so accustomed to—stirs up the sentimental yearnings in them.

Despite the fact that this disarming young man covers enough territory to bring pangs of envy to the breast of a Bluebeard, Jimmy is not a wolf. It is not enough for him that a girl fills her dress enticingly. No matter how fetching her torso, a dimwit wouldn't stand a prayer with the intense Mr. Dean. His many dates do not bespeak so much an appetite for conquests as they do a yearning—and a deep need—for companionship.

Jimmy's idea of a good time — except when he packs his lady fair into his new white Porsche, (a dazzling, foreign built sports car) for a breathtaking ride in the country—is to dine in a quiet restaurant and philosophize the evening away, or to curl up on a couch and rediscover the lost art of conversation. He likes nothing more than to be able to relax and be himself with a girl who is not afraid to be *herself!* He has no desire for the glamor side of Hollywood. What he seeks in girls, and what they have offered him abundantly, is friendship.

This is not idle speculation. It is the inescapable conclusion that comes from long and earnest conversations I've had with many of Jimmy's girl friends. He never has been as much in love with any lass as he was with Pier Angeli, but there are many candidates who are trying to succeed to his affections. He dug Pier the most—was captivated by her bubbling honesty, her native intelligence, her vitality, her unquenchable enthusiasm and a curiosity about life and people that matched his own. He even watched Pier's wedding, sitting on his motorcycle, alone, across the street from the church.

Dean at twenty-four may be pretty young to be despondent about an unrequited love, but he wears it well. Whether his many dates represent a subconscious seeking for another Pier Angeli, a harmless — and normal — social activity, or a groping for the Dean dream girl, no one could be certain, including Jimmy himself.

The notion that Jimmy might be casting around for another Pier Angeli found dramatic support in the recent whispers that he was dating Pier's comely sister, Marissa Pavan—a two-some that has irony coming and going. For the gossip was that Marissa had been carrying the torch for Vic Damone when he married Pier.

But of course this could be wishful thinking. Many of Jimmy's casual friendships have been exaggerated as full bloom romances by trigger-happy gossip columnists. If Jimmy has been seeing Marissa, as some syndicated peepholers have informed their readers, it could be, and most likely is, nothing but an expression of their friendship. In any case, the speculation about Jimmy and Marissa is just another example of the romantic legend that has been growing around him. Every time he looks at a girl, someone conjures up dreamy visions of romance.

His almost fanatical devotion to his career would give pause to almost any husband hunter, for it would seem that her position as his wife would be secondary to his first love—acting. Unappealing a fate though this may be, there is no shortage of girls willing to run this risk.

Jimmy's gals seem to sense and respond to his deep-seated loneliness. They have made pretty much of a fad of mothering him and understanding him. They are constantly on guard against doing anything that would annoy him, and they are remarkably patient with his shortcomings and lapses—his late arrival at dates, his last minute phone calls and the long spells during which he doesn't keep in touch at all. They don't think he has any failings, and if any are pointed out, they are quick to make excuses for him.

Even those who know him casually find themselves immediately protective in his behalf. I spoke with Johnny Ray's ex-wife, Marilyn Morrison, following a rash of gossip column items hailing her as Jimmy's latest steady.

"He's a nice, nice boy," Marilyn conceded, pained by all the fuss over her dates with Jimmy, "but there's no point even in mentioning our names together. I've met him and that's it. I have nothing against him, but I don't want my name linked with James Dean. Just because I've spoken to him a few times, I don't think it would be right."

Marilyn went on to explain to me that she was not thinking of herself, but that she was anxious to be fair to Jimmy!

"I kinda hate people," she summed it up, "who grab hold of a celebrity, and get a lot of publicity just because they've dated him. I wouldn't like it to be done to me if I were a name. It seems presumptuous."

As for the rumor that she and Jimmy were a real hot romance, she shook her head and said softly:

"It's nothing."

But when I pressed Marilyn and asked if that meant it couldn't lead to anything serious, she laughed and parried:

"That's kind of a leading question, isn't it?"

Marilyn isn't the first divorcee in Jimmy's life. The other is Vampira, née Maila Nurmi, the girl who has known Jimmy longer—and possibly better—than anyone else in town, and who is less in awe of James than any of her competitors. While most of Jimmy's dates listen like spell-bound disciples at his feet, Vampira would just as soon tell him off, and does with gusto. The fact that Jimmy doesn't date Vampira exclusively would suggest that he isn't keen on a steady diet of such feminine independence.

Once when I mentioned that Jimmy had been quoted as saying she didn't know anything about satanic forces, the field in which she specializes, Vampira blew her pretty top and said, "He can go to - - - -!"

After she cooled down, however, she refused to say anything nasty about Jimmy —for fear he would be put out with her!

"I was mad at him a while," she later told me, "but I'm all right now."

Vampira is very intimately identified with Jimmy's success and her interest in him dates back to when he was an unknown who had not yet made his debut on the Broadway stage.

"My ex-husband, Dean Reisner," Vampira explained, "got him in 'See the Jaguar' in New York and that's how he was discovered, you know. I seem to be in a rut. My ex-husband's name was Dean, and now this Dean!"

Maila is a spirited girl who likes to get a rise out of people. Although she is overwhelmed with admiration — and affection — for Jimmy, one of her favorite sports is to needle him by telling him what's wrong with him.

But where most girls are concerned, Jimmy can do *no* wrong. He's just the most. His photo occupies a station of honor on Lili Kardell's bureau in her modest but neat North Hollywood apartment, where she and Jimmy while away many an evening in earnest conversation, wolfing an occasional sandwich, sipping an occasional cocktail and giving way to an occasional one-man concert by Jimmy beating away on his bongo drums.

Lili, a Universal-International starlet, is one of Jimmy's favorite girls. She lives by herself, came to the United States on her own after a brief fling in Swedish films, has her own ambitions in movies, and understands—and sympathizes with—Jimmy's ambitions. She has Jimmy sized up as a lad of burning integrity and deep compassion. They both are relaxed in each other's company and their friendship is strengthened by deep mutual respect.

Oddly enough, although Jimmy seems to bat close to one thousand per cent with the girls themselves, he doesn't appear to score so perfectly with their mothers. Lori Nelson's mother and dad—exceptions to that rule—both raved to me about what a fine, natural, unpretentious boy they have found Jimmy to be, but on the other hand, Jimmy ran into strong opposition with Pier Angeli's mother, whom he once had the indiscretion to tell to mind her own business.

Nor was Pier's mother the only parent who did not approve of Dean as readily as her daughter. Natalie Wood's mom is another. Natalie, who dated Jimmy even before they were cast as sweethearts in "Rebel Without a Cause," still has a crush on him, but it has been a long time since Jimmy has taken her out.

"Natalie is only eighteen," a close friend of her family told me, "and her mother objects to her going with boys so much older. Not that Dean is old, but at this point Dean is a boy of the world, and Natalie's mother didn't think it wise for her to see him too much."

Her mother may prevent Natalie from seeing Jimmy, but she can't stop Natalie from raving over him.

"He's the greatest!" Natalie enthuses. "He's not only talented, but he's a wonderful boy. While we were making 'Rebel Without a Cause,' Jimmy taught me so much I didn't know. He couldn't have been nicer."

But Natalie's yen for Jimmy was not restricted to their moviemaking chores. They had met months earlier when she did a TV film with Jimmy. They went to several teen-age parties after that meeting, but they did not resume dating although their being cast together in a movie gave them the opportunity.

At one time, Jimmy was supposed to take Natalie to the Hollywood premiere of "East of Eden," but for some reason it didn't pan out. Nevertheless, the last may not have been heard of this romantic possibility. Warners are thinking of co-starring Jimmy and Natalie in another picture, at which time she would be older, perhaps even more infatuated with Jimmy, and very possibly more independent.

"She likes everything about Jimmy," her friend told me significantly. "She's crazy about his looks and his personality. It may be only a passing fancy, but she's got a heavy crush on him."

While Natalie's mother may be wary of Jimmy on the theory that he's a man-of-the-world, to others, Jimmy is just out-of-this-world!

There's no doubt about it. Hollywood's gals are on a great Jimmy Dean kick. Where it will end—at the altar or in frustration—nobody knows.

But this much is sure. As long as Jimmy continues to be a moving target, that old sharpshooter, Dan Cupid, will have to bide his time and hold his fire. END

DICK AND JUNE

(continued from page 31)

children are two of the most attractive children you can find anywhere.

What happened? Why were the rumor-mongers having such a happy time linking June's name with Alan Ladd's and, a year or so ago, with Dean Martin's?

The ways of the world are strange, and if they are strange in the rest of the world, you can imagine exactly how complicated they can get in the glamor-town of the world. Of all the people in Hollywood, Dick Powell is about the most business-like and least "stage-struck." He has his own ideas about how long a star stays in the eyes of the public if they get tired of him, and he takes himself less seriously as an actor than he does as an ordinary human being.

It can't be quite the same thing with June. She fought too hard and against too many odds to get to the top, to ever take the whole thing quite so casually.

When June first got to Hollywood, she was just a clear-eyed kid with not such a clear idea of what she was worth as an actress. She had a tiny part in "As Thousands Cheer," and she thought that was just fine. She didn't hound the night clubs, dress in satin, sex-lined clothes and she didn't get her name linked with all the hopeful Hollywood swains. As far as she was concerned, she had made it. She was in the movies and that was where she wanted to be.

That was just about the time that Dick, who was making a sort of a comeback in "Meet the People," met June. At that time, Dick had more or less given up on the movies—and felt that he ought to be pretty cagey with women, too. It was just after his divorce from Joan Blondell, and, it may be, he was in his most cynical mood about everything.

But June was appealing. And she appealed to him for a little more attention than he was giving her. Lots of people who knew June at the time understood, had seen her two blue eyes brimming with tears everytime she mentioned Dick. The last one to catch on was Dick. It was only after some of the memories of his broken marriage had thawed out of his heart that he was able to look around and notice that June Allyson, who had been following him for months, could mean more to him than just a girl who had a part in his movie.

June had to do a little convincing with Dick. He had been burned once. He had *had* it, and was not intending to get married, especially not to a little girl who was twenty years younger than he and looked and acted as though she wouldn't know how to manage marriage if she had it.

All this might sound strange to us, who have seen June in one picture after another acting like one of the best little

JIMMY holds no bitterness over his loss of Pier Angeli, but he rarely dates a girl twice now.

Genius or Jerk?

He's been severely censured, wildly acclaimed. What is controversial Jimmy Dean really like?

By JAN JAMISON

TODAY in Hollywood everyone has something to say about that non-conforming newcomer, James Dean. Some of it's good, some bad and the lion's share is horrid.

Up to a pernicious point, this controversial character is just about the only person who manages to remain passive and indifferent to the chaos he causes. He prefers to harness his energies and direct his interests into more productive channels—*unless* his integrity is challenged. When this happens he can explode higher, farther and faster than those "cup cakes" they tossed at Bikini. However, turbulent or tender as the case may be, his reasoning remains philosophical.

"If a choice is in order," he portends, "I'd rather have people hiss than yawn. Nothing can be more deadly than boredom and this applies if one is either the cause of it or its victim. It has never been my desire or intention to provoke criticism and create ill-feeling. But while it may be less hazardous to be accepted generally, only a supreme egoist could hope and expect to please everyone.

"My purpose in life does not include a hankering to charm society. Such dedication would limit my progress and I hate anything that limits progress, or curtails growth. I hate institutions that do this, as well as a way of acting, thinking and feeling that is bounded by limitations.

"Of course I am well aware that there are those who think a net should be dropped over me. But any public figure sets himself up as a target and this is a chance he takes. Most of us have more than one choice and I chose to

continued on page 22

NEITHER praise nor blame deters unorthodox Jimmy from his main purpose—acting. He's currently in "Rebel Without A Cause."

Jimmy. But his acting has earned wholesale cheers

leased a house recently. Those who respect his interests knew what would invariably happen. The house would become a meeting place for hungry, out-of-work actors—the same ones who have a little habit of dropping by the Villa Capri where they know generous Jimmy has a charge account! He listened to reason, forfeited his $150 deposit and returned to his over-a-garage apartment in the Hollywood hills.

JIMMY moved there when he was courting Pier Angeli. Although their broken romance left no visible scars, a framed picture of pretty Pier still stands on his desk. Jimmy's current interests include girls, acting, reading, music, bull-fighting, bongo drums, racing his Porsche speedster and riding his palomino which he stables in Santa Barbara "where there is more freedom." Since Pier left his life, he takes a girl out once and rarely repeats a date. "Because," he says, "I know all about them after that!"

Back in 1950, James Dean appeared in one scene with Martin and Lewis in "Sailor Beware." No one thought he was a genius then and the whole truth is, he wasn't important or impressive enough to be called a jerk! Since his terrific trouping in "East Of Eden," however, everything he says and does provokes contention. In other words—James Dean is *now* hot news!

While he was making "Eden," a prominent columnist happened to be in Warners' Green Room at lunch time when Jimmy walked in. His usual coterie of odd-ball buddies dogged his footsteps. Slumped, surly and looking like he'd dressed on a four-alarm fire truck, eccentricity oozed from every pore. The columnist witnessed the unsubtle exhibition at Jimmy's table, went back and blasted the dungarees off the ribald individualist.

A few months later, the studio sneak-previewed "Eden." Hollywood looked, listened and fanned itself into a flame of frenzy over the (quote) "fabulously creative and talented newcomer." So what happened? Jimmy received a message from the acidulous columnist inviting him to her big Hollywood party. Later she repeated her invitation, this time hoping Jimmy would escort her to our annual Academy Awards.

Conveniently or otherwise, Jimmy wasn't "available." Neither was he amused, bitter or the least bit resentful. To the contrary and in typical fashion, he automatically turned his thoughts in the general direction of things he considers important.

"We've all got to live," he shrugged non-committally and from that moment on, he never thought about the incident again. **END**

25

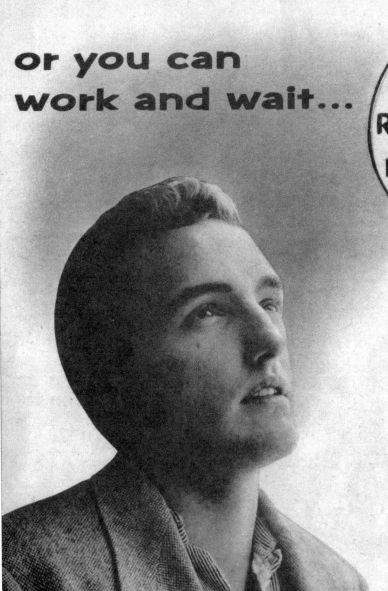

or you can work and wait...

"Please don't call me another Jimmy Dean..."

Dennis Hopper has come a long way since 1953. After working as a member of the stage crew at the famous La Jolla Beach Playhouse, Dennis got some encouragement from actress Dorothy McGuire and so he went to Hollywood. No one cared until Hopper did a few larger TV roles . . . then he had 3 major studios bidding for his services. Warners' won. Dennis did parts in "Rebel Without a Cause," "Giant" and is now one of the stars in "The Story of Mankind." Dennis is a very sensitive person. One of the most precious things in his life was his friendship with the late James Dean. But ironically the press and studio moguls call him *another* Jimmy and, every time they do, Dennis shrinks a little inside. He desires nothing more than a successful acting career—but he wants it as Dennis Hopper and not as a carbon copy of his best friend —when he says, "Please don't call me another Jimmy Dean," he isn't being brash . . . it's just that Dennis knows if he's going to make it it has to be on his own talents!

THE SEARCH FOR MR. X

AFTERLIFE IN THE MOVIE MAGAZINES

Many of the one-hundred-forty movie magazine articles featuring James Dean between 1955 and 1958 specialized in spirited attacks on "malicious, unfounded rumors" that, for the most part, the magazines themselves had initiated. Is Jimmy Dean's ghost haunting the set of the James Dean story? Did James Dean hate his father? Stepmother? Children in general? Did he die a pauper, leaving a pregnant widow? Stay tuned.

Another favorite theme was the ongoing search for Mr. X. Who is going to take James Dean's place? Are his fans deserting him for Tony Perkins? And — complete with ballots — who should play the part of James Dean in *The James Dean Story*? (Elvis was the big favorite.)

This errant quest provided a convenient pretext for introducing facts and photos of a number of rising young stars. They told us that Elvis, like Jimmy, owned a motorcycle and had a tragedy in early life. That Dean Stockwell and James Dean both wore horn-rimmed glasses and had been unhappy at college. One magazine complained that "some people" even "claimed that James Dean and Dean Stockwell were both rebellious, sloppy, and off-beat." Who? Who are they? I want names!

Thus, "Can Dean Stockwell Shake Off the Jimmy Dean Jinx?" — a long Mycenaean laundry list of nutty comparisons — is as crafty and demented a piece of reasoning as you're likely to find this side of the Albigensian heresy. By means of a goony separated-at-birth syllogism the writer manages to get in some pretty arcane statistics about Dean Stockwell. We get the stats on Stockwell and Dean all for a single price: our sanity.

The beauty of this sort of approach is that it can be effortlessly extended to encompass, say, Machiavelli and Twyla Tharp. There's a lobotomized logic in it that at its sublime nadir approaches Samuel Beckettry: Elvis peeking through a curtain, paired with a shot of Jimmy looking through the viewfinder of a camera; Elvis putting the wrong end of a trumpet up to his eye and, odd coincidence, Jimmy sticking his finger in his eye.

Gossip is, of course, the scandal goddess, the plankton of the star/fan food chain. Still, it's hard to imagine how they came up with these airy concoctions month after month. Endless variations! Even Charlie Parker would be hard pressed to come up with this many riffs. And all this before bubbleheadedness could be chemically induced.

"And in walking away, he hadn't just walked away from an accident; he had also walked away from a jinx — a jinx that had been haunting him for three years, ever since the tragic death of Jimmy Dean."

melancholy genius

The Life Story of James Dean:

■ When *East of Eden* opened in New York last winter—replete with tickets selling for $150 each for the benefit of the Actors' Studio, and celebrity-ushers in snappy uniforms to lead the celebrities to their seats—the man who created the greatest stir was someone who wasn't there: James Dean. Studio representatives tore their hair in private, smiled sweetly in public, and admitted both privately and publicly that Jimmy had been brought to New York expressly to make friends and influence the press, but they hadn't the slightest notion of where he was.

While Warners' New York office kept the telephone wires humming all that week in a vain effort to track him down for the dozens of newspapermen and magazine writers who wanted to interview him, Jimmy spent a quiet week in New York virtually in hiding—visiting friends at the Actors' Studio, where he'd once been a student, taking in the shows, and catching up on fun he'd missed with old friends Bill Gunn, the Negro actor who appeared on Broadway in *Take A Giant Step,* and Marty Landau, a TV actor. The three of them sauntered past the Astor one day, and stood quietly gazing up at the marquee with Jimmy's name emblazoned in lights on it: just looking up at it with the proper amount of awe. When Jimmy spotted the manager (who was wearing a full-dress suit in broad daylight, as theatre managers do) the triumvirate slinked off as though they'd been trespassing on an estate that said "keep out" and had been caught.

His behavior may have astonished the studio and astounded reporters, but it needn't have. On the record, Jimmy's friends will tell you that he doesn't go for those after-the-show congratulations, that he doesn't think they're sincere. But off the record, they'll admit that "he's probably the most sensitive guy in the world" and allergic to both criticism and praise. Big crowds frighten him. Strangers asking personal questions make him ill at ease. He's been labeled anti-social by some, rebellious by others, and just plain shy by those who think they understand him—but he's attracted some very loyal friends. And Hollywood, viewing the sets closed to visitors, the motorcycle, the sneakers, and the complete disregard for publicity, calls him "another Marlon Brando" and lets it go at that.

Jimmy counters that "People were telling me I behaved like Brando before I knew who Brando was. I'm not disturbed by the comparison, nor am I flattered." (To which Louis Sobol wryly added the aside, "Dear boy, neither is Brando.") By way of dismissing the subject for all time, Jimmy adds succinctly, "I have my own personal rebellion and don't have to rely on Brando's."

That should be that. But it isn't. Jimmy Dean is an actor who creates controversy—and perhaps a little of the riddle of his complex behavior is to be explained rather simply in terms of his past, and the fact that he was uprooted from a happy home before he was able to cope with it.

Jimmy was the only child of Winton and Mildred Dean, an Indiana couple who'd met, courted and married not far from Mario, Indiana, and who had moved to the West Coast when Winton Dean got a job as a dental technician in a hospital there. When Jimmy was 9, his mother died suddenly of an incurable disease. Jimmy's father had known that Mrs. Dean's death was imminent, and tried to comfort the youngster despite his own bereavement and loss. "I tried to prepare him, to make him understand," Jim's father declares. "But I just couldn't get through to the boy." Death, which sometimes brings people closer together than before, succeeded only in adding mileage to the emotional distance between Jim and his Dad. Mr. Dean, feeling that he might not be able to give little Jimmy the love and affection he needed, sent him off to Indiana to live with his aunt and uncle. Robbed of his father as well as his mother, Jim discovered very early in life what it meant to be lonely. . . . (CONTINUED ON PAGE 45)

the boy who lost his mother

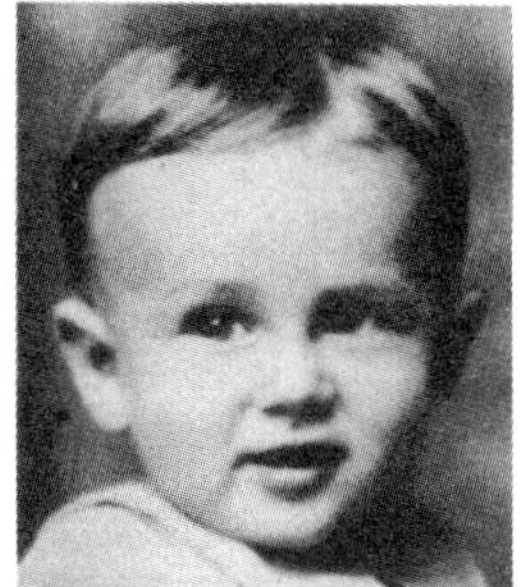

The Dean boy, age 2

Motherless at 9

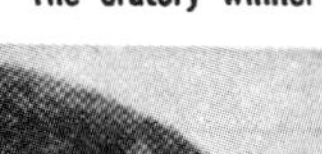

The oratory winner

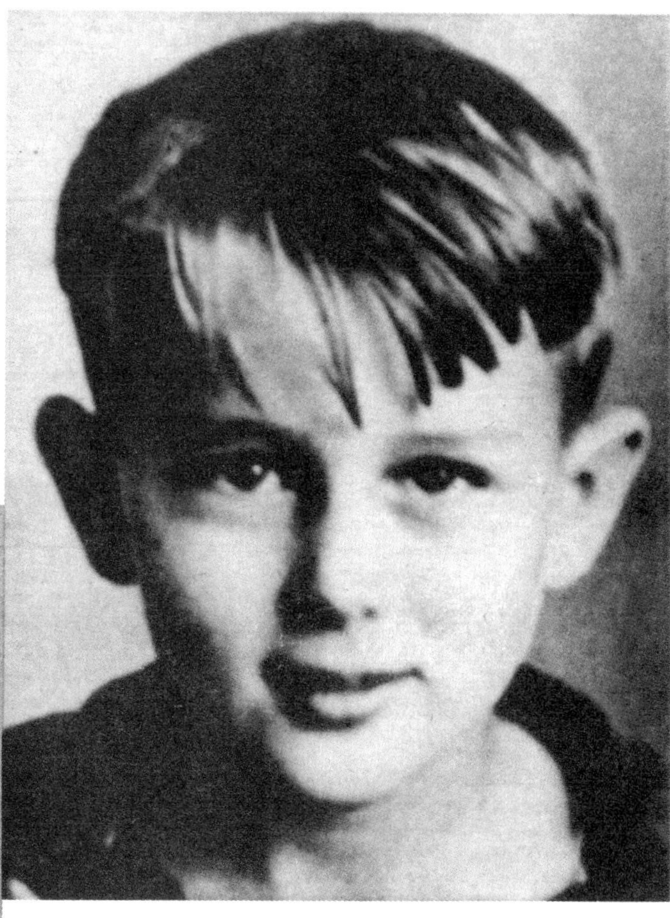

■ Life in Fairmount, Indiana proved somewhat better than a frightened child of 9, traveling back there with his grandmother, might expect it to be. His Aunt Ortense and Uncle Marcus Winslow welcomed him with warmth in their hearts and understanding in their souls. Though they have two children of their own, they tried to make him feel as though he belonged, and that their home was his. His Aunt Ortense describes him as having been "full of mischief, running over with pep, and into something all the time. He could do anything he set his mind to—stir up candy, bake a cake, help his uncle with the livestock. He was very determined, and lost himself completely in his current enthusiasm." Current enthusiasms during high school were many. He was a "sensational guard" on the basketball team, a member of the F Club, the band, and the Thespians.

About those green years, Jimmy now says, "Whatever abilities I may have, crystallized there in high school, when I was trying to prove something to myself—that I could do it, I suppose. One of my teachers was a frustrated actress. Through her I entered and won a state oratorical contest, reciting a Dickens piece called *The Madman*. It begins with a scream." And the school yearbook records that he "scared the wits" out of the audience by his portrayal of Frankenstein in *Goon With The Wind,* the class play. Shocking audiences was always fun for Jimmy.

Graduation brought the end of a comparatively carefree interlude. Quite grown up, Jimmy went out West to Los Angeles, to join his father and the woman who was now his stepmother. At Santa Monica Junior College he majored in theatre arts, and had his heart set on becoming an actor. His dad countered with, "Suppose you do have acting ability? Will you be happy leading an actor's life? Why don't you study law? That way, your acting will come in handy."

The desire to please was strong—strong enough for him to enter U.C.L.A. and sign up for pre-law. But compliance wasn't easy. Jimmy tried, but he couldn't quite fit himself into the mold. "I even joined a fraternity," he recalls, "but I busted a couple of guys in the nose, and got myself kicked out. I wasn't happy in law, either."

By the coincidence of geography, U.C.L.A. is also close to the film studios in Hollywood—and Jimmy found himself running away from campus and studies to get bit parts in films. He had small parts in *Fixed Bayonets* and something called *Has Anybody Seen My Gal?* but if anybody saw Jimmy, they overlooked him. Another Jimmy, James Whitmore, suggested he go to New York for stage experience. This was the kind of advice he enjoyed taking: it was something he'd always wanted to do. And if he had any misgivings about rebelling against his Dad's wishes, he stifled them. At 19, a boy is almost a man

James' father (left) with Aunt Ortense and Uncle Marcus Winslow

The well-tailored Winslow farm in Fairmount, Indiana

"GOON WITH THE WIND" AND FRANKENSTEIN

The play "Goon With the Wind" and Frank[illegible] appearance October 29 at the annual Halloween Carnival held at the high school. Characters in the play were Joan Jones, Jim Dean, and [illegible] Nall. Jim Dean as Frankenstein, [illegible] "scared the wits" out of the audience.

Two plays presented by the Thespian Society during National Drama Week included "An Apple from Coles County" and "Junior Prom."

Formal initiation for new members was held during the year. Those initiated were seniors: Edith Thomas, Ethel Thomas, Virginia Payne, and Earl Velon, David Worl, Kathleen Titus, Paul Smith, Rex Brown, and Janet Sue Nose; and sophomore, David Nall.

The plays were under the direction of Gurney Mattingly.

From Fairmount High Yearbook: Jim (inset) as Frankenstein

45

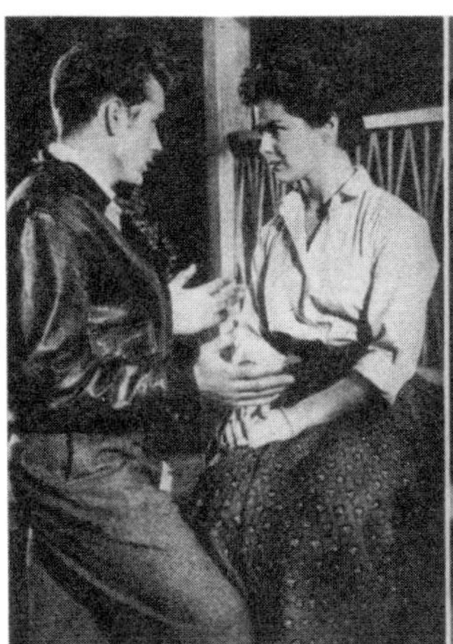

On TV theatre with Pat Hardy

On Broadway with Geraldine Page

In **East Of Eden** with Julie Harris

With Marlon: they get along

■ New York is a huge and a lonely place—particularly if you don't have a job. To keep from being engulfed by depression, Jimmy used to see three cheap movies a day (and even those got to be expensive). Just about the time he was running out of money, he was tested by CBS. They liked him, and kept him busy as a "stand-by," rehearsing jackpot stunts for *Break The Bank.* He was paid about $5 an hour, and they were dollars from heaven.

Quite accidentally, he landed a crewman's job on a sloop cruising the Atlantic, and the skipper had a friend who was a producer—a good friend. Jimmy won an introduction, and a part in *See The Jaguar.* The play lasted a fast five performances, but that was enough for Jimmy to make an impression. He went back to TV (as an actor this time) and appeared on *Studio One, Danger, The U. S. Steel Hour,* and *Kraft TV Theatre,* specializing in "heavies" and character parts before he got his first really big break on Broadway as the blackmailing Arab in Billy Rose's *The Immoralist.* Elia Kazan saw him, and brought him West for *East of Eden.*

In Hollywood, Jim lived through his first big success (in pictures) and his first big failure (in love). The *East of Eden* set may have been closed to visitors, but there was one big exception—and her name was Pier Angeli. If it wasn't the real thing, it was the closest Jimmy'd ever come to it. They visited each other's sets every day, and dated each other every night. He took her home to meet his dad, and for her 22nd birthday he gave her a gold bracelet and matching necklace.

But then one night he brought her home after curfew, and Pier's mother got angry. One look at his dirty leather jacket, his T-shirt and sneakers, and Mama put her maternal foot down! Another man might have set out to ingratiate himself with his gal's mother: toned down his behavior, and dressed up his appearance. But not our Jimmy. You either take him or leave him—as he is. And Mrs. Pierangeli left him.

Soon after, when Pier announced her engagement to Vic Damone, Jimmy was shocked and shattered. "Oh no, please say you're kidding me," he moaned. And when she was married, he stood across the street from the church and watched a beaming Pier make her getaway after the ceremony on the arm of her brand-new husband. This had been his first Big Romance, and he was hard hit. Of course, there'd been a succession of girls in New York. Actresses, for the most part. But Pier was the only girl who had touched his heart in a long time—and he felt the scars deeply.

They were scars too painful to be glossed over quickly or easily—but he tried. He started dating so many girls you'd need to fill your fountain pen before you could make a list. There were Pat Hardy, Ella Logan, Susan Strasberg, Vampira, Julie Robinson and Lilli Cardell, to name a few. If his heart was broken, he may have found a little salve with which to heal it in the extent of his success. Money hasn't brought him happiness, or even the imitation of it, but it has paid for visits to a psychiatrist (Marlon Brando's), a new white Porsche (which the studio won't let him race any more) and a Laurel Canyon hideaway where he can play the bongo drums or listen to Bartok in the "complete isolation" he wants.

His father, his family and his friends enjoy his newfound prominence, but it's been harder for Jimmy. Proud, defiant and essentially lonely despite his frequent dates, he prefers to keep his distance from people, and is plagued by a restlessness that he buries in dozens of hobbies. "I wouldn't like me if I had to be around me," he declares candidly. That's the melancholy genius talking. James Dean doesn't really think that little of himself—and one of these days, when he's good and ready, he'll let someone in to share his loneliness—and won't be lonely any more.

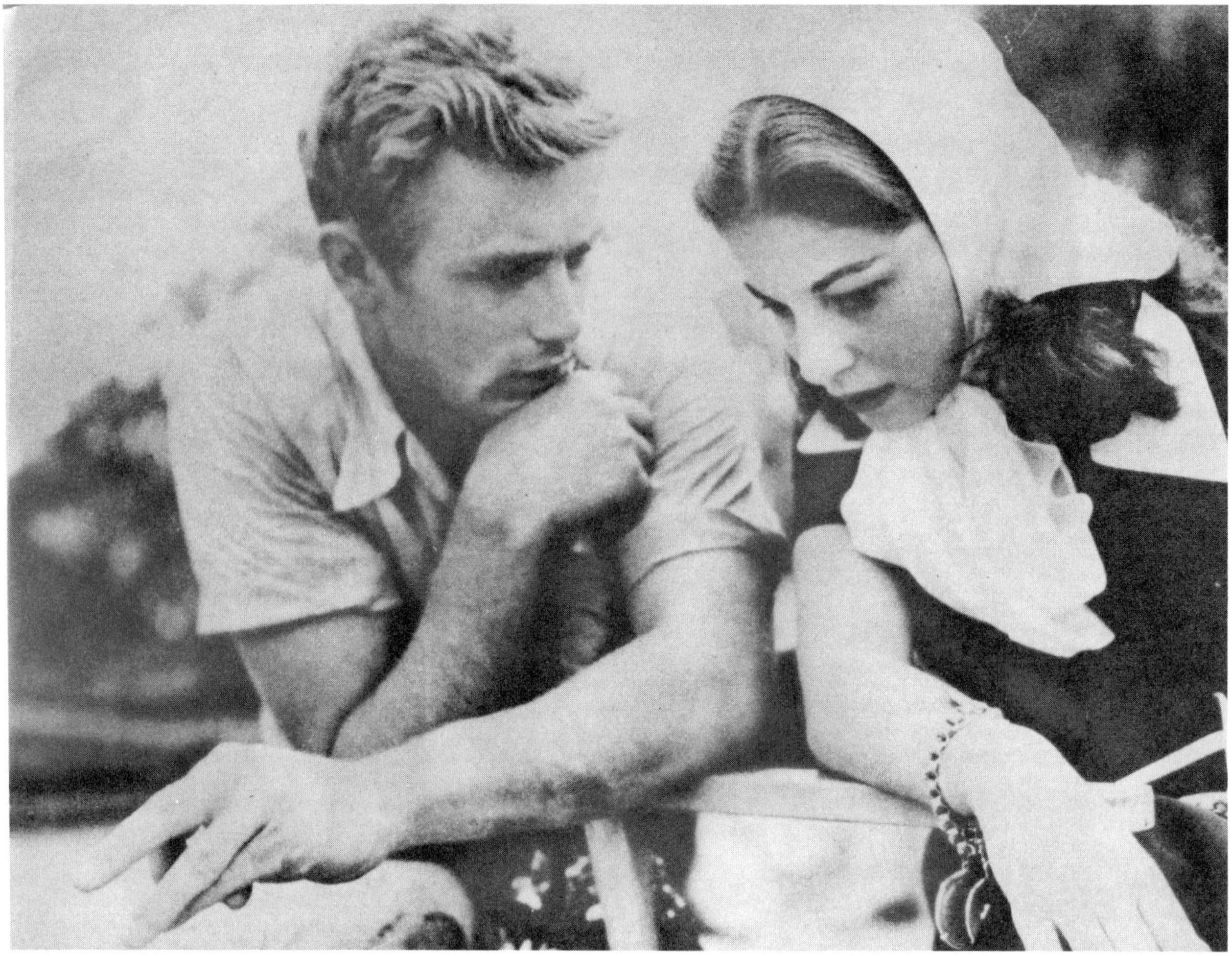

HIS SEARCHING HEART

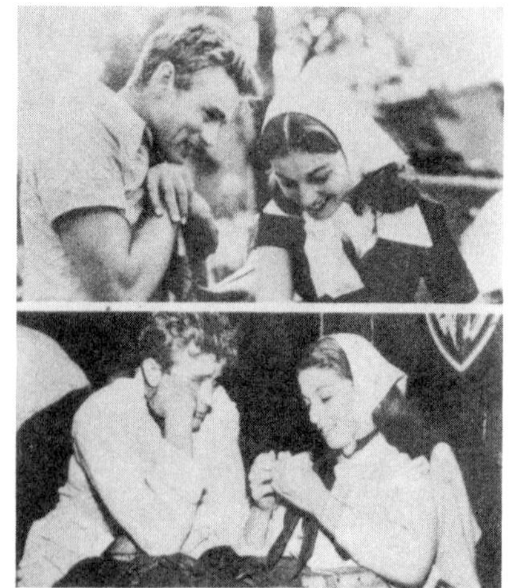

With Pier Angeli, it was real love . . .

They met on the *East Of Eden* set and before long it was an open secret their commissary lunches were more than friendly meetings. Jimmy, seeking something he had lost years before, found his wordless longing answered by Pier. Then one night Pier announced this was their last date, she'd accepted Vic Damone's proposal. The day she wed, Jimmy stood across the street from the church, crying. Friends say the break-up was caused by her mother, who objected to him because he was a non-Catholic; in fact, they'd had to sneak around to see each other. Though he dated many girls after that, none replaced Pier in Jimmy's heart.

With Vampira, it was friendship.

A good deal older than Jim, Vampira first attracted him with her eccentric charms. Well-known on the west coast for her weird TV program and ghoulish costumes, she frequented Googie's Restaurant —Jimmy's favorite spot. Knowing firsthand the lonely climb up the ladder to success, she befriended him in the same way she'd befriended Marlon Brando a few years earlier. He'd go to her apartment for advice, professional and romantic —nothing more. Contrary to an article in a recent scandal magazine, which tried to paint a sordid picture of their dates, the only relationship they had was on a platonic basis.

He confided in Ursula Andress . . .

Jimmy needed advice and the 19-year-old startlet from Germany tried desperately to help him. Though they fought like cats and dogs, Jimmy admitted it was fun making up. He liked her way of telling rock bottom truth, of not taking any nonsense from him. But it was this same lack of patience on her part that made them incompatible. Ursula tried, but when she felt it wasn't working out, she switched her affections to John Derek. Moody and sullen, Jimmy dogged her footsteps for weeks afterwards, peering in car windows at her and John, confronting them at restaurants, calling her at odd hours. But he was left out in the cold.

But with Natalie Wood he had fun.

On *Rebel Without A Cause* set, Jimmy and Natalie formed a bond of friendship that gave the lie to the people who said he was peculiar and only attracted "characters." Natalie at 17, is well-adjusted, popular and well-read. They both loved to listen to records, have deep talks. But most of all they shared an intense interest in their careers. After a day of grueling shooting, they'd meet for coffee and discuss the next day's scene. For Natalie, this was not just a bobby-soxer's crush; she's much more sophisticated than that. For Dean, it could have been a chance to open the shell that always seemed to enclose him.

(Continued on next page)

can

DEAN

Stockwell shake off the

Three years ago, James Dean smashed up his Porsche and died. A few months ago, Dean Stockwell smashed up his Renault—and walked away alive!

In those hours after he climbed out of the twisted wreckage of his car and left it behind . . . in those hours Dean Stockwell started taking his first steps in the long walk away from a shadow . . .

The shadow of Jimmy Dean . . .

The shadow that has followed him and haunted him since that day of September 30, 1955, when Jimmy died . . .

Now what made me think of that? Dean thought, cruising in his Renault that bright summer day. He felt the hot Hollywood sun warm the side of his face and neck. Traffic was light; the road ahead was clear. From his radio, he could hear the beginning of a Bach cantata. The music's like acting, Dean thought. Like working with Connie Stevens, Mark Damon or Millie Perkins, in the theater group. Building together. Finding the elusive themes of a great play and slowly fusing them until the play really lives—and *you* live because it does.

Aw, come off it, he thought. Stop sounding (*Continued on page* 81)

by JIM HOFFMAN

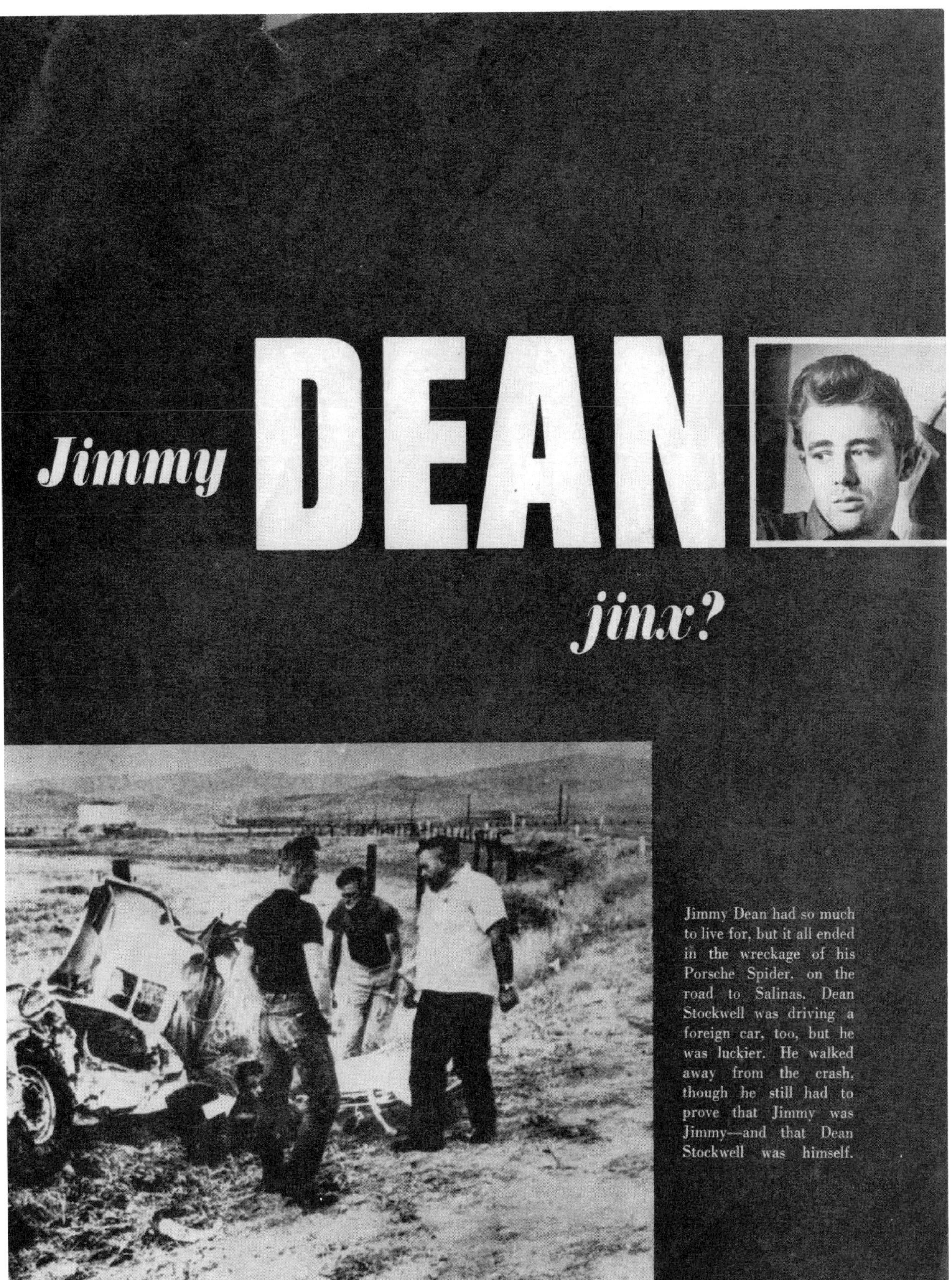

Jimmy DEAN jinx?

Jimmy Dean had so much to live for, but it all ended in the wreckage of his Porsche Spider, on the road to Salinas. Dean Stockwell was driving a foreign car, too, but he was luckier. He walked away from the crash, though he still had to prove that Jimmy was Jimmy—and that Dean Stockwell was himself.

DEAN STOCKWELL

Continued from page 62

like a hammy philosopher. Or worse yet, like the sound-track of one of his movies. Twenty-three movies, he thought. *And all of them before he was fifteen.* Dean laughed to himself. And then he concentrated on the road ahead.

Automatically, he slowed down at an intersection, even though the light was with him. A sudden blurring squeal on his right made him clench the wheel and slam down on the brake. But it was too late. Something blotted out the sun on his right. Something that didn't stop but kept on coming. Then the horrible jarring crash . . .

Dean opened the side door of his car and got out. He wasn't hurt. He saw that his car was only slightly damaged. And the other driver seemed okay. A minor accident, yes; but a major event in the life of Dean Stockwell. He had been in a collision, he had been uninjured, he had walked away. And in walking away, he hadn't just walked away from an accident; he had also walked away from a jinx—a jinx that had been haunting him for three years, ever since the tragic death of Jimmy Dean. . . .

A jinx. . . . it didn't matter that Dean Stockwell had never met Jimmy Dean, had only seen him in pictures. After Jimmy's death, people began to accuse him of aping Jimmy, of copying his acting style and personal habits. It was silly. Sure, there were some likenesses; but there were more differences than similarities. But this didn't stop magazine writers from trying to get Stockwell into the Jimmy Dean mold. And it hurt. Stockwell had the highest respect for Jimmy Dean, the actor—the only Jimmy he had ever known—but he wanted to be accepted for his own abilities as an independent, unique human being.

But the magazines wouldn't let him. They harped on the similarities between the two, manufactured others where they didn't exist.

There was the business of their physical appearance. Articles were published stating that they looked very much alike. But anyone who took the trouble to *really* compare their photos could see that this just wasn't true. A faint resemblance, yes; but 'twins' (as one magazine put it), no.

And their height: A magazine claimed they were both five-foot, ten-inches tall. Stockwell was five ten, but Jimmy—although the studio biographies claimed he was that height, too—was *actually* only five seven. And Jimmy weighed a good deal less that Dean.

True, they both wore horn-rimmed spectacles, and for the same reason. Neither could see very well without them. In fact, Jimmy was blind as a bat without glasses, although he didn't wear them onstage. And once, because of this, in the middle of a play he almost tumbled into the audience. Stockwell, on the other hand, doesn't wear glasses at all any more, except when he's driving or reading. He *needs* them all the time. But he doesn't wear them in public 'cause he doesn't want people to say he's copying Jimmy.

A jinx. . . . Copying Jimmy . . . Once a critic, in reviewing Stockwell's performance in the picture "Gun for a Coward," accused him of "incredible mimicry of Jimmy Dean." Kind of a funny accusation, a friend of his pointed out, when you realize that Stockwell had been an actor long before Jimmy dreamed of being one.

A jinx. . . . One writer pounced upon the fact that both boys had been unhappy at college, that both had left before graduation. The writer was right, but he neglected to point out that they had left college for exactly the *opposite* reasons. Jimmy left after two years because he *wanted* to be an actor, not a lawyer. Dean left too, after one year, because he *had been* an actor. It was because his fellow students remembered him as a famous child actor, and treated him like a celebrity instead of just another fellow, that he gave up college. Quite a difference.

A jinx. . . . Some people claimed that Jimmy Dean and Dean Stockwell were both rebellious, sloppy and offbeat. But these people never bothered to say *exactly* what they meant by these words.

"Rebellious," for instance. When they used this word in describing the two boys, what they should have been saying was "honest." If you ask Dean Stockwell a straight question, he'll give you a straight answer. If he has a strong feeling, he'll express it—directly. He's bluntly honest.

And Jimmy was the same way. When Pier Angeli married Vic Damone, Jimmy was still head-over-heels in love with Pier. So he stood outside the church while the wedding was taking place. Exposed and painful as an aching tooth. No attempt to hide. Hurt. Suffering for all to see. What mattered wasn't what *others* thought. He *had* to be there. He had to be true to his own feelings, to *himself*.

Sloppy? That's a funny word to apply to Dean Stockwell. And the word was first used about him when someone didn't bother to find out *why* he was doing what he was doing. And what was he doing? Wearing light, seersucker pants in New York in the middle of winter. And why? He had come to New York to rehearse for a play. In California he wore the usual summer suits. But in New York he was so busy rehearsing during the day and studying his lines at night that he hadn't found time to buy warm winter clothes. So somebody wrote that he was sloppy and compared him to Jimmy Dean. To Jimmy—who also threw himself so fully into what he was doing that sometimes he just couldn't be bothered to worry about such things as suits and ties.

Offbeat? Well, maybe. In their taste for music, at least. Unusual stuff. Stockwell digs Charlie Parker and Miles Davis the most. But also he's seriously studying the piano and is crazy about Bach, Beethoven, Brahms and Mozart. A columnist said that the night his picture "The Careless Years" premiered he went to a concert.

Jimmy also seriously studied the piano, with the composer, Leonard Rosenman, in the winter of 1953. Like Stockwell, he was crazy about Bartok. But his first love, as everyone knows, were the bongo drums.

Jinx. . . . The one thing that Jimmy and Dean Stockwell had most in common, according to the magazine writers, was speed. True, Stockwell was once crazy about fast cars and drove a flame-red racer with the throttle wide open. Off he'd go, alone, not caring where he was heading, passing everyone on the road. Fast. But today, all that is over. He's outgrown his need for high speed.

If Jimmy had lived, he would have outgrown it too. . . .

Yes, one day three years ago on the road to Salinas, Jimmy Dean ran out of luck, smashed up his Porsche and died. And after his death, another Dean—Dean Stockwell—seemed jinxed, jinxed to always walk in the shadow of Jimmy Dean. But a few months ago, when Stockwell was in a minor accident, he was lucky. He walked away from a collision—and from a jinx. A jinx that will never haunt him again. THE END

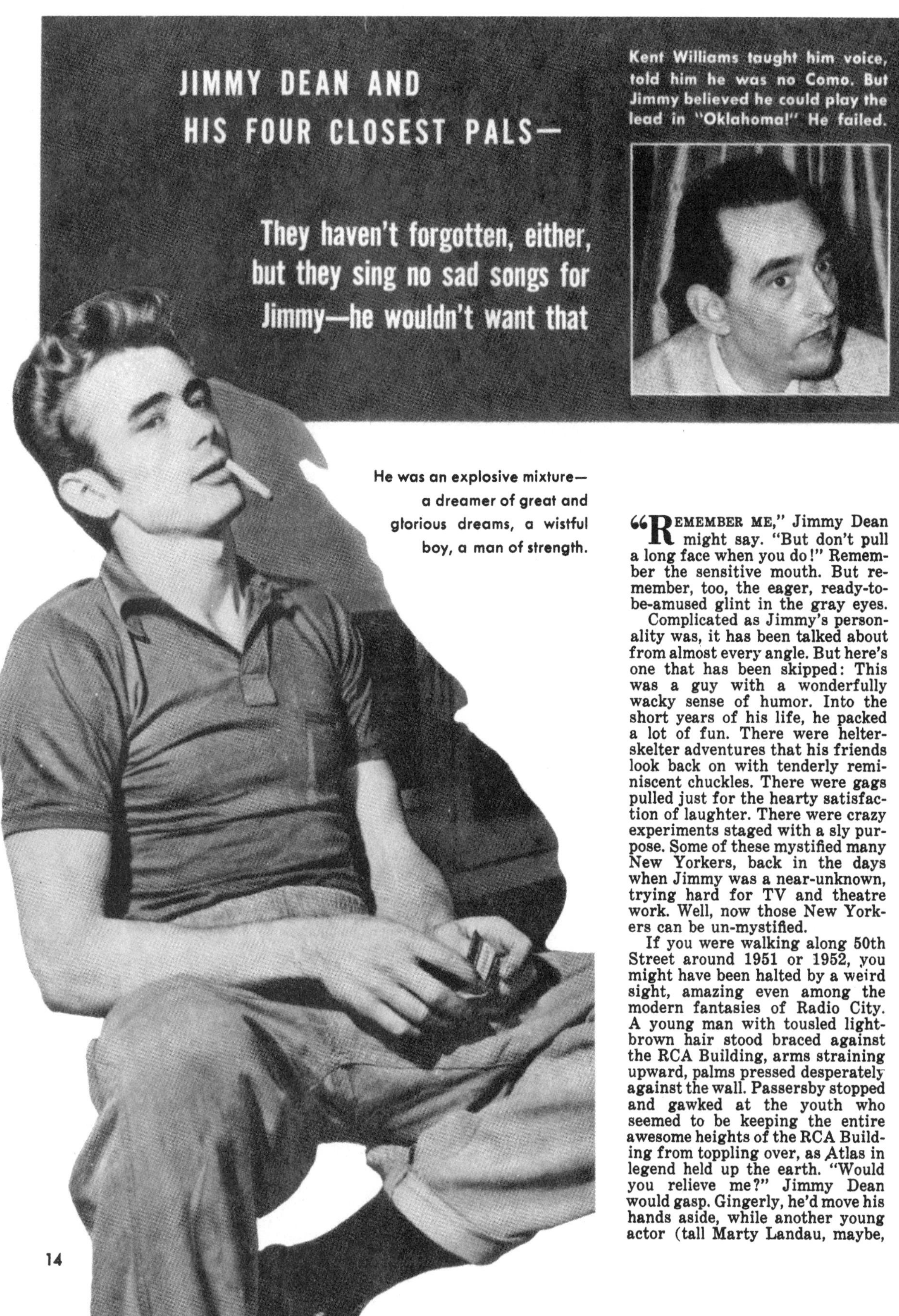

JIMMY DEAN AND HIS FOUR CLOSEST PALS—

They haven't forgotten, either, but they sing no sad songs for Jimmy—he wouldn't want that

Kent Williams taught him voice, told him he was no Como. But Jimmy believed he could play the lead in "Oklahoma!" He failed.

He was an explosive mixture—a dreamer of great and glorious dreams, a wistful boy, a man of strength.

"REMEMBER ME," Jimmy Dean might say. "But don't pull a long face when you do!" Remember the sensitive mouth. But remember, too, the eager, ready-to-be-amused glint in the gray eyes.

Complicated as Jimmy's personality was, it has been talked about from almost every angle. But here's one that has been skipped: This was a guy with a wonderfully wacky sense of humor. Into the short years of his life, he packed a lot of fun. There were helter-skelter adventures that his friends look back on with tenderly reminiscent chuckles. There were gags pulled just for the hearty satisfaction of laughter. There were crazy experiments staged with a sly purpose. Some of these mystified many New Yorkers, back in the days when Jimmy was a near-unknown, trying hard for TV and theatre work. Well, now those New Yorkers can be un-mystified.

If you were walking along 50th Street around 1951 or 1952, you might have been halted by a weird sight, amazing even among the modern fantasies of Radio City. A young man with tousled light-brown hair stood braced against the RCA Building, arms straining upward, palms pressed desperately against the wall. Passersby stopped and gawked at the youth who seemed to be keeping the entire awesome heights of the RCA Building from toppling over, as Atlas in legend held up the earth. "Would you relieve me?" Jimmy Dean would gasp. Gingerly, he'd move his hands aside, while another young actor (tall Marty Landau, maybe,

Billy Gunn: he helped his pal hold up the RCA Building, and "wound him up" for sale. Sometimes he couldn't follow Jim's imagination.

Chris White: she went in search of sweaters, but found only a mountain of peanut butter. "He wanted to be a cowboy hero."

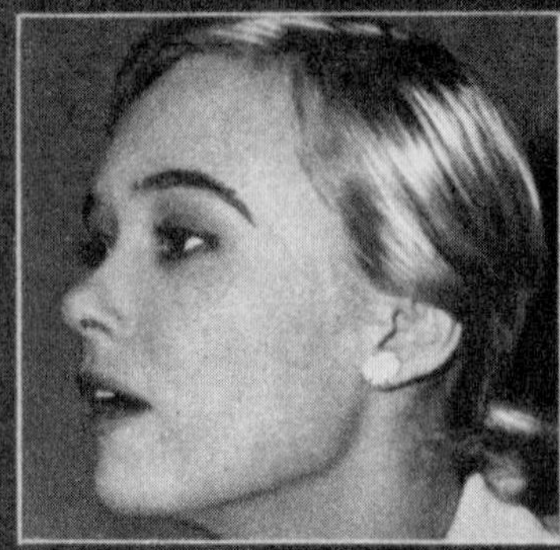

Marty Landau: he saw him last just before "Giant," his greatest role. Like the other pals, he shares the glow of special laughter.

or sprightly Billy Gunn) would ease delicately and quickly into position to take up the burden of the building.

More people would gather, mouths innocently open. "My arms are getting tired!" Marty or Billy would complain.

And Jimmy, standing by, would say casually, "Ah, let it go!" Then there'd be a breathless moment of suspense as Atlas took his support away . . . For some reason, the RCA Building never fell down.

"Remember the headless midget?" Billy laughs. That was another favorite Jimmy Dean gag. Jimmy would bend double; his friends would fasten his coat around him backwards and solemnly plant a hat on top of the unexplainable monstrosity. Thus they'd parade along the street, some pal leading a Jimmy who looked like José Ferrer playing Toulouse-Lautrec in "Moulin Rouge"—minus a head.

New Yorkers are blasé characters. They don't give a second look to a lady in a sari: "Probably from the UN." Or to a gaudily turned-out cowboy: "From the rodeo." Or to a shapely damsel patrolling Times Square in leopard-skin bra and shorts: "Must be advertising something." But Jimmy's "headless midget" stopped them cold!

That was the whole idea. Jimmy was an actor, avid to learn everything he could about human emotions, about the expressions people have when they're caught unawares. So he set out to catch them, with his friends' cooperation. "All these tricks," Billy says, "were done entirely for the purpose of observing people's reactions. When they saw strange things, how would they react?"

While Jimmy Dean was around, strange things kept happening. Walking nonchalantly past a fire hydrant, he'd suddenly flap his coat back at both sides, as if blown by a blast of air. With pretended puzzlement, he'd stop and stare at the hydrant, while the inevitable crowd gathered. In its midst would be Billy or Marty, dutifully playing stooge, but apparently a total stranger to Jimmy, asking, "What happened?"

Jimmy would shrug, "In this city, anything can happen!" And he'd stroll off down the street, leaving the crowd to gape at the hydrant and go on wondering. Sometimes, he'd pull the same gag with a passing truck, reeling back as if the draft from its speed had nearly blown him over. That might not have seemed so incredible to the harried pedestrians of New York City. But most of Jimmy's capers were more imaginative.

Often, he'd be a wind-up man, with Billy as his vendor. Like a sidewalk pitch-man who tries to sell mechanical toys to home-bound commuters, Billy would wind an imaginary handle in the middle of Jimmy's back, and off Jimmy would go, dead-pan, walking compulsively, not to be stopped, with Billy trotting after him. A stranger asks Billy for a light. Pausing to bring out the matches, Billy turns his head and shouts "Hey!" as Jimmy marches tick-tock across the street, without his vendor. Billy hails a cab and opens the door for his wind-up man. Jimmy bends stiffly, goes in the door and right out the opposite door, marching away.

So whole-hearted and convincing was Jimmy's happy make-believe that even his friends occasionally were fooled. He and Marty Landau had a secret pact: Close as they were, they swore they'd never go in for enthusiastic greetings after a long separation. They kept to their agreement—and that's putting it mildly. One day, when Marty had just returned from a tour with a road company of the play "Stalag 17," he was walking along the street with Billy Gunn. "There's Jimmy," Billy said suddenly.

"Don't say anything," Marty whispered. Rushing toward Jimmy, he bent black brows and roared, "You stole my watch!"

Jimmy cringed guiltily away, like a juvenile delinquent caught with a hot car. "I didn't!" he whined. And he bolted across the street, with Marty in outraged pursuit. Flabbergasted, Billy looked on, wondering whether a beautiful friendship had ended in violence or whether both his friends had gone off their rockers.

"We were just doing an improvisation," Marty explains blandly. Again, Jimmy was using an apparent practical joke to learn his profession. Actors of his school are often asked, as part of their training, to make up scenes on the spur of the moment and act them out. This Jimmy always did with the ardor that deceived Billy.

Whatever Jimmy tackled, it was

(*Continued on page 64*)

with the unconquerable urge to win. He played high-school basketball that way; he became a movie star that way. And his boundless energy was ready to meet any challenge, however frivolous. En route to a party, Jimmy and his two pals were walking along Sixth Avenue, when Marty spied three cardboard cartons on the pavement ahead. Lanky, long-legged, he turned his stride into a leap and cleared them easily. Dancer Billy, whose walk has plenty of bounce, had no trouble jumping over the boxes. Jimmy, with no thought of his own slight stature, valiantly played follow-the-leader—and fell over the obstacle. The three of them were stuck on that spot for hours, it seemed while Jimmy doggedly set about the feat of clearing the boxes. He finally made it, but he missed the party, because he had a charley-horse—from broad-jumping on Sixth Avenue!

Of course, the will to win isn't always enough. With fond amusement, his friends remember a couple of Jimmy Deans who *didn't* make the grade: Jimmy the cowboy star; Jimmy the singing star.

Early in his TV career, he played a famous figure of Western legend, Bob Ford. In the ballad of Jesse James, Bob's "the dirty little coward who shot Mr. Howard" ("Mr. Howard" being Jesse's alias at the time). That taste of adventure in the wide open spaces seemed to whet Jimmy's appetite for more. He found a paper-back book about a good boy who became a frontier outlaw. Sure that it would make a splendid movie—with Two-Gun Dean in the lead—Jimmy promptly began practicing lightning draws with an imaginary six-shooter. Well, he does start "Giant" in the guise of a cowhand, but nobody could call Warners' epic the horse opera that Jimmy had his heart set on.

Music, too, was an overwhelming interest of his, but he wasn't grimly serious about it, and he wasn't content just to listen. At one time, he was crazy about a wild record called "You Ain't Nothin' but a Hound Dog!" He phoned a young lady of his acquaintance and, without saying a word, put the receiver next to the phonograph. Hearing the lyrics howled forth, the girl didn't have to ask a single question. "Hello, Jimmy!" she laughed.

As for his own singing, to Jimmy that was no laughing matter. He consulted an actor-singer friend, Kent Williams, to ask earnestly what he could do to improve his voice. "In the years that I knew him," Kent says, "I was able to see his development in all directions—except in the field of singing. He loved it. His voice quality was okay. But he might really have established a record of a sort if he'd become a singer—he could sing in more different keys during the course of one song than anybody I've ever heard."

When the movie version of "Oklahoma!" was about to get under way, Jimmy's two off-beat ambitions converged into one solid resolution: The role of the singing cowboy *Curley* was for him! He confided this decision to an actress friend, Chris White. "You must be out of your mind!" she exclaimed. Chris had a profound admiration for his acting ability, and the two would often take advice from each other. But this time Jimmy wouldn't listen to her.

He charged into Cromwell's Drugstore and commanded Marty Landau: "Come outside!" On the sidewalk, Marty listened dazed to Jimmy's carefully rehearsed rendition of "Oh, What a Beautiful Mornin'." (As Marty mimics the quavering tones, Kent says with affectionate humor, "I don't believe he ever stayed on pitch that long!") The determination to land the role of *Curley* got no encouragement from Marty, either. In all Jimmy's friendships, there was so strong a tradition of frankness that none of his real comrades would insult him with compliments they didn't sincerely mean. Besides, he had too many talents and qualities that they could respect and love in utter honesty.

Marty's amused disapproval made absolutely no impression on the would-be singing cowboy. Jimmy wanted that part. He *had* to win it. Hearing that Fred Zinnemann, set to direct "Oklahoma!," was in town, he called and made an appointment to see him. By chance, the rodeo was also in town. Conscientiously intent on soaking up the proper atmosphere, Jimmy put on old jeans and a beat-up jacket and dropped in at various hangouts near Madison Square Garden, to observe all the mannerisms of the rodeo riders, the way they talked and stood and walked.

Then he went on to the Astor Hotel to keep his appointment with Zinnemann. He happened to be carrying a package, and this fact, combined with his intentionally sloppy outfit, brought him an offhanded order from an attendant in the lobby: "Go around to the delivery entrance."

Jimmy didn't put up an argument; he went meekly to the delivery entrance and told the doorman that he was headed for Mr. Zinnemann's suite. The doorman called the suite to announce, "There's a boy here with a package for you."

"No, no!" Jimmy protested. "I'm James Dean. I have an appointment with Mr. Zinneman."

No reaction from the doorman, who simply turned from the house phone to report: "He says, 'Bring it up.' "

Package under his arm, Jimmy went to keep the appointment. Of course, Zinneman gave him a sympathetic hearing, being familiar with his fine work. (P. S.: Jimmy didn't get the job; fellow named MacRae did.)

Jimmy and Chris White were at a party on an evening when he was due to catch a plane around midnight, returning to Hollywood to start "Rebel Without a Cause." Suddenly, Jimmy remembered that this particular flight left not from LaGuardia Airport (as most domestic flights do), but from Idlewild, a longer trip from Manhattan. "And I haven't even packed!" he despaired.

"Don't worry," Chris told him. "I'll take care of that and send it all out to you."

Jimmy was concerned for his new set of luggage — about the only new belongings he had. "Pack one suit," he asked hurriedly. "Sweaters! And as many white shirts as you can find. Only make sure that they're mine, not Lonnie's." (He was referring to his New York apartment-mate, actor Lonnie Chapman.)

This detail settled, off they went on a frenzied dash for Idlewild—and a couple of hours of waiting at the airport. Getting thoroughly confused while juggling calculations of Eastern Time and Pacific Coast Time, Jimmy had the plane's schedule all mixed up.

As soon as he was winging westward, Chris went to his apartment to carry out her commitment. "Going up the steps was like climbing a ladder," she says. "The narrowest stairs I've ever seen! And when I got in, I couldn't see a thing. There was only one light in the place—a naked bulb in the bathroom. I fumbled around in the kitchen and finally found a candle—right next to the peanut butter. There was peanut butter all over the place!" Working by candlelight, Chris managed the packing. About the white shirts: probably some of those she sent *were* Lonny's. And she decided that Jimmy needed an extra sweater; so she bought him one and packed it, too, enclosing a card.

Off to the Coast went the handsome new bags, neatly packed. Back from the Coast, for several months after that, came nothing but silence. Eventually, Chris got a note: "Thanks for the sweater. Thanks for sending the bags."

Remembering Jimmy Dean, his friends pull no long faces, make no show of sobby sentimentality. They still can share his laughter, the laughter that brightened his life and cast a reflected glow on theirs. Jimmy would like it that way.

THE END

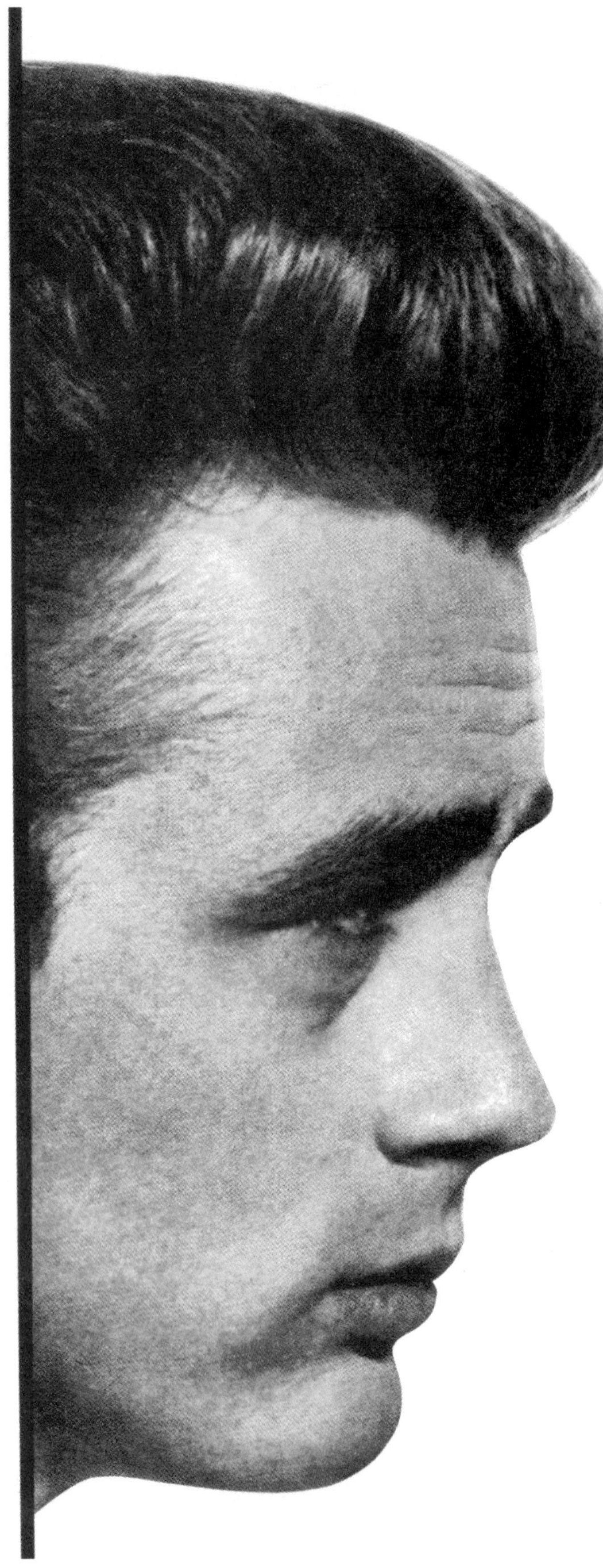

The Search for Mr. X

Elvis, Paul, Sal, Tony, Cliff, Don . . . is Jimmy Dean's successor among them? . . .

★ It seems inevitable that the throne left vacant by Jimmy Dean will be inherited by one of a number of likely prospects now busy making names for themselves in Hollywood. Whether that throne *can* be filled, this is another matter. As to who *should* or will fill it, this, too, is merely conjecture. We as editors are not drawing conclusions, but rather we are commenting on a situation that now exists. We are setting down the facts, presenting the case before you the jury. And, in the final analysis, it is YOU the moviegoer—you the public that will decide whether Dean's throne should be filled or left empty in silent tribute to a memory. On the following pages we have selected the six young men who at this moment seem closest to being heir apparent to a legend. We will point up their similarities to Dean—their differences. We will examine and reexamine what it was that made Jimmy what he was . . . And then we will leave it to you. Who is to be Mr. X? Read on—then let us know what you think.

MORE➔

ELVIS PRESLEY....

THIS IS ELVIS PRESLEY . . . the singer. . . .

These are his ardent, frantically loving followers. When Elvis sings . . . they're gone.

18

Should He?

Most frequently mentioned as the new teen-age idol . . . can he bridge the gap between sensationalism and serious acting?

MORE ➤

Elvis signs on the dotted line—once for fame and fortune, with Hal Wallis of Paramount; secondly for some of his fans, to whom he's devoted.

ELVIS PRESLEY

★ In discussing the role of the modern day hero in the lives of the nation's movie going public one late entry has, for the moment, seemed to zoom ahead . . . Elvis Presley—the actor. In regard to Elvis' possible success as the new teen-age idol we come up against one basic problem SHOULD ELVIS PRESLEY inherit the throne of James Dean? Should a figure as controversial as EP inherit a crown so recently put down by the tragedy of James Dean's death? Well, let's examine the record, keeping in mind that just as Jimmy is still the idol of millions so, too, is Elvis. Let's, for the moment, put aside all personal feelings about Elvis—pro or con. Let's forget for the moment his "unique" type of talent—a style and presentation that has had parents' groups, educators, clergymen and a great segment of the nation's population up in arms. Let's just take Elvis the boy versus Jimmy the boy—for that actually is the question at hand. Does Elvis have the stuff that will send him to the heights as a matinee idol, perhaps without the aid of a guitar and his "perpetual motion"? Well, those who have seen Elvis act claim that he's the hottest dramatic prospect since both Brando and Dean. People like Hal Wallis at Paramount and Buddy Adler, executive head of 20th Century-Fox, sing Presley's praise to the skies. Adler was quoted as saying he was "proud to have Presley on the lot." Wallis, after shooting Elvis in a straight dramatic test, agreed that Presley had a natural talent that could well develop into great acting ability. The cameramen and the crew who shot Presley's test were frankly skeptical—but even they had to agree that "the kid has something!" The consensus of opinion is that Elvis Presley is one of that rare breed of people who are, for want of a better word, "naturals." The same word is applied to the musical side of him, that innate ability that has allowed him, sans any musical training, to play the guitar, drums, piano, accordion and to compose music that sells records into the millions (Elvis' latest song, "Love Me Tender" sold a million copies before it was released through advance orders). Okay. Then assuming that Elvis is a natural, where do we go from here? What similarities exist between Jimmy and Elvis that bear comparison? Well, for one thing, they both came from small rural areas, both were products of a basic environment that may account for their unique public acceptance. Both convey a shy, casual attitude and independence that comes with being raised up fairly "free and easy." There was a tragedy in both families at an early age. With Elvis, an identical twin died at birth, and for the rest of his life his parents have devoted all their love and lavished all their attention on their one and only son. They gave Elvis as many material pleasures as they could afford; this wasn't much at times, but the love that he received and still receives, can never be measured. Jimmy's early tragedy came when he was 8 and his mother died—instead of his father completely devoting himself to Jimmy, Mr. Dean, in a sincere effort to give Jimmy the opportunity for a "normal" childhood sent him to the home of Jimmy's aunt and uncle, the Marcus Winslows, who raised him to all intents and all purposes as their own son—until they had a child of their own. Then, somehow, through no fault of the Winslows, Jimmy felt like he was an outsider again. With Jimmy, the urge to be *somebody* stems back to his childhood, when he felt he was *nobody*. With Elvis, the urge to succeed can be traced to the days when the Presleys knew great poverty. When Elvis' father couldn't work because of illness and his mother accepted a job as a nurse's helper to bring in some money for their food. Elvis, as a child, sensed the longing for security his parents yearned for and he promised that he'd be successful someday and help them—and he has—tremendously. So both boys strove for success with a fierce determination bordering on frenzy because of childhood misfortunes. Jimmy was and Elvis is basically a quiet, introvertish type of person, a person who, if not in the spotlight, would probably have been content to brood alone and be alone and who, had fame not tapped him

MORE ON PAGE 22

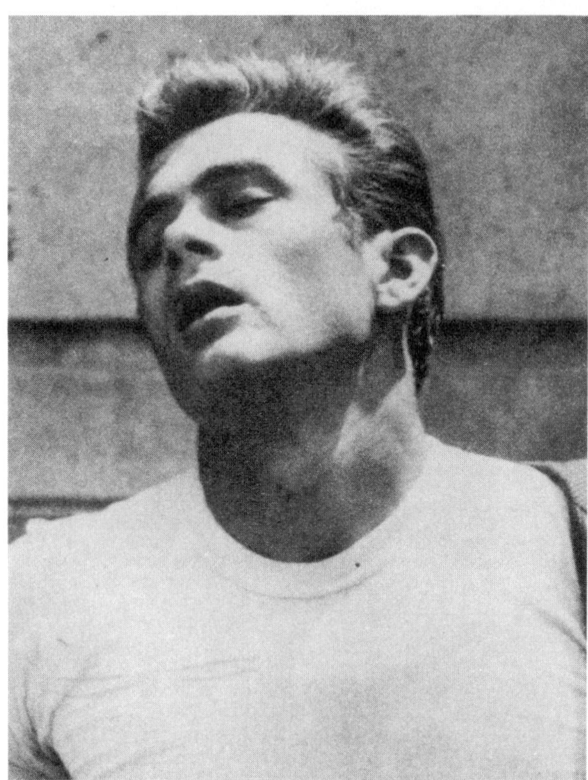

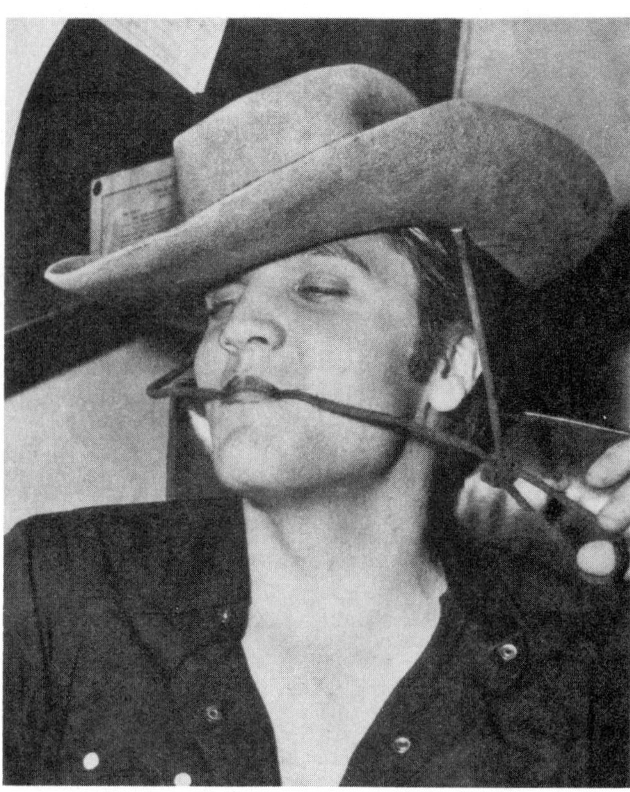

Two separate studies of the late James Dean as contrasted with Elvis . . . do you see any similarity in these pictures of them?

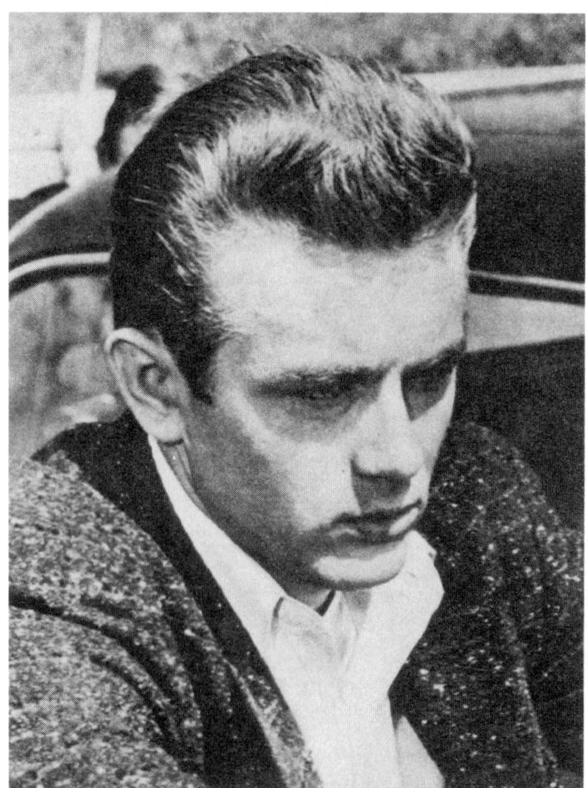

on the shoulder, might have even been considered the world's "outsider." Presley likes and Dean liked solitude, although these days Elvis rarely gets it. Then, there's this mania for cars. We don't have to go over Dean's fanatical love for speed, his desire to win races, to drive as fast as his high-powered motor and a favorable wind could carry him, his unquenchable desire for speed, speed, danger and more speed. Well Elvis, too, uses this means for release. Since the days when he got his first old jalopy, a car that was so old it had to be pushed to get it started, he too loves to tinker with cars and to dream about soaring down a highway free and fast . . . Elvis owns four cars and a motorcycle and indulges in sportscar talk and admiration. Perhaps to these two speed is symbolic—a means of trying to escape—to escape from a dream world they only dared think about but which became for both of them a reality. To get out in the open spaces and drive fast . . . fast . . . faster . . . Aside from this Elvis is as Jimmy was a controversial figure. When Jimmy first came to Hollywood the good words of praise written about him were few and far between. Dean was described as a leather-jacketed, sloppy, mumbly mouthed carbon copy of Marlon Brando. None of the columnists gave him a break. If this seems unbelievable now, go back and read the magazines and columns several years ago . . . look for the stories called "Jimmy the Rebel," "Jimmy: Little Boy Lost," "The Unhappy Dean," etc., etc. It was only death that brought Universal love to Dean. Only the grave that made him immortal—for now round the world the legend of Dean grows. Instead of being called sloppy, Dean is now referred to endearingly as "individualistic"—instead of being called rude, his lack of social graces is now called "Jimmy's desire for solitude", instead of calling him a mumbler, Dean is now referred to as a genius! Isn't it rather a sad commentary on life that some people have to die to be appreciated? Today Elvis Presley is getting, for the most part, the same treatment by the press. His show has been thrown out of towns, he has been branded sinful from the pulpit and from the typewriter. As we said before we are not here as his judges. But isn't it perhaps fair that now that hysteria has reached its peak and that Elvis Presley has become the most talked about celebrity in the world, we ease up and give him a chance to prove himself. He wants to be an actor, a serious actor. Some say he has it, others say impossible. Well, 20th's "Love Me Tender" will prove some wrong and some right. Either Presley is a phenomenon that will fizzle and fade away or else he will show his detractors that he can be a serious artist. Should Elvis Presley fill Dean's shoes? Should Elvis get his desire to play the life story of James Dean? Well, that's up to you, the public. As for us, we say there are enough things about both boys that could make for comparison and yet the difference between them is distinct. Jimmy, however, was just as "sensational" in his bout with social conformity as Elvis in his battle with parents and critics. So though they're alike—they're also different as day from night. As Jimmy beat his sad solos on the ominous skins of bongo drums and Elvis tinkers with a solitary piano when he's in the mood, these boys reflect one thing—they are definitely individuals. Whether Presley can fill Dean's shoes and win artistic integrity, whether the comparison between the immortal Dean and the sensational Presley is justifiable, this only time will tell.

THIS IS ELVIS . . . the actor . . . in camera studies taken on set of his very first film, "Love Me Tender," for 20th Century-Fox. Notice any contrast between these and the typically "frantic" Presley pictures?

Jimmy Dean fights back from the Grave

Jimmy Isn't Really Dead! He Is Dead, But Is Communicating With a Medium from the Spirit World! He Hated His Father And His Fans! He Deliberately Broke Girls' Hearts, Was Secretly Married! Rumors, Rumors, Rumors. What's the Truth About Them?

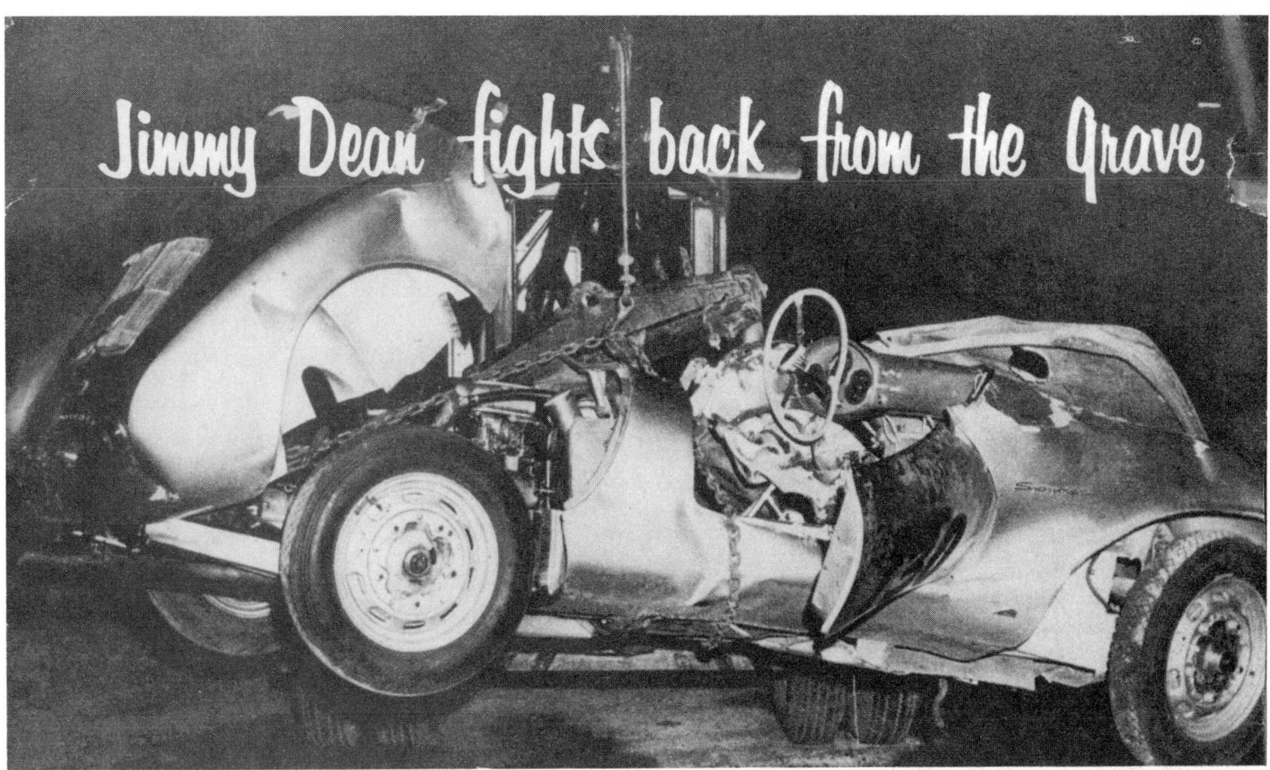

Jimmy Dean fights back from the Grave

BY NELL BLYTHE

■ EIGHT MONTHS have passed since all life was drained from James Byron Dean as he was being rushed to a Paso Robles Hospital following his disastrous auto crash on California Highway No. 41.

Eight months have passed. But James Dean cannot rest in peace.

His soul stirs restlessly in his cold Indiana grave. And his spirit rebels—with cause—against the legends, rumors and claims about him which have been circulating far and wide since his death.

Had Jim lived, many of these fantastic stories never would have sprung up. If a few had appeared, the distorted facts would have been set right, or perhaps even shrugged off with a "Man, that's the gonest."

But Jimmy's character, the kind of a man he really was, talks back from the grave. The facts about this boy, the qualities which remain so strong in the memories of his friends, make it possible for us to set the record straight for once and for all—to answer for him the questions in the minds of his many admirers who are deeply disturbed by the stories they have heard or read within these past eight months.

RUMOR: Jim was NOT killed in that auto wreck, but he was so badly mutilated and disfigured that his family and studio decided that he should be pronounced dead to the world. Jim is instead a patient at a private sanitarium for incurables. The boy buried in Indiana is a hitchhiker whom Jim and his buddy picked up enroute.

FACT: Jim was pronounced dead at around six p.m. on September 30, 1955. Later that evening his father went up to Paso Robles to claim and identify the body. Jim was brought back home to Indiana to be laid at rest alongside his mother. Rolf Weutherich, the German mechanic who was with Jim on the ill-fated trip to Salinas, says that at no time did they pick up a hitchhiker. Motorists who saw the car a few seconds before the crash testified in an investigation before a coroner's jury that there were just two people in the car.

RUMOR: Jimmy Dean hated his father and stepmother and tried to avoid them whenever possible. This hatred stemmed from the fact that he couldn't forgive his father for remarrying and sending him back to Indiana to live with his uncle Mark and Aunt Ortense Winslow.

FACT: Jim, not quite nine at the time of his mother's untimely and tragic death, never fully recovered from the shock of losing her. He loved his aunt, however, and in time even began to call her "Mom." Jim stayed in Indiana until graduation from high school. He then returned to the Coast where his father and stepmother were living in order to take a pre-law course at U.C.L.A. It is true that he found "communication" with his dad extremely difficult. A ten-year estrangement is a long gap to bridge even for someone less reticent than Jim. But there was no open breech or enmity between the two. During the months just preceding his death, Jim grew closer to his dad than he had ever been and was finally beginning to feel that he "belonged." If Jim had hated his father it would have been unlikely for him to have taken out a $100,000 accident insurance policy—of which Mr. Dean was sole beneficiary.

24 JUNE, 1956

◀ **This is the death car. Did James Dean—horribly disfigured—really live through the crash?**

This is James Dean's father and stepmother. Did Jimmy resent her, hate him? ▶

RUMOR: James Dean hated children and swore never to have any of his own because of his own childhood experiences. Furthermore he was exceedingly rude to his young fans and would never sign an autograph.

FACT: Nothing could be further from the truth. Jim longed for a son of his own more than anything in the world. In fact he spent hours trying to decide on names for his future children. He once worked as a counselor at a boys' camp in Glendora, California, and got along exceedingly well with youngsters. He wanted to give a child of his own all the love he himself was deprived of as a child. As for his treatment of his fans, he infuriated a contingent of N. Y. newspapermen by refusing to talk to them and spending his time instead with the youngsters who hung around the Marfa location of *Giant*. Neighbors' children were always welcome and well-treated when they dropped in at his home in North Hollywood.

RUMOR: Maila Nurmi, professionally known as Vampira, cast a hex on Jim because he rejected her in favor of younger and more glamorous dolls like Ursula Andress and Lili Kardell.

Continued

◀ **This is George Stevens, director of *Giant*. Did he and James Dean feud irrevocably?**

These are some of Jimmy's fans. Did he secretly loathe them? ▶

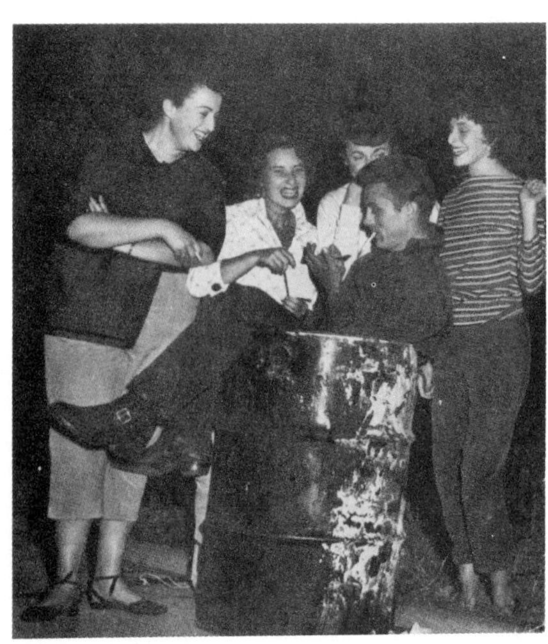

Jimmy Dean fights back from the Grave *Continued.*

FACT: Maila, when she washes off her weird theatrical makeup, emerges a striking and warm-hearted young woman. She knows less about witchcraft and hexes than Lassie, and her supernatural powers are limited to those conjured up for her by the trick photographers of her television show. Shortly before Dean's death, Maila told a friend that her position in Jim's life was that of a pal who advised and consoled him when he had romantic problems. "And I advise and console the girls he is having the problems with too," she said. There was absolutely no bitterness or resentment in her attitude. During her association with Jim, Maila forfeited a great deal of publicity—and cash—by refusing to do stories about him for leading national magazines.

RUMOR: Jim took a fiendish delight in making girls fall in love with him so he could jilt them in the same manner in which he was jilted by Pier Angeli. And after losing Pier he vowed never to become seriously involved with anyone again.

FACT: Jim wasn't ready for either marriage or another serious romance. He was too involved with his career. When he felt that Ursula and Lili were taking his dates with him too seriously and possibly were becoming a little too possessive, he deemed it advisable to allow the relationships to cool off a little. He did this not to hurt either girl but rather to *prevent* their being hurt in any way. This attitude is not original with Jim. Men from Tampa to Timbuctu have used the same gimmick when they felt the firm hand of Cupid pressing down upon them too tightly. About Pier Angeli: It is true that Jim cared enough for her to mope outside of the church on the day she was married. None of Jim's friends, however, can remember his saying that he had either proposed to or was intending to marry her or anyone else. In fact, the reason Pier broke up with Jim was because she was unwilling to wait until he was ready to settle down. Discussing the subjects of love and marriage, Jim told a friend: "I'll get married when I find the right companion. Marriage would be a very delicate subject with me. I have a lot to learn. I fall short in the human department. I expect too much of people. Tolerance comes with maturity and I guess I'm sort of a baby where women are concerned. Besides, there's no rush. I think thirty is a good age to get married. So I've got six more years to look!"

RUMOR: James Dean left a pregnant widow. Because they were secretly married she cannot come forth and claim his estate for herself and their child.

FACT: A young woman from northern California has swamped magazines and newspaper offices with letters stating that she was Jim's "wife" and several months with child at the time of Jim's death. MOVIE LIFE, intrigued by this girl's lengthy letters and the subsequent rumors that Jim had a secret bride, investigated thoroughly. We found these rumors to stem from the fanciful imagination of a childish mind. No marriage license bearing Jim's name and/or the name of the girl claiming to be his "wife" exists. Furthermore, at the time she claims to have become pregnant Jim was many hundreds of miles away in Marfa, Texas, on location with *Giant*. James Dean was never married—secretly or otherwise, according to all records available.

RUMOR: Jim's father is writing a book about him in order to "cash in" on the interest in his son's life and death.

FACT: Mr. Dean is writing Jim's biography. However, he is not doing so for material gains. As mentioned above, he was amply provided for by Jim's insurance policy so that it is not necessary for him to want or need royalties.

RUMOR: Jim was under the care of a psychiatrist at the time of his death and this kind of therapy may have caused him to have conscious or unconscious suicide compulsions.

FACT: Jim had become involved in psychoanalysis. Psychologists and psychiatrists are among the first to admit that during the early stages of this painful soul-searching many patients are exceedingly suicide-prone. These people prefer to face death rather than their real selves. Jim's doctor refuses to discuss whether this could be true in his case. Jim did leave cryptic messages to many of his friends. However if he had any conscious suicide impulse or death-wish or premonition of disaster, he gave no indication of it to his New York agent and close friend Jane Deacy. He

Continued on page 67

Did Vampira put a hex on Dean when she couldn't win him?

Did Pier Angeli (left) break Jimmy's heart, spark his vow never to love again? Did he set out to hurt every girl he dated, like Ursula Andress?

Jimmy Dean Fights Back from the Grave

(*Continued from page 26*)

lunched with Jane on the afternoon of September 30, a few hours before he took off for Salinas. And he was as excited as a little boy with his first electric train at the prospect of his forthcoming trip to New York to star as Morgan Evans in *The Corn is Green.* He was thrilled also at the plan afoot for him to play *Hamlet* in a revival of that Shakespearean classic. His own personal scrapbook was filled with reviews of *Hamlet.* It didn't matter to him who played the role or where it was played; anything pertaining to it he loved. And it was a life-long dream to play the part himself. Professionally, Jim was booked solid for all of 1956. And each role scheduled for him was one he desperately wanted to play. For the first time in his twenty-four years, Jim had a real design for living.

RUMOR: Because of his extravagant spending on automobiles and other luxuries, Jim was many thousands of dollars in debt at the time of his death. Although he was drawing a large salary he refused to compensate the friends who had loaned him money during his needier days. He even refused to talk to them or answer their letters.

FACT: Jim did owe sixteen hundred dollars to a New York agent (not Jane Deacy), who lent him the money to finance his trip to California for *East of Eden.* Jim had planned to return this money personally to the man as soon as he got to New York for his telecast. He had no other personal debts. On the contrary, he had a savings account amounting to about $10,000. Aside from the Spyder and his collection of records, Jim had few luxuries. He was not a lavish spender.

RUMOR: During production of Giant,

Jimmy Dean Fights Back from the Grave

Continued

director George Stevens said that Jim was impossible to work with and vowed never to do another picture with him so long as they both should live. Stevens, furthermore, shed no tears over Jim's death and later tried to persuade Warner Brothers to eliminate as many of Jim's scenes from Giant *as possible without destroying story continuity of the film.*

FACT: George Stevens was fighting mad at Jim because he didn't show up on the set one Saturday morning and didn't notify the studio where he was or why he had no intention of coming to work. Thousands of dollars of production cost were lost and the other stars, Rock Hudson and Liz Taylor, were forced to remain idle all morning because Jim was crucial to the scene. When Stevens discovered that Jim was loafing at Ursula Andress's apartment and didn't report to work because he was annoyed at having been kept waiting on set the day before, the director blew his top. Before the picture was finished, however, Stevens and Jim were completely reconciled. Stevens, in fact, has said that although at first he was deeply disturbed by Jim, he was now devoted to him because of his strong sense of fairness and his deep regard for performance value. Jim's scenes in *Giant* were not tampered with—either by Stevens or by the studio.

RUMOR: Jim's death was no accident at all. He was a victim of a fiendish Communist murder plot. A mechanic was hired to execute the dreadful scheme and Jimmy's car had been mysteriously tampered with before he took it out that fateful night. The party wanted to do away with Dean because of his anti-Communist activities.

FACT: Jim, as all good Americans, disliked everything that Communism stood for, but his anti-Communist activities were no greater than the majority of the stars in Hollywood who despise this form of government. None of his friends knew Jim to be politically absorbed in any way.

CLAIM: A mid-western "medium" has recently claimed to have made contact with Jim's spirit at a seance she held at her salon six months to the minute of the anniversary of Jim's death. She further made the startling announcement that Jim, crying out for his unlived days and uneaten bread, "told" her that he would come back in some other "form" and during some other generation to resume the life which was so abruptly snuffed out.

FACT: Such claim was made. Fortunately it got no farther than the small community in which the "medium" lived—Fortunately, because even there it created havoc. What of this claim? Fantastic? Possibly. The majority of mediums who have boasted of having made contact with the spiritual world have been exposed as frauds. There is no way to prove this woman's statement. But is *her* story any more fantastic than the best seller about Ruth Simmons who, in hypnosis, declared herself to be a reincarnation of an Irish girl of another century named Bridey Murphy?

Shortly after Jim's death a good friend of his said, "I wondered sometimes if Jim lived subconsciously in resentment of a life thrust at one with the injunction that you *had* to live it. He was fascinated at the thought rather of being able to *select* a life. I can't describe it exactly, but no one who ever met Jimmy can forget feeling that he was on his way to that life."

Whether Jim will come back in that life—twenty, fifty, or a hundred years hence—is a question no one can answer. But the reincarnation of James Dean is a provocative thought.

DID JIMMY DEAN'S SPIRIT HAUNT THE STUDIO?

BY JANE WILLIAMS

No one wanted to believe it—but too many strange things happened!

Filming *The James Dean Story*, Producer George and Photog Stoumen talked with Jim's cousin Markie Winslow in Fairmount, Ind.

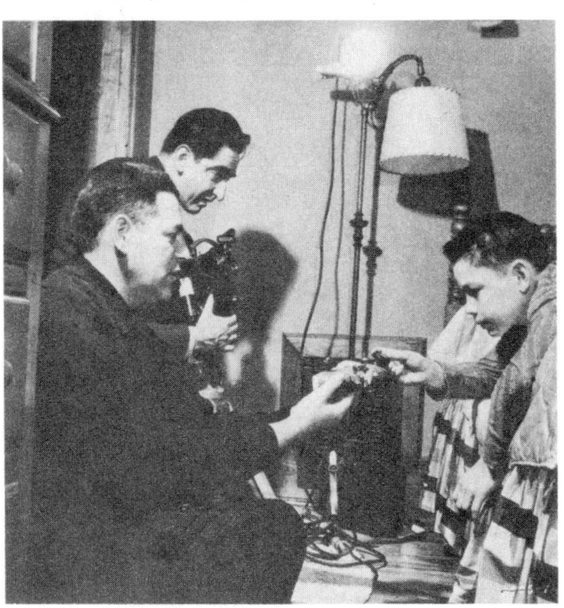

■ It happened just before midnight. The three men, tensely hunched over their work, at first didn't hear the door open. They were cutting and editing a sequence which had to do with a time when Jimmy Dean arranged to have his cat looked after while he was gone.

Quietly, Mrs. Lombardo entered the room. She'd dropped by to take her husband, Louis, home. Suddenly, as she was walking towards him, she stopped dead in her tracks.

"Bob," she breathlessly asked one of the other men present, "what's that cat doing on your shoulder?"

Bob Altman, one of the two producers of *The James Dean Story*, looked up with a strange expression on his face. "Cat?" he muttered nervously. "What cat?"

Mrs. Lombardo walked over to him and she looked embarrassed. "I'm sorry," she said. "I'd have sworn there was a large black cat on your shoulder, right there, when I came in. I guess it was just the way the light and shadows played on you."

Well, this is just coincidence, I tried to convince myself as I heard the story, the natural result of too much work and strain. But George George, co-producer of the movie, shook his head. "No," he said, "this was only one of the many strange incidents that piled up during the making of the film. At first we wouldn't believe it either, but after a while it almost seemed as if the spirit of James Dean was hovering over every step we took, watching, waiting, you could almost say haunting everything we did. Some (*Continued on page* 54)

james dean

(*Continued from page* 23)

of the coincidences were so eerie they suggested the supernatural.

"For instance, after Mrs. Lombardo saw the cat on Bob's shoulder, a big stray black cat joined us at the studio. He hung around the building and cutting rooms almost the entire time we worked on the picture!"

Ordinarily, I wouldn't have taken George seriously, but one look at his earnest, please-believe-me expression and I knew he wasn't kidding. Besides, even the interview itself had commenced in such a weird way that I was beginning to wonder whether or not I, too, was experiencing the Dean jinx.

Less than an hour earlier, I had been sitting with guests in my living room. We were sipping tall, cool drinks and discussing the strange events that surrounded the making of *The James Dean Story.* Why that particular subject? Because—and you won't believe this!—among the guests were young George George and his pretty screenwriter wife, Judy. The reason this was surprising is—in the midst of our conversation the doorbell rang. It was a special delivery letter for me from the editor of MOVIE LIFE. She asked me to get in touch with George George and ask him what unique, unusual things might have happened in connection with producing *The James Dean Story!*

Amazed, I passed the letter around for the others to read. George didn't seem as surprised as I. "This is the sort of thing that kept happening all the time we were working on the picture," he said, "from the start."

There was no possible way for the editor to have known whether or not I'd ever met George George. Yet her request to interview him came as he was a guest in my living room. Strange? Yes, but not as strange and eerie as the things he told me about the making of this picture. Take the recorder incident.

When the film was first assembled in rough-cut form, mention was made in the picture of Jimmy Dean's pleasure in playing the recorder, a little-known musical instrument. But, of course, the producers had no picture of him playing it. Then, when Warner Bros., where Dean made all of his pictures, bought the distribution rights to the new documentary, certain live-action sequences from their files were added.

Imagine George and Altman's amazement, in running off Jimmy's original screentest for *East of Eden,* when he walked over to a chair, picked up a recorder and started to play.

But they really began to think Jimmy was watching them when they heard WHAT he played. The first four notes that Dean sounded were the exact four notes of the theme music Lief Stevenson and Ray Evans had composed as the *Dean Story* background music!

"'Most everyone who sees the picture will naturally assume that we have dubbed in the music of the recorder," Altman told me. "They'll never believe that Lief and Ray composed the score quite apart from Dean's film test."

And then there was the strange case of the falling screen . . .

Among those interviewed for *The James Dean Story* was Jimmy's friend Arthur Wall. He told of an eerie sort of gag that Jimmy was always pulling on guests at Wall's apartment. The apartment was on two floors and when things became a trifle dull during the evening, Dean would excuse himself and disappear upstairs to the bathroom. Five or ten minutes later the front doorbell would ring and there would be Jimmy on the front stoop, waiting to be let in. When the bemused, surprised guests trouped upstairs, it was to find the bathroom door locked from the inside.

Dean had simply shinnied dowr the rain spout from the second t the first floor. He would always re place the screen on the window o of which he crawled, but not lock i Sooner or later in the evening t wind would dislodge it and it wou go rattling and banging to th ground.

One night, when the picture was about midway in production, George and Altman were busy at work in a Hollywood cutting room, assembling footage on the film. Suddenly a gust of wind came up. The screen on the window above their heads began to rattle and shake. Then with a crash it blew right in and fe on top of the movieola machine.

"Okay, Jimmy, okay," Geo quipped. (*Continued on page*

Another incident almost caused George and Altman to abandon night work on the production. They had been working for hours and decided to take a coffee break.

"Working on this morning, noon and night, I can't think about James Dean any more," George griped.

The two men went out the back door, locking the cutting-room door behind them. Suddenly, they looked back to see the lights in the locked room go out.

"But there's no one in there," George gasped. Quickly, they dashed back inside as chills ran up and down their spines.

Then they saw what had happened. A big poster illustrating the animated scenes they were using in the film was scotch-taped to the wall. The tape had loosened and the poster had fallen sideways hitting the light switch and shutting it off.

The men looked at each other shakily.

"Maybe we'd better knock it off for tonight," Bob said. He went over to the movieola machine, picked up the splicing knife, moved it once and the blade fell out onto the floor.

"Yep, we knock off," agreed George.

For months the group working on the picture had been so immersed in the Dean saga that when it came time to recreate the scene of the fatal car crash, they all felt jumpy about it.

Without intending it, as they neared the actual crash scene it was growing dusk. It was just about the time of day that Dean's accident happened. Nobody let on to the others what he or she was thinking. The only show of outward tension was Judy George's periodic requests, "Please, drive slower."

As they neared the corner, that country intersection where the life of James Dean was snuffed out in a split second, they could see an old jalopy approaching. It came closer, its noisy motor shattering the peaceful twilight. Then, as they reached the corner, the jalopy turned off onto the side road.

Bob Altman heaved a great sigh. "Turnipseed's early tonight," he quipped, easing the tension a little.

In recreating the crash, by the way, the producers were able to prove that Jimmy would have been saved had his split-second driving decision been different. He apparently thought his best chance to avoid the other car was to circle to the right. If he had spun his car and circled off to the left and to the rear of the other car, he would be alive and at work in Hollywood today.

As the picture neared completion, the strain told more than ever on George and Altman. Their nerves were rubbed raw.

One afternoon, a friend who accompanied Altman to his new Brentwood apartment after a tennis game, noticed the odd way Bob had of continuing to look out his window while making a telephone call.

When the call was completed, the

friend asked what was the matter.

"Do you see what I see out that window?" Altman asked. "Look in that tree, there."

The friend could see nothing.

Altman explained. "Ever since I've moved in, I keep looking out that window at night when I go to bed. The way the branches and leaves are formed in the center of the tree makes an outline of Dean's head. It's uncanny. It's crazy, I know. But there it is. He's watching me. Or so it seems."

When George George traveled to Fairmount, Indiana, Dean's home town, he found everyone in the community preparing a celebration. It turned out that it was Jimmy's birthday. George scratched his head. "Friday night, Jimmy's birthday," he grinned. "Why, say, that's my birthday, too!" Not an unusual coincidence, yet in view of all that had happened before, it made George wonder.

Though they themselves couldn't throw aside the morbid thought that they were being directed by Jimmy's invisible hand, George and Altman tried to avoid all traces of the macabre in making their picture. For this reason they cut out many real-life incidents which happened to Dean. Such as this one with Vampira: Vampira is a professional actress named Maila Nurmi, who specializes in ghost pictures and vampire assignments. She and Jimmy were close friends although she was a number of years older than he. A couple of days before Jimmy's crash, Vampira had gone to Forest Lawn, the famous Los Angeles cemetery, to have some publicity pictures made. One of them showed her dressed in her usual jagged black gown standing above an open grave with her long-fingernailed forefinger pointing down into the depths. As a gag, Vampira took one of the pictures over to the Villa Capri restaurant the night before Jimmy went to Salinas.

Dean hadn't come in yet and Vampira had to hurry off for a job assignment, so she left the picture

Jimmy's uncle, Marcus Winslow (with calf), does film sequence for *James Dean Story*.

for him. But first she autographed it jestingly, "Wish you were here —(signed) Vampira."

There was also no reference in their movie to a party given three months after Jimmy's death which may have been the origin of all the reincarnation stories about Jimmy.

A group of young Hollywoodites had gathered at the apartment of Dennis Hopper. There were numerous Dean pals, among them Natalie Wood. On the wall was an inscription about how to become a man, that Jimmy had always admired. As the story goes, someone at the party remembered how Jimmy had liked it and those in the room saw the inscription move. Or thought they did.

Later in the evening, a guest examined the little toy monkey on the fireplace mantle. It was the same one shown with Jimmy beneath the opening titles of *Rebel Without a Cause*. As the group discussed Jimmy, the little toy monkey started to clap his hands. It must have been the wind from the open window that caused it, but all the young people were so startled—and even a little frightened—that they ran out of the room.

But perhaps the strangest coincidence of all concerned the sequence with the speeding Porsche Spyder. To create this illusion, George and Altman needed an authentic miniature. They finally settled on the closest thing they could get—a model Austin from a Westwood department store's toy shop.

The toy model was numbered "38." It wasn't until after all the animation sketches for the picture were completed that they were compared to actual photos of the car Jimmy was driving to the race. The number of Dean's Porsche was "38."

Neither George George nor Bob Altman attempt to explain away all these coincidences and happenings. They can't. But they do ask themselves frequently, "Why did they happen? Was Jimmy really watching us make that picture? Was his spirit haunting the set?" What do you think? THE END

NEWS FROM THE DEAN FOUNDATION

JULY 21. 48 students were graduated from the James Dean Theater School.

AUGUST 13. A monument was dedicated to Jimmy within 100 feet of his grave.

AUGUST 21. The Foundation announced two two-year winners to the Neighborhood Playhouse School of Acting in New York City.

SEPTEMBER 30. There will be religious services at Jimmy's grave in Fairmount. (Last year's attendance exceeded 5,000.)

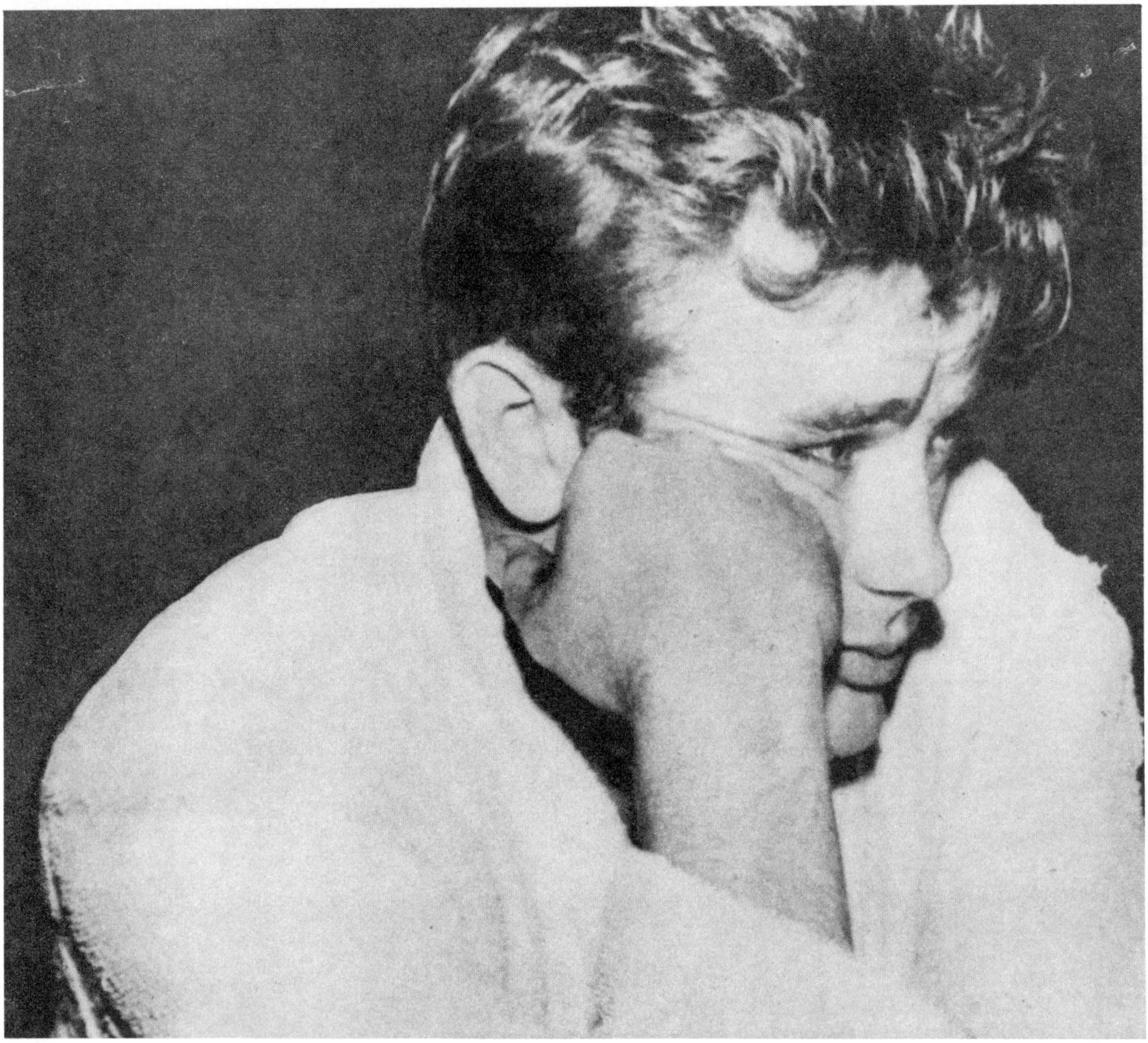

the untold story of the

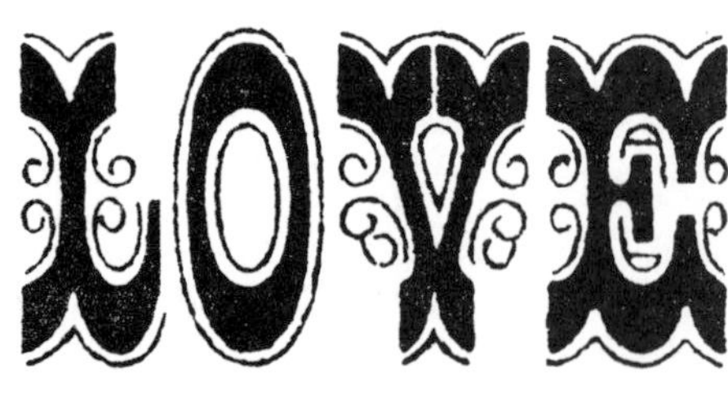

Jimmy lost

BY NELL BLYTHE

■ It was springtime, 1954.

But if you opened the door leading from sound stage five of Warners' Burbank lot, you'd never have known it. It was one of those grey, murky days, the existence of which Californians prefer not to acknowledge.

Crouched in a corner of a set from *East of Eden,* Jimmy Dean was too engrossed in preparing for his next scene to even give a passing thought to the weather.

So far as he was concerned, it was a warm night in the Salinas, California, of 1917.

Thus was he deep in concentration, when he felt the silent presence of someone standing nearby. Reluctantly he looked up from his script into (he told friends later) what appeared to be the face of a Madonna.

And he forgot all about the script, all about the forthcoming scenes. And suddenly the sun seemed to be blazing forth in all its glory.

"Hello," said the girl. "I do not mean to take you from studying. But I hear so much about this picture. And I am not needed on my set for an hour—so I come to watch. I am Pier Angeli."

"James Dean," he answered. And he rose to his feet.

"Yes," said the girl. "I know."

And for the next few minutes, they just stood there, facing one another, saying nothing.

A member of the *Eden* crew who watched all this could hardly believe his eyes. Later he told us:

"If anyone—and I mean ANYONE—interrupted him when he was getting 'into a mood' for a scene, there'd be all hell to pay. He'd be in a snit all afternoon. Even his agent, Dick Clayton, who was a close friend, would stand around for hours waiting for Jim to disentangle himself from a character before he would talk to him.

"When I saw Pier standing there, I was scared to death that Jim might do or say something rude. But once I saw him rise to his feet and watched the two of them standing there, smiling at one another shyly—I breathed easy again.

"They seemed like two helpless youngsters, who suddenly had found something wonderful added to their lives—but who still weren't at all sure as to what that 'something wonderful' was."

Within a week's time Jim and Pier were pretty much sure.

Always, on the days he wasn't working, Jim drove across into Burbank just to watch Pier shooting *Silver Chalice.*

And whenever she was off you'd find her the lone visitor on the tightly closed (*Continued on next page*)

the LOVE Jimmy lost *Continued*

(it was to everyone else) set of Warners' *East of Eden.*

When both were free you could find them in some sunny spot: Jim with his camera, taking picture after picture of Pier—and not objecting at all when a studio photographer interrupted this private session to grab some shots of them together.

Instead of scowling at the still-man, he'd be much too absorbed smiling at Pier—or just looking at her, very, very tenderly.

Warner Brothers was delighted, particularly when the two met for lunch in the Green Room.

Prior to his meeting Pier, Jimmy was the commissary's "problem boy." Important members of the press—like Hedda Hopper, for instance—would be lunching at the studio, and he'd slough them off by putting his feet up on the table, his hat over his eyes, and pretending he was fast asleep.

On another occasion, while paying his lunch check, he saw a framed portrait of himself, hanging on the wall together with other pictures of Warner Brothers stars. Oblivious to the crowded roomful of people, he yelled out, "I told them I didn't want this stuff. I told them no pictures on the walls. No pictures of me anyplace. Can't they understand, I don't want it!"

And then he tore the picture from the wall, smashed it to the floor and stomped out.

Then there were all the times when he'd come to a table, pull his jacket over his head and his head to his plate and literally slurp down his food—to the shocked annoyance of everyone at surrounding tables.

These were his rebellions against fancy Hollywood trappings—childish and inexcusable, perhaps, but his only way of expressing them.

That he knew better is obvious. But at the time few people thought so.

When he lunched with Pier, there was a radical change in Jim. His table manners were impeccable. Gone completely were the pranks and outlandish remarks with which he enjoyed shocking people. It was as if she brought out everything that was good and beautiful about Jimmy Dean.

As the relationship with Pier grew, other changes in Jim became apparent.

He had long resisted Dick Clayton's suggestion he meet some of Hollywood's "younger set." Suddenly he thought it would be a "wonderful idea." Dick, delighted at this change of heart, threw an intimate party for Jim.

Tab Hunter was there, Lori Nelson, all of the top up-and-coming players.

One of the guests remembers the evening vividly.

"I looked forward to the party for days," she said. "I had heard nothing but James Dean this and James Dean that for weeks: from Dick, from studio people, from friends. I was dying to meet him—and to tell you the truth, perhaps wangle a ride home or future date. I was plain intrigued.

"But five minutes after I arrived at the party, I knew I was a goner. Jim was polite and all that, but he didn't give anyone a tumble. We all could have disappeared in a spiral of smoke and he wouldn't have known the difference, and probably wouldn't have cared. He was thoroughly absorbed in Pier: Was she comfortable? Did she want something to drink? To eat? Was she having a good time? That's all that seemed to matter to him that evening."

For the next few weeks things went beautifully.

Pier and Jim went on long rides to the beach, to quiet little restaurants, to the movies, and finally, at her insistence, to the gala premiere of *A Star Is Born.*

"Aw, Anna"—he always called her by her real first name—"must we?" he groaned, when she first told him about it. And when he found she had had her heart set on it, he agreed, and went out and rented a much-hated tux.

And at the premiere itself, he stood in the spotlight he detested, smiled at the press he always felt should be avoided, and was miserably ill-at-ease in an over-starched shirt and tight jacket. But if his being there with her meant happiness for his Anna, then that was all that really mattered.

Thus through Pier's love Jim (*Continued on page* 64)

THE LOVE JIMMY LOST

(*Continued from page* 50)

earned the meaning of true unselfishness, the ability to give of oneself for the happiness of another. Now he could give *of* himself—but of his *entire* self was still an impossibility.

On June 19, Jim was the most excited young man in town. For days he had searched the city for a suitable birthday present for "his girl." It was her twenty-second birthday and he wanted something "special." He spent hours roaming through department stores and jewelry shops without success, until finally he stumbled on a gold necklace and matching bracelet which were "just right."

Perhaps they *were* just right to express Jim's feelings. And Pier *was* delighted with them. And also a little disappointed. It was obvious to friends that she was hoping for another kind of present: One that would indicate they would have many birthday celebrations. . . .

But all Jimmy said was, "We'll work something out. But we won't get married."

When Pier heard those words, something in her kind of died.

No longer could she fight as hard in Jimmy's defense—as she *had* fought many times. No longer could she overlook the problems their love had caused in her home life.

And it had caused plenty of problems. Mrs. Pierangeli had been against the relationship from the very first evening Jim came to the house to call on her daughter. She took one look at his clothes, his dirty sneakers, his disheveled hair, and immediately decided this was a young man *not* to have around the house.

On other occasions when Jim would just drop in unexpectedly, driving into the Pierangeli property on his motorcycle, Mama burned. And on the night he brought Pier home from a date way past curfew, she was downright furious and gave the couple a tongue-lashing neither would soon forget.

Still her arguments against Jim fell on deaf ears. "He is not for you, Anna," she said. "He will not marry you."

The last five words Pier would not allow herself to believe. She couldn't believe them until she heard them from Jim himself.

And when he said, "We'll work something out. But we won't get married," she knew the time had come to make a decision.

It was the hardest decision she ever had to make in her life. And yet the only one she could make. Her background, her religion, her belief that two people very much in love should marry without fear or hesitation made up her mind for her.

Driving home one evening, she told Jimmy that as much as she loved him it would have to end. They were not to see each other any more. He was not to contact her. Goodby.

And she rushed into the house and up to her room and cried her heart out that night.

Jim didn't cry. Men are not supposed to cry. But for weeks he brooded about it, because as he told his friends many times, "Pier is the only woman for me."

Jimmy, even more than Pier, wanted and needed security with all his heart. He felt, however, that he couldn't achieve it merely by marriage. Nor, on the other hand, was he able to offer it to Pier—or to any other woman at the time.

The fact that he himself was emotionally insecure was but one factor. There was another, equally important.

At the time Jim and Pier's romance flourished, Jim had no idea where he was going, career-wise.

When he arrived in California to make *East of Eden*, he was just a few dollars away from being totally broke. His salary at the studio, contrary to any other reports that may have been published, came to a few hundred dollars a week, and how long that salary would continue was anyone's guess at the time.

He couldn't foresee his tremendous impact in *East of Eden*, nor could he be aware of the fact that the old contract would be torn up and another substituted assuring him of hundreds of thousands of dollars. To Jim, who often had the tendency to look on the pessimistic side of things, his option could just as well have been dropped after the first year, sending him back to New York—and a perpetual struggle to make a buck. (And such a fate *did* befall Richard Davalos, who had the same deal as Jim when he signed to play his twin in the picture.)

Until Jim knew what was ahead of him, in his career and finances, he felt it foolhardy even to think of marriage and a home and children.

The tragedy of Jimmy's and Pier's romance was: by the time he *did* know—it was too late.

Jimmy didn't cry when Pier told him Goodby.

Nor did he cry when a friend told him of Pier's out-of-the-blue announcement of her engagement to Vic Damone. He just stood there, shattered, begging: "Oh, no. Please say you're kidding me."

He did, however, cry on the morning of November 24, 1954, as he stood alone across the street from the church and watched a radiant, happy Pier holding tightly to the arm of a deliriously happy bridegroom.

For he realized with stunning impact that the man could have been he. He realized that he had lost the girl "with the most beautiful soul I have ever known"—forever. And he realized how very, very much he *had* lost.

He rarely talked of Pier after that day. But through newspaper columns and magazines he kept track of her every doing.

And when she was in that plane accident en route to Palm Springs, he called the hospital almost every day to find out how she was. But always when he was asked, "Who's calling?" he merely replied, "A friend."

Any other guy would have started looking around for another girl, one just like Pier.

Not Jim. He went to the opposite extreme and started dating women as different from Pier as night is from day.

Pier was innocent and childlike and wise. Jim's new companions were chicks "who had been around," who were fast and hard, whose only wisdom consisted in what's generally called "knowing the score."

With Pier, Jim always watched his language and his manners, and rarely took anything but a soft drink. But with these women, it didn't matter. After one or two evenings he didn't care if he ever saw them again. And certainly to none of this ilk could he ever lose his heart.

And *that* was important: Not losing his heart again, not for a long time.

There were exceptions to the rule of one-or-two-dates and to the kind of girl he'd take out. Ursula Andress was one. But even with her, he called halt before the friendship developed into anything that could possibly be serious.

Natalie Wood, he saw a lot of. But that was different. With Natalie he could laugh and have a ball. They were true pals. Could this palship have turned into love? There's no real way of knowing. But it seems unlikely.

For there was one bad effect the romance with Pier had left on Jim.

It is true that while seeing her he was afraid of the responsibilities of marriage. He didn't feel he was ready for them. But afterwards he became afraid of love, and even more afraid of losing the object of his love.

And so when he left for the Salinas races on September 30, 1955, he was a boy unloving—and one who felt himself unloved.

But on the latter score, he was wrong.

He was so terribly, terribly wrong.

THE END

Jimmy's last role before his tragic death and his last chance to win the coveted Academy Award is as Jett Rink in Warners' *Giant* (below). Will he be neglected again just because he's no longer alive? His death lost him the Oscar for his magnificent job in *Rebel Without A Cause*. Don't let it happen again.

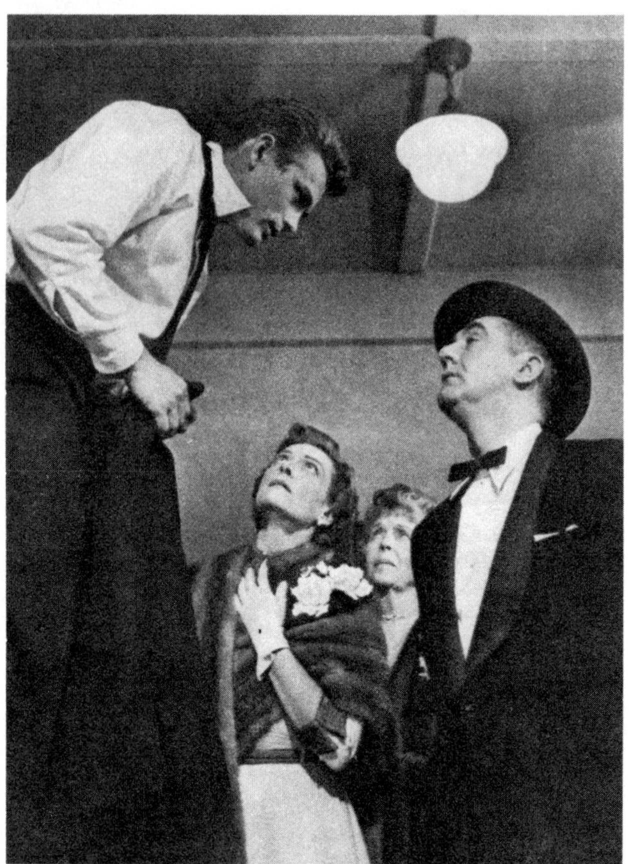

will they cheat jimmy again?

When Jim first appeared on-screen (*East of Eden*, above), a whole nation applauded one of the most outstanding talents the world has ever seen. Help him get the Award he merits.

This Is Jimmy's Last Chance For the Oscar He Deserves—Here Is How You Can Help Win It

■ It was the night of Wednesday, March 21st, 1956. All through the country hundreds of thousands of people were glued to their television sets to watch the great ceremonies of the Hollywood Motion Picture Academy of Arts and Sciences, to share in the excitement of the giving of the treasured awards for the best acting performances of the year.

Came the moment when lovely Grace Kelly opened the envelope containing the magic name of the man designated as the year's greatest actor. It was Ernest Borgnine acclaimed for his *Marty*.

A great collective sigh rolled through the nation. Tears came to the eyes of many of us. Not because of the man who won the award—but because of the man who didn't, who, it seemed, had been forgotten because he was dead, but who wasn't dead in the hearts of those who loved and admired him.

Immediately the mail began to barrel up in publication offices. Our MOVIE LIFE mail room was swamped with anguished letters the tenor of which was, "Unfair! Jimmy Dean deserved the Award!" "Why did they forget Jimmy?" Suddenly the fame of (*Continued on page* 67)

JIMMY DEAN

(*Continued from page* 41)

Jimmy Dean was even greater than before because it seemed that he was being discriminated against simply because he was dead.

Right now, even as you are reading this magazine, members of the Screen Actors' Guild are making their nominations to the Academy for the best acting performance for the awards in March, 1957. Right now, even as you are reading this, the Board of Governors of the Academy are considering whether or not to create a special posthumous award for Jimmy Dean.

Our suggestion is that if you honestly feel that Jimmy deserves an award for his performance of Jett Rink in *Giant*, for this, his very last role, that you send a postcard or a letter to the President of the Motion Picture Academy of Arts and Sciences, 9038 Melrose Avenue, Hollywood 48, California, saying, "Please see to it that James Dean gets an Academy Award. He deserves it because . . ." At the same time write a note to your favorite actor, at the same Academy address, urging that Jimmy's name either be placed in nomination or definite arrangements be made to make a special posthumous award.

Naturally, members of the Screen Actors' Guild, the president and board of governors of the Academy and its members will vote conscientiously and according to their true belief, but it might help them to make up their minds for Jimmy if you were to indicate *your* belief, if they were to see the public's great interest.

So write today. Let's make sure Jimmy Dean gets his Academy Award. It's his very last chance. THE END

Why Are Jimmy Dean Fans Switching To Tony Perkins?

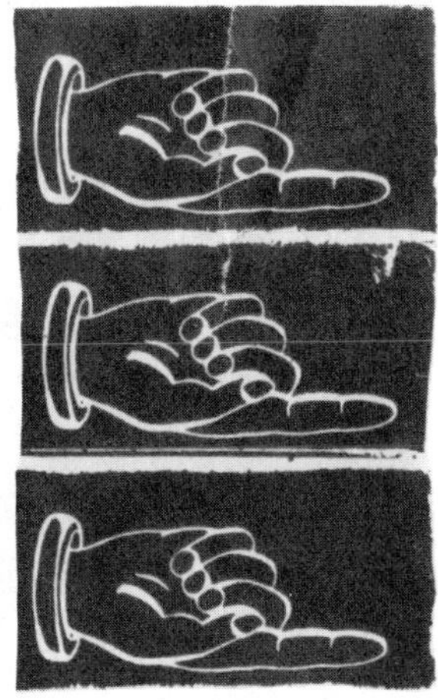

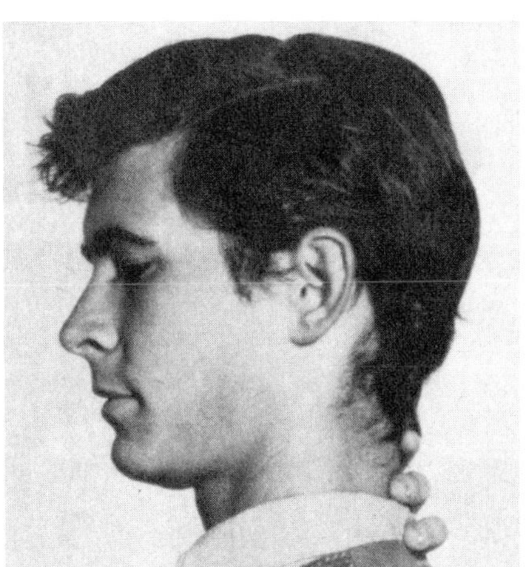

EVERY MORNING AT MAIL TIME we get a new batch of mail and most of these letters concern various personalities in the limelight.

We put these letters in pigeon holes (when we can get the pigeons to leave) under their various headings such as "Hound Dog Letters," "Love Letters to Tommy Sands," (sung by Pat Boone) and so forth.

Because of a recent splurge, we've opened up another file for *"Letters From James Dean Fans Who Have Switched To Anthony Perkins."*

Most of the letters indicate that Anthony has the same shy, unassuming, almost bashful set of features that Dean possessed. No one has switched from James Dean to Marlon Brando, for instance. And the letters lead us to believe that no one has switched to Tony Perkins from, say, Tony Curtis. It's always from James Dean to Tony

Tony undoubtedly must stir up the same kind of emotions in the same people that Dean did. As a result, the file of "Letters From James Dean Fans Who Have Switched To Anthony Perkins" keeps
50 growing.

WHEN JAMES DEAN DIED he left behind a dull, aching emptiness in the heart of America's youth.

The quiet, erratic rebel from the mid-West was a walking, talking symbol of the unrest and commotion that bubbled inside the teenager's body. When he died, it was as if part of each of his fans had died along with him.

What brought him so close to everyone was his depth and awareness of all the problems that bother all youngsters in the troublesome process of growing up. He lived the difficulties, breathed the problems and fought to be free and honest with himself and not be subjected to the whims of a stiff-backed society that frowned on off-beat behaviour. Simply, he wanted to do what he wanted whenever he wanted.

Dean wanted to be understood, yet he resented anyone prying. He wanted to be popular and likeable but he resisted if someone tried to force him to smile politely at a certain moment. You knew this. You could see it by the way he sat and sulked and bit out salty comments that his acting reflected his general attitude on life.

Teen-agers saw this and felt better. He was someone you could suffer with. Someone who had the same problems and who was fighting the same battle.

Then he died.

Extreme elements of his fandom insisted he was still living. Morbid rites were conducted to bring him back to life. The weird nature of these goings-on received bad publicity and brought a distorted picture of Dean's warmth and ability to those who didn't understand him.

But those who saw him and loved him were crushed. Their James Dean was gone. The mirror he held up to life's problems was shattered. They had lost a close friend. And that's the way it stayed. Fans were convinced that no one could ever take his place. They resented a newcomer being called "another James Dean." They wouldn't hear of it.

Now, another high-strung, moody young man has appeared on the scene, taking strong, silent steps to the hearts of the fans who were committed to James Dean.

Tony Perkins.

This slim, gangling, dark-haired star has the same boyish yet brooding features that distinguished Dean. He can be friendly or aloof, affable or stubborn, intense or carefree, depending on his mood at the moment.

Tony resents being called "another anything." When told he was being termed another Marlon Brando, he replied. "Not me. I never wear a T-shirt."

Whether or not he is "another James Dean" isn't important. The important thing is that he seems to be filling the vacuum

PERSONAL
ROMANCES
PDC
TEEN-AGE
DEVIL
GIRL
PERSONAL ROMANCES/APRIL 25¢
I WAS
JIMMY
DEAN'S
WIFE
HORROR IN OUR HOME
MARRIED
TO A
BRUTAL
RIVER RAT
Ideal
MAGAZINE

SEX AFTER DEATH

IN SCANDAL AND ROMANCE MAGAZINES

We're in Scandal Land, domain of tough-talking, no-punches-pulled exploitation magazines. Right from the opening salvo of "Did James Dean Really Die?" you know you're not in movie magazine fantasyland anymore.

"One day last December, the denizens of Hollywood, U.S.A., were shaken from their stupor by a weird event [which sent] showers of loose coconuts on the phony yogis basking on Sunset Boulevard. Though Cuckoolanders didn't know it, the cause of the phenomenon was very simple. . . . At the same moment, thousands of miles away, a striking blonde stood in an obscure Indiana cemetery mumbling prayers, and the sound they heard, that rumbling of the California earth, came from Rudolph Valentino turning in his grave."

The new star/old star comparison formula has a sneaky new twist: This time they're *both* dead!

"I Was a Friend of Jimmy Dean" is pinup girl Lynne Carter's kiss-and-tell story of how Jimmy picked her up while he was doing out-of-town tryouts for *The Immoralist* in Philadelphia. The stilted tone and formal language trigger the sort of "girls like I" dumb-but-sexy non sequiturs that Anita Loos specialized in.

"We sat discussing things: psychiatry, Marlon Brando, music. He laid his head on my lap and asked me to massage his temples. He recited Shakespeare . . . tried to kiss me several times and told me I knew nothing about art."

With "Did James Dean Leave a Son?" and the tale of the pretty carhop, Mary B., we enter the realm of Dean's Ghost Wives. "More and more, he turned to working girls like Mary B., who could give him more genuine sympathy and understanding than the glamorous starlets who were at his beck and call." True, it's a sordid tale, but we're hooked. Unfortunately, "until the mysterious Mary B. opens up and decides to talk, the truth of the most fascinating angle of his brief love-life may never be known." Thanks a lot!

"He started to look through my cheesecake pictures. He told me I must be very talented to take such lovely pictures. Jimmy loved art in every form and only saw the beauty of things."

Things get progressively more preposterous with "The Girl James Dean Was Supposed to Marry," a shameless, full-blown, farmer's-daughter fantasy. While "I Was James Dean's Wife" is simply a true romance story using James Dean as the mysterious, handsome stranger. This nine-thousand-word novella from *Personal Romances* magazine is heady stuff. It induces the emotional vertigo of a powerful gender-bending mood elevator. "I sat on the stool in the kitchen, sipping coffee, listening to Sinatra's 'That Old Black Magic.' Even now I can tell you everything about that moment—the way the coffee smelled, the yellow color of the cup, the feel of the breeze through the open window and the faint sound of traffic outside. . . . I was as happy as a girl can be." Alas for Mrs. Dean, it was September 30, 1955.

DID JAMES DEAN REALLY DIE?

Why the luscious dolls he left behind won't let the handsome ghoul rest in peace . . .

ONE DAY last December, denizens of Hollywood, U.S.A. were shaken from their stupor by a weird event. Suddenly, a high-pitched, piercing sound came from thin air and the ground trembled slightly, sending showers of loose coconuts down on the phony yogis basking along Sunset Boulevard.

Though Cuckoolanders didn't know it, the cause of the phenomenon was very simple.

At that same moment, thousands of miles away, a striking-looking blonde stood in an obscure Indiana cemetery mumbling prayers — and the sound they heard, that rumbling of the California earth, came from Rudolph Valentino spinning in his grave.

After thirty years of being the world's #1 ghoul-magnet, Rudy was suddenly discovering that he has a real tough competitor in the late James Dean.

THEY ALSO SERVED

If Rudy Valentino could become a legend, why not Jimmy Dean?

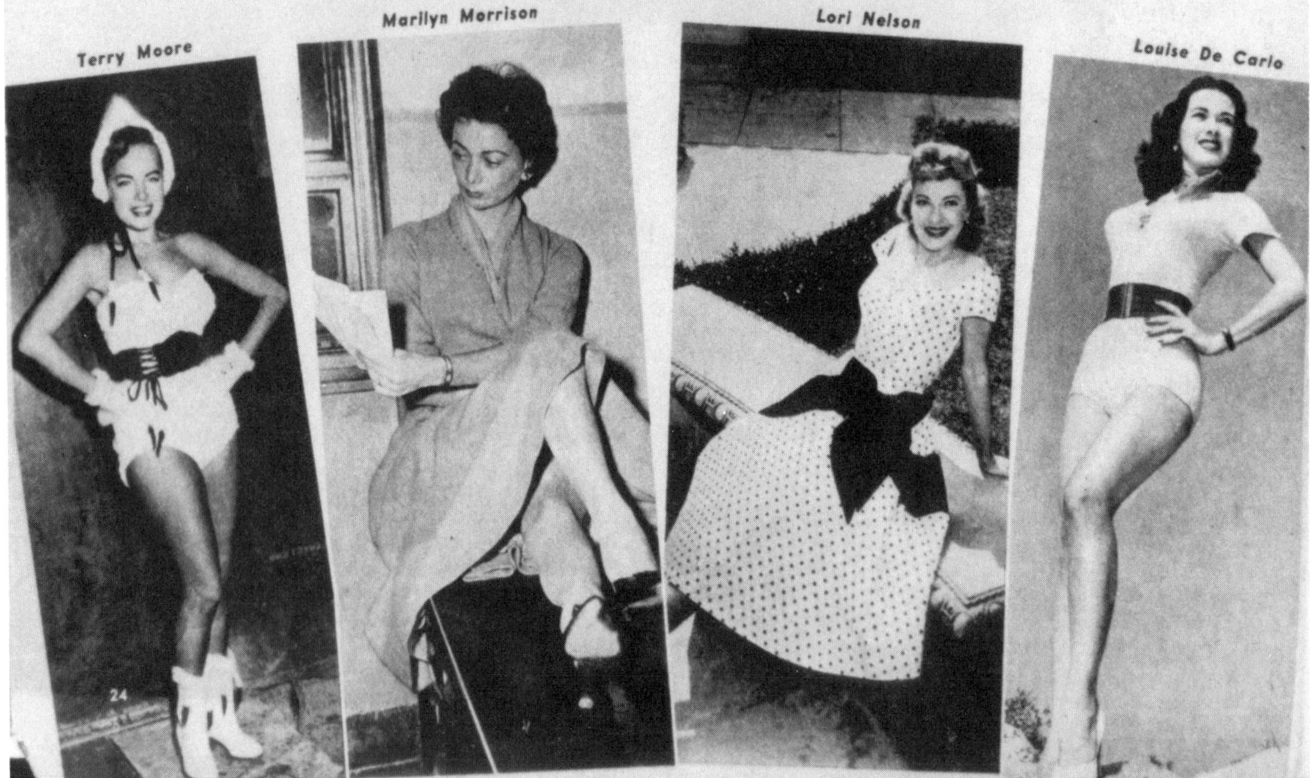

Terry Moore — Marilyn Morrison — Lori Nelson — Louise De Carlo

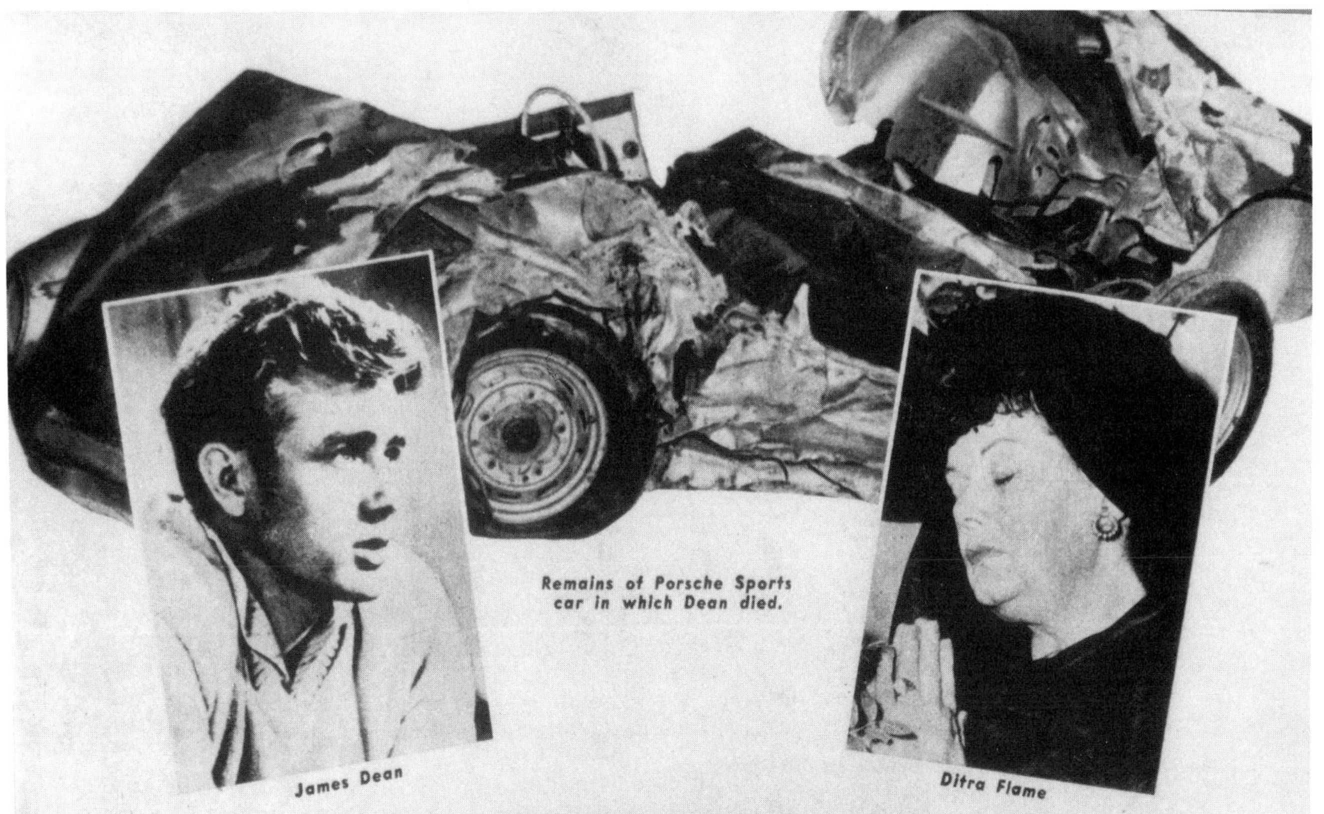

Remains of Porsche Sports car in which Dean died.

James Dean

Ditra Flame

THE GHOUL & THE FLAME

The sound they heard was Rudy spinning in his grave . . .

It was August 23, 1926, when Valentino kicked off, supposedly after a too-torrid night of amour (RAVE, August 1954), and the antics that his fond female fans have gone through ever since are nutty even for Hollywood. Aside from the mysterious "Woman in Black" who shows up to mourn at his graveside each August 23rd, there are women who send flowers every week—and at least two demented dames have gone to join the Great Lover via the suicide route.

It's still too early, of course, to tell how Jimmy Dean will last over the long haul—but Hollywood insiders report that he's gotten off to one helluva fast start.

Item: When word of Dean's car-wreck death came through last September 30th, pretty Liz Taylor was so affected she had to be lugged off to the hospital.

Item: On the same date, nifty Leslie Caron vowed to a pal that she'd never dance again.

Item: That striking-looking blonde who mumbled prayers beside Dean's Indiana grave was Maila Nurmi, erstwhile Vampira of West Coast TV and erstwhile girl friend of Mr. D., who'd traveled thousands of miles out of her way just to stand at the sacred plot of ground.

When you toss in the millions of idiotic teen-agers who drizzle tears into their coke at the merest mention of their screen idol's name, any guess as to how it'll wind up is enough to make the hair of the MGM lion stand straight on end.

RUDY VS. JIMMY

Impartial laboratory tests reveal that the greatest difference between Rudy's ghouls and Jimmy's is the superior quality of the latter. To put it mildly, the dames who revere Valentino are the choicest collection of fruit and nuts outside a Christmas plum pudding.

Number One of the motley crew is that famed "Woman in Black" herself, whom we referred to earlier as "mysterious"—mysterious only if you don't know Hollywood. She goes by the flossy name of Miss Ditra Flame and shows up regularly at Rudy's grave, entirely undeterred by cynics who doubt that she ever even *met* Valentino. Back in 1943 she wangled a charter for a "religious" outfit called *The Hollywood Rudolph Valentino Memorial Church*, and any RAVE reader who thinks that this is a pretty loony racket is entirely correct.

After one of her tombside circuses, staged for benefit of bored photographers, Ditra tossed a fourth-rate vaudeville act which she described as a "Memorial Show." The piece-de-resistance was her personal rendition of a lousy song called *Candlelight*, described

25

Leslie Caron

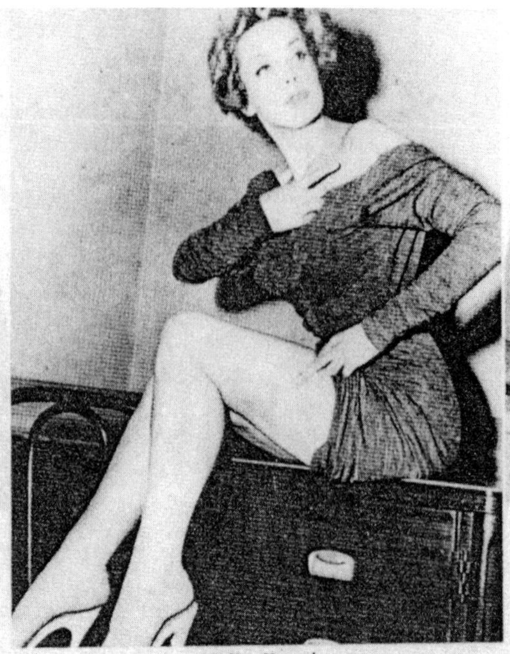
Maila Nurmi

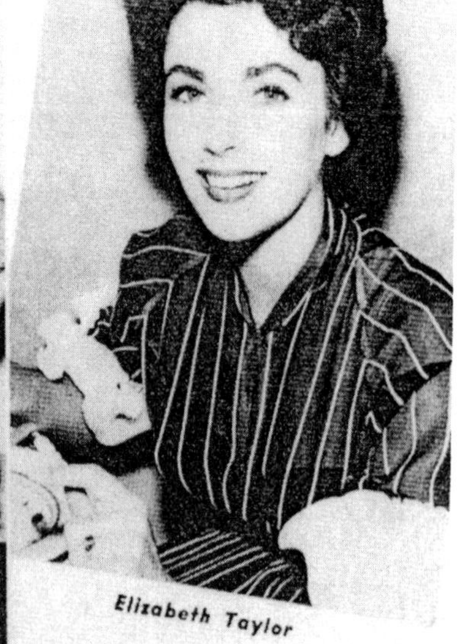
Elizabeth Taylor

THEY ALSO SERVED (CONT'D)
Any, or all, may join the crew of grave worshippers . . .

DID JAMES DEAN REALLY DIE?
CONTINUED

on the sheet-music version as "From a poem by RUDOLPH VALENTINO to DITRA FLAME." The whole affair was such a shambles that even Ditra's press agent quit.

Another of Rudy's self-styled "secret loves" is one Carol E. McKinstrey, who took out a charter for a set-up called *The Valentino Memorial Church of Psychic Fellowship*. When last heard of, this strangely-feathered bird was holding seances at Rudy's old hacienda and waiting for him to finish dictating a screenplay via some sort of psychic Western Union.

The real trouble with Valentino, from the female-worship point of view, is that there's considerable evidence he didn't give much of a damn about gals. The same cannot be said about James Dean.

Though dark, broodsome Jimmy struck out more often than he scored, strangely enough, it certainly wasn't from lack of trying.

Whether Liz Taylor was overcome simply because she'd just finished making *Giant* with him, or from some more intimate reason, is shrouded in the mist of history. But insiders point out that the shooting of *Giant* coincided with some very spicy turmoil in Liz's married life. The Taylor-Michael Wilding wedlock has long been considered shaky, but since Dean's death it's been like a skyscraper erected on a foundation of strawberry Jello.

RAVE's international spy ring recently sent us word of billing-and-cooing between luscious Liz and hambone Vic Mature, while Michael was seen enjoying himself in foggy London with Anita Ekberg.

JIMMY & VAMPIRA

If there's some mystery about Liz Taylor's upset over Dean's unhappy demise, there's none whatever about Miss Maila Nurmi's. Better known as Vampira, she had a friendship with Jimmy which ended only when the sultry actor switched to starlet Ursula Andrews.

And there were a raft of other beauties in Dean's short, unhappy life—any, or all, of whom may well join the crew of grave worshippers.

At one time he was prominently linked with Marilyn Morrison, luscious ex-mate of weeping Johnnie Ray. There's no evidence that Marilyn is anything but a 100% healthy American girl, but a hitch of holy deadlock with Mr. Ray, followed by a spell with Mr. Dean, might be enough to make any healthy American girl turn oddball.

Others who fell under Dean's spell were pretty Lori Nelson; a well-rounded chick named Louise De Carlo, who adorns the chorus line of *Guys and Dolls;* Swedish lovely Lili Kardell; and teen-age beauty Natalie Wood, who shimmered with him in *Rebel Without a Cause.*

26

A TORCH FOR PIER ANGELI

There are well-informed folks who believe that Italian Pier Angeli, now Vic Damone's ever-loving, was James Dean's only true love. It has even been said that it was his torch for pretty Pier which made him take up the sports-car racing which led to his death. Be that as it may, it's a fact that Dean did have the hots for Miss Angeli and went into something of a tailspin when Miss A.'s suspicious Mama forbid her chick to see the guy. Jimmy went around crying in his beer that no one loved him, and acted so broodingly on the set of "Giant" that mild-mannered director George Stevens once blew his top at him in front of the whole company.

The picture of all these luscious females arriving at Dean's grave in Indiana each September 30th, draped in black and depositing fond wreaths on the headstone, is surely enough to give poor Rudy Valentino conniption fits when he considers his own crop of bags like Miss Ditra Flame.

But the worst of all is yet to come.

Among the gals who gave Jimmy the eye was that supreme bore—publicity-mad Terry Moore.

Maybe Terry hasn't yet thought of the possibility of appearing at James Dean's Indiana grave in a sombre veil, daintily covering a bunny-fur Bikini. But give the girl time and you can bet that she will!

ANITA EKBERG *(ABOVE)*
A skyscraper erected on a foundation of Jello?

COOING TWOSOMES
The trouble with Rudy was that he didn't give much of a damn about girls . . .

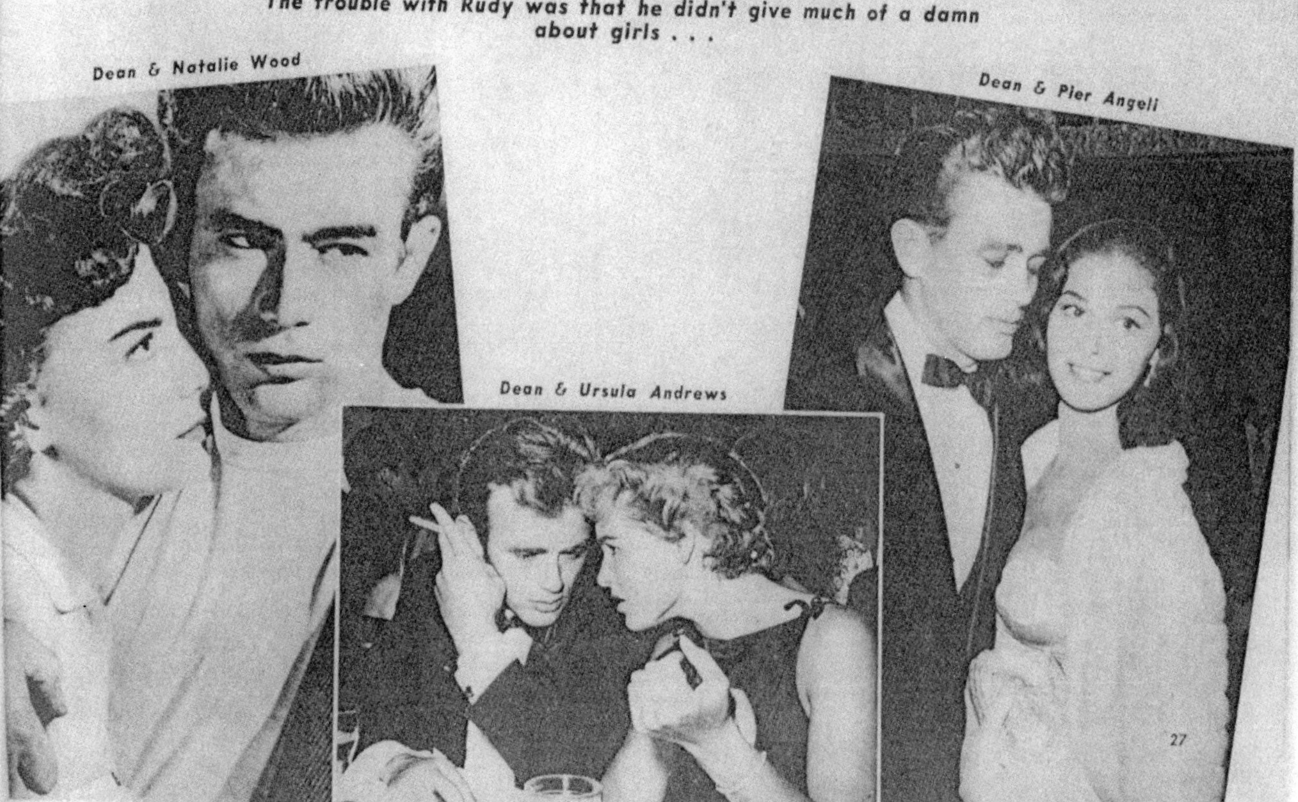

Dean & Natalie Wood

Dean & Ursula Andrews

Dean & Pier Angeli

27

"I WAS A FRIEND OF JIMMY DEAN"

A fresh impression of the late great idol by one who knew him intimately

I am writing this story in the early hours of the morning. It is the best time to talk about a boy who has become a legend surpassing even that of Valentino.

As I watch the dawn breaking, I can find the words I have been desperately searching for to describe my relationship with Jimmy Dean. New incidents keep popping into my head—incidents that were so deeply buried in the back of my mind it has become a pleasure to recapture them.

Before I begin, let me assure you that this is a completely honest account of our friendship. I am not attempting to color this story by describing myself as a "secret love." I am only trying to give a true and faithful picture of Jimmy as I knew him. What we had between us I consider beautiful and rare, and I am proud to put it into words.

Jimmy wasn't ready for love when I knew him. Even if he fell in love, he would have been afraid to declare it for fear of being rejected. He was tormented by insecurity and attempted to conceal it with an air of superiority.

This is our story – his and mine. Through it you will meet and appreciate, as I did, the true Jimmy Dean.

LYNNE CARTER

IT'S BEEN two years since his passing that I first met Jimmy. It was one of those rare accidents where you find yourself face to face with someone you have admired from afar—like having a date with your favorite movie star.

THE AUTHOR: LYNNE CARTER—SHE KNEW JIMMY DEAN
"I noticed how well-built he was . . . he didn't seem a bit shy about appearing half-nude in front of me . . . "

JIMMY & LYNNE
"Jimmy laid his head on my lap and asked me to massage his temples . . . he tried to kiss me several times and told me I knew nothing about the art. He said he would teach me."

I had seen Jimmy many times on TV. I always made it a point to catch his shows. He was my favorite actor.

It was a rainy Saturday afternoon in Philadelphia and I was returning home after making some modeling rounds. I stepped into a doorway on Chestnut street to adjust my umbrella and accidentally brushed shoulders with someone. When I turned to apologize, I found myself staring at the face which had become so familiar to me on my TV screen. Automatically, I ended my apology with the words: "Mr. Dean."

He smiled, a boyish grin with dimples. His clothes were shabby and he wore boots, which seemed to be a trademark with him.

We struck up a conversation about the play he was appearing in – *The Immoralist* – with Geraldine Page and Louis Jourdan. I had purchased a ticket for the following Monday evening and Jimmy invited me backstage after the performance.

After the house lights dimmed, I was reluctant to go backstage alone. I had always been shy and when something intrigued me, all I seemed able to do was retreat. Slowly, I turned the corner to the backstage entrance, trying to talk a little spirit into myself.

It had been snowing and the streets were icy and sloppy. The only other person waiting inside was a boy with glasses – a "milquetoast" type, but very sweet and sincere. He said he was waiting for a glimpse of the actors, that he wanted to act himself. When I told him I was waiting for James Dean, he lit up like a Christmas tree.

Suddenly, I heard Jimmy banging outside the upstairs window, shouting hello and something about having his picture drawn. I suppose he thought the boy and I were together, for he told us to go to the Russian Inn and he would join us.

31

"I WAS A FRIEND OF JIMMY DEAN"

CONTINUED

When Jimmy did join us, we had one of the most stimulating and colorful conversations I have ever engaged in – chiefly about the theatre.

Jimmy's constant use of four-letter words shocked me at the time. He was full of fire and intensity as he blurted his opinions on his favorite subject. He spoke highly of Miss Page's talents and called Louis Jourdan a French pain-in-the-ass. He felt Jourdan was only adequate in a part which someone more capable could have done great things with. He expressed contempt for Jose Ferrer for his exaggerated artifices in "Cyrano de Bergerac" and insisted that he was only an expert in fooling an audience. He scoffed at the idea of Dan Dailey competing with Sir Lawrence Olivier for an Oscar in the Hollywood Academy Awards competition. He considered Laurette Taylor and Olivier as the greats of the acting profession.

He was direct and honest and eloquent, and we might have remained in the restaurant forever had the manager not requested us to leave. We had become so absorbed we were the only customers left, having conversed for four straight hours.

HIS CHANGING MOODS

We went to the Hickory House, where Jimmy indulged in a huge banana split. He always had a good appetite although he was a little on the thin side. He was amusing, trudging playfully along in the snow and pulling my hand along in his. This was typical of Jimmy's many moods, changing from one extreme to the other.

When the other boy said he hoped to go to New York and become an actor, Jimmy told him never to permit the big city to frighten him, to feel that he was in full control – like walking into a drug store with the thought that "this is *my* drug store, it is here at my disposal so long as I have sufficient funds"– which was confidence in one's abilities.

Jimmy delivered this lecture on the steps of his hotel, where I had given him my phone number, written in eyebrow pencil – for he had expressed a desire to visit Philadelphia's museum the following Sunday afternoon and wanted me to accompany him.

The following Sunday he called and cancelled our date, saying the play was being rewritten and a rehearsal was scheduled for that afternoon. I was disappointed, for I had anticipated inviting him home

32

for dinner. We made a date for Tuesday evening after the play. This time I felt much braver on approaching the stage door and was shown to his dressing room.

Jimmy hadn't arrived backstage, so I sat meekly waiting. When he appeared, he apologized and said the cast had been kept after the curtain calls for a pep talk. He seemed irritated.

On his dressing table I saw two telegrams. One was addressed "To my Immoral One" and was signed "Bobbie." He said she was an actress he had been dating. The second telegram referred in part to "now being able to afford those new curtains" and was signed "Jane." Jimmy said she was his agent and one of his close friends.

He spoke as I watched him remove his makeup and strip off the garb he wore as an Arab boy. He didn't seem a bit shy about appearing half-nude in front of me, so I attempted to conceal my uneasiness by constant chattering. It was the first time I noticed how well-built he was and commented on his muscles. He said he had been active in sports during his college days.

He put on his boots, dungarees, a patched sweater, and a pea-jacket, and we started walking towards the Hotel St. James, where he was staying. He said he had forgotten his wallet. Being naive, I accepted his invitation to accompany him upstairs, and my naivete couldn't have been more appropriate. Once in his room, he made no physical pass of any kind, but proceeded to show me his new charcoal-grey suit and even tried on the jacket for me. I think it was the only suit he owned. He disliked conventional suits and said he felt much more comfortable in an old pair of pants and a jacket.

He called the desk clerk for phone messages and was told that "Blanche" had called again. He explained to me that a character who called herself Blanche Dubois kept leaving messages for him and annoyed him with phone calls. Blanche, I knew, was the name of the nymphomaniac in *A Streetcar Named Desire.*

He showed me some pictures taken at a party in a friend's apartment in Greenwich Village. One showed him with a big-breasted blonde whom he said was French. He commented on her outstanding features in earthy language. Then he said he was hungry and we went to the Hickory House again, where he had a large meal and discussed acting. It was the only subject he liked to talk about.

He would end a serious talk by tickling my nose or giggling boyishly. In the midst of a meal, he would try to balance a knife and fork, or perform a similar feat at the table, with the intensity of a groundhog.

Before he put me into a taxi, he slipped a bill in my hand to cover the fare. When I refused it, he gave it to the driver. Then he kissed me goodnight – the first time he ever kissed me.

We made a date for the next Friday night, but the

next day he called to cancel it – and since the play was leaving the following Saturday, he told me to call him in New York if I were ever in the city.

Four months later I went to New York, intent on making it my new home. I phoned Jimmy at the theatre where he was playing. He asked me if I were free later that night and I suggested he call me at my hotel. However, I spent the evening sightseeing and didn't return until 2 A. M. I was sure I had missed Jimmy's call, but when I asked my roommate she said there had been no calls.

This was my introduction to Jimmy's indifferent attitude toward time – for as I was preparing for bed at 3 A. M., he phoned me. He asked me to accompany him on a motorcycle ride and told me I could wear a pair of his pants.

I went to his apartment on the top floor at 19 West 68th Street. The hall was dark and it was difficult for me to find my way up the rounding flight of stairs. Jimmy met me halfway up and led me to his apartment — which consisted of one medium-sized room, candle-lit, with a few pieces of battered furniture. He had several shelves full of books on acting, bullfighting, and philosophy, plus some foreign publications. At one side of the room stood his bed and an object which resembled the insides of a radio. It was a radio, but he attempted to play it without any luck. An occasional squeak was all he could get.

On one wall was a huge white sign with black letters reading, "Please Keep On The Grass," with a green mat on the floor directly beneath it. He said he was so annoyed at public signs telling people what *not* to do that it was refreshing for him to gaze at one offering a positive command.

He didn't mention the motorcycle ride at all. He commented on my dress and offered me a glass of wine. We sat discussing things: psychiatrists, Marlon Brando, music. Jimmy laid his head on my lap and asked me to massage his temples. While I did it, he recited Shakespeare. He tried to kiss me several times and told me that I knew nothing about the art. He said he would teach me.

As dawn crept through the windows, Jimmy suddenly recalled that he had a morning rehearsal for a show he was doing in the Village and was annoyed at himself for not knowing his lines. As we walked down the stairs, his landlord appeared and screamed at Jimmy for keeping a woman in his room all night. I was embarrassed and hurried on while Jimmy casually told him to "Go to hell."

He told me not to worry about the incident, hailed a cab, and slipped some money into my hand to cover the fare – something he never neglected to do.

Two mornings later I called Jimmy and to my surprise, he simply said "Hello" in a muffled voice and

LYNNE AS A MODEL
" . . . his landlord appeared and screamed at Jimmy for keeping a woman in his room all night."

"I WAS A FRIEND OF JIMMY DEAN"

CONTINUED

hung up. Apparently, I had awakened him and he was in no mood to converse. This was typcial of Jimmy, and sometimes I thought he carried his honesty too far.

A week later he called and asked me if I were in the mood for a movie. We went to Forty-second Street and ate hamburgers.

As always, we talked — and I learned that his great dream was to be a writer. He felt that writing was the most challenging of the creative arts, for the actor had something to work with and his chore was mainly one of interpretation, whereas the author created out of nothing.

He rarely spoke of his family and not once did he mention that his father was living. He gave me the impression that both parents were dead. He referred to his aunt and uncle as his parents. Only later did I discover that his father was alive. I don't think a true father-son relationship existed between them. But then, Jimmy was a difficult person to understand and his father evidently failed in this respect.

He spoke of his California days and of James Whitmore, the movie actor. He told me his family was Quaker and that he practiced no religion, but firmly believed in a higher power.

He never engaged in small-talk and rudely reminded me of this several times. It was customary for him to hang up in the middle of a phone conversation if he didn't feel like continuing it and only when I began to give him the same treatment did he call back and apologize. Somehow, I found it easier to forgive Jimmy than to remain angry at him.

AND THEN HOLLYWOOD

One evening, while I was visiting Jimmy in his room, he showed me a manuscript bearing the title, *East of Eden.* As I started to open it, he seized it from me and said no one was to read it.

He nonchalantly told me that he was going to do his first film under the direction of Elia Kazan. I think I was more excited than he was; at least I reacted that way. However, I've always felt that Jimmy was more impressed with the situation than he cared to reveal.

He spent the entire evening explaining the story. It was fascinating to hear him speak, he was so full of fire as he described several scenes — particularly the

34

JIMMY SEES LYNNE . . .
"He drank the half bottle of Scotch I had saved for the occasion . . ."

death scene with the father. When I saw the movie version of the scene, I couldn't help but smile to myself.

The following morning I bought a copy of the novel and read it that afternoon. I felt that I was participating in a very great secret. I knew Jimmy would be fine in the film.

That evening, on the phone, we discussed the novel and exchanged ideas. Several times Jimmy encouraged me to become an actress.

I didn't see or hear from Jimmy for a couple of months after that. Then I read in the gossip columns that a New York actor was in Hollywood for his initial role in an Elia Kazan film.

Subsequently, I read the excited reaction to Hollywood sneak previews of the picture, and the predictions that he would be a great star. Thus, began the accumulation of stories tagging him as an eccentric and odd-ball. I suppose he was, in a way.

I never thought I would hear from Jimmy again — but when I read in the New York papers that he was in town for a TV show, I decided to phone him. He said he was glad I had called, as it was difficult for him to reach me (I had no private phone and could only be reached on the hall phone).

I fired a barrage of questions at him about Hollywood and the publicity I had been reading about him, and teased him about being a full-fledged movie star. He seemed completely unaffected by his success.

When I said I wanted to see him on TV but had no set, he suggested that I go to Jerry's Restaurant and watch him from there. He told me to tell the bartender that I was a friend of his. He said he would call me on his next trip to New York, as he was leaving for Hollywood right after the show.

The next time I heard from Jimmy was a week or two before the New York premiere of *East of Eden.* He called and asked if he could come right over. I suppose he was lonely and in the mood for company. Sudden moods were common with Jimmy. Sometimes he would find a girl's company annoying and would be inexcusably rude, while at other times he seemed to crave it.

I'll never forget the last time I saw Jimmy. As I heard him coming up the steps, I opened the door to greet him. He was just rounding the corner of the hallway and the dim light fell on his face. He wore the same shabby clothes, the same boots and horn-rimmed glasses. I shall never forget that glimpse of him. That is how I shall always remember him.

We had much to talk about that evening. He lay on my bed and answered all my questions about Hollywood. He said he found Hollywood women "dumb" and that I was not to feel alone in warding off "makers." It seems a noted producer was discussing a movie with Jimmy and, after attempting to fill him with liquor, made a play for him. To use Jimmy's own words, his reply was "Man, this is where I cut out."

As for the slimy insinuations that Jimmy himself was a sex pervert because he frequented certain Greenwich Village hangouts, I find them ridiculous and unfounded. He never felt it was his right to openly judge any one person or thing. He accepted people on the basis of their character and not their color or class.

He drank the half bottle of Scotch I had saved for the occasion and we celebrated the success of his movie. Then he proceeded to play my collection of mambo records. He seemed to be on a dancing kick, and when he learned that I was a mambo dancer, he urged me to teach him the steps. We made a date to take mambo lessons together at the Palladium every Wednesday night when he returned to New York.

While the music was playing, he ran into the kitchen and seized two of my large pots and sat on the floor with a cigarette hanging from his lips, beating out the rhythm.

I don't think I ever enjoyed an evening more. Jimmy was warm and affectionate and more approachable than he had ever been since I knew him. I liked him more than ever. He laughed frequently, a silly cackle that he possessed. He decided to take a shower, and reappeared with a towel around his waist and, as ever, wearing his boots. He said he was going out for a pack of cigarettes and stood in the open doorway. He said, "Modesty is for the birds." I noticed the absence of his underdrawers and he explained that he had been going without any because they were all dirty and he hadn't bothered to wash them.

He started to look through my cheesecake pictures. He told me I must be very talented to take such lovely pictures. I think Jimmy loved art in every form and only saw the beauty of things.

He decided to nap for an hour and told me to wake him. He slept with his boots on. In jest, I said: "I'll bet you'll even die with your boots on." He slept so peacefully I decided not to wake him and at 3 A. M. he jumped up and rushed out, saying he had an important Hollywood call he had to make and promising to call me in a few days. He flew down the stairs and out of sight.

I didn't know it, but that was to be the last time I would ever see Jimmy Dean.

On September 30th, 1955, at about 1 A. M., my roommate telephoned me from Philadelphia. She told me that a news flash announcing Jimmy's death had just been released over television. I was stunned. I told her she must be mistaken. But, when other friends called, I knew it was true.

Knowing Jimmy Dean was one of the most vibrating experiences of my life. Perhaps he has found the peace he was so desperately searching for. The mysteries of nature remain boundless, but none could be more unique in life than the mystery of James Dean.

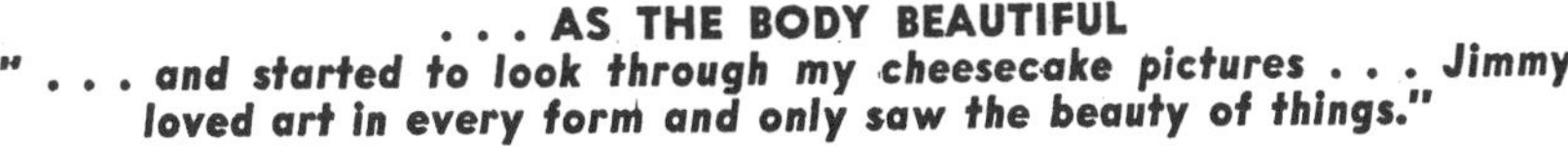

. . . AS THE BODY BEAUTIFUL
" . . . and started to look through my cheesecake pictures . . . Jimmy loved art in every form and only saw the beauty of things."

I Learned About LOVE From Jimmy Dean

The shapely photographer's model who was intimately acquainted with the late great idol reveals his romantic secrets

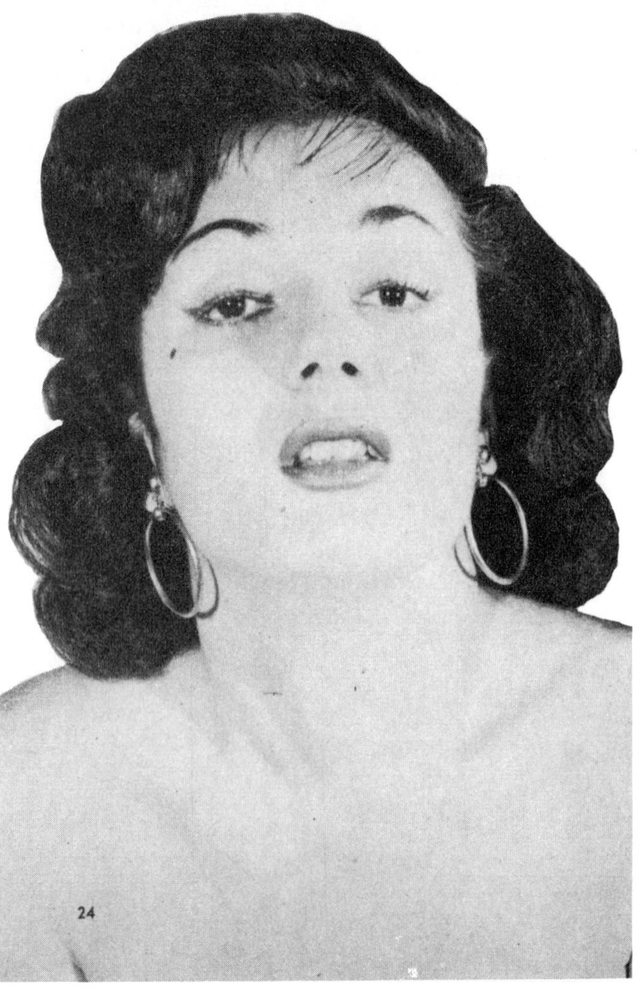

by Lynne Carter

Sir:
I have known James Dean all my life and I think you are a — — to print anything about James Dean like you printed. . .

Camille Laverne Dean
2242 West Franklin, Chicago, Ill.

Dear Mr. Phillips:
The article that was printed in your January issue is an outrage. This girl, Lynne Carter, should try and do some work to earn her living instead of lying to get her money. Anyone who would say that about Jimmy is his enemy instead of his friend. . .

Maria J. Campo
2509 S. Lambert St., Philadelphia, Pa.

Dear Editor:
If I had been in this girl's place, even if I had no respect for myself, at least for Jimmy's sake I would have kept those things to myself . . . instead of publishing them to the whole world. There are times when silence is golden. . .

Viola Miller
Dayton, Ohio.

DEAR IRATE READERS:
The hundreds of letters you sent me attacking my article on James Dean in the January issue of RAVE compels me to deliver an immediate answer.

The lack of intelligence displayed in most of these letters is ludicrous. The ignorance and pettiness of Mr.

PORTRAIT OF THE AUTHOR
She first met Jimmy in Philadelphia when he was shopping for a pair of boots. . . .

JIMMY & LYNNE
Many psychiatrists feel that the undying interest in Jimmy is a result of some form of self-identification. . . .

Dean's so-called "fans" is obvious. I could analyze your illiterate manners, but I'm sure it would accomplish nothing and the lead in my pencil is too valuable to waste on such advice.

When I decided to write an article about Mr. Dean, I did so with the idea of combating the morbid hysteria about Jimmy that has crept upon the American scene.

JIMMY LOVED LIFE

As I said in my article, I first met Jimmy during the winter of 1952 when *The Immoralist* was having its premiere in Philadelphia. He was shopping for a pair of boots at the time. His disdain for the conventionalities of life intrigued me. I had never met anyone like him.

Our first date was at the Russian Sun, a small restaurant in midtown Philadelphia frequented by theatrical people—and we later went to the Hickory House. This was also the scene of our second date, that same week. Jimmy ate a large meal and discussed acting. He never seemed to tire of the subject.

The next time I saw him was in his New York apartment at 19 West 68th Street, about three months later. Other dates consisted of impromptu phone calls, resulting in Forty-second Street movies, conversations lasting into the early morning, and listening to mambo records.

Jimmy loved to sit by candlelight. He seemed to find it relaxing. At our last meeting, when he

I Learned About LOVE From Jimmy Dean

CONTINUED

called and asked if he could come to my place, his first move was to light two candles I kept on a small table. Candlelight is a habit I have kept up ever since.

Jimmy was no ordinary person; he was fascinating. He had a way of leaving me confused and in a state of pleasant shock at the same time. He was a combination of many things: maturity and adolescence, meekness and rudeness.

On his last visit, he spoke of returning to California and his future role in *Giant*. When he didn't call after that, I went to his apartment to congratulate him on his fine performance in *East of Eden*. He wasn't in, and his landlord told me he had left the previous morning for Hollywood.

It was one year after his death before I revealed my friendship with Jimmy. The idea of making our relationship public never even occurred to me. Only after I was urged to do so by people who knew about the friendship, did I decide that sharing my experience with Jimmy would serve the interests of good taste and understanding.

It's quite natural for people to develop an abnormal interest in someone they've placed on a pedestal, particularly after his death. But my reflections on Jimmy's qualities, his faults as well as his virtues, cannot be regarded as defamation—as so many of you imply.

You so-called "fans" seem to possess an allergy to the truth, which is what Jimmy constantly searched for. Perhaps you should follow his example. You accuse me of lying and of desiring publicity simply because your immature minds refuse to accept reality. In denying my story you are unwilling to admit that Jimmy possessed human frailties. I wrote an honest account of Jimmy as he appeared to me. My only purpose was to reveal a colorful, complex character of paradoxical moods—moods which, in all probability, were a source of his greatness.

For an even more detailed account of Jimmy's life, I suggest that you read his biography by William Bast (Ballantine Books, 35c) a close friend of his, who gives a vivid account of his days with your idol. I have never met Mr. Bast nor did I ever hear Jimmy speak of him. He never discussed his friends with me, never engaged in small-talk of any kind.

There can be no denying Jimmy's talent (and I would be the last to do so), but the distinction between his creative ability and his personal shortcomings seems to confuse you. I should like to quote some passages from Mr. Bast:

> "I had never known such lack of communication as existed during his fits of depression. For my own peace of mind, I found it wise to ignore him, or avoid him completely. . . Very often the situation would become unbearable and anger would grow in me."

I recall that during one visit to his place on 68th Street, Jimmy showed me a few fan letters he had received from women who had seen him on television. His attitude implied indifference, even embarrassment. He had no desire to play the "television idol" and did not consider it a true reflection of his acting abilities.

I think if Jimmy were alive today, he would be shocked and disgusted at the hero worship displayed by over-emotional morons. To admire a person's work and applaud him for his contributions is one thing, but to let it overwhelm you to the extremes set forth in your letters is the real discredit to Jimmy's memory.

I desperately hope, in due respect to Jimmy, that his talent appealed to a better calibre of people than the illiterates who wrote to me. Jimmy always made it a point to surround himself with learned people. Anyone from whom he felt he could learn, he sought

It's natural to develop abnormal interest

out. Whether they were obscure or famous, he respected their intelligence. He could not tolerate ignorance or pettiness of any kind. He constantly tried to improve himself intellectually.

When I first met him, he bluntly told me I was infantile and recommended that I read several books. He suggested Stanislavski and Chekhov on acting, everything written by Shakespeare and Oscar Wilde, *The Little Prince* by Antoine de Saint-Exupery, Andre Gide's *The Immoralist,* and the dictionary.

Mr. Bast explains Jimmy's intellectual interests thusly:

> "It was no longer sufficient for him to be merely acquainted with the works of such artists as Matisse and Klee, writers like Colette, geniuses like Cocteau, now he had to understand the significance of the literary and intellectual movements that influenced their thinking. With amazing speed he was absorbing an understanding of art, literature, music and the professional world about him . . . he refused to stop at any limitations in his quest for experience. He insisted upon absorbing all there was for the human mind, soul and body."

In reference to his personality and desire for *truth* we find:

> "Through the years, Jimmy's personality characteristics had not changed, nor had his disposition. His moods had, as a matter of fact, become more and more frequent and each time seemed to be deeper and more complex. It seemed the more he found out about the world the less he liked it, and the more he pitied it . . . and when he saw himself, he was sometimes puzzled, sometimes sickened . . . what was real was real; what existed existed. There could be no denying the truth. His one major battle with that aspect of his own psyche was all too human. It was that which made him slip into patterns of thinking and behaviourism which he himself so violently opposed. There were instants when he would face himself candidly, the first to admit his faults and shortcomings. There were more when he turned a defensive back on his indiscretions and mistakes."

Many psychiatrists feel that the undying interest in Jimmy Dean is a result of some form of self-identification. If this is the case, it's about time you put a stop to this self-flattery. The very idea of any comparison is odious.

As for my own feelings about Jimmy, I can think of no better words to express them than by calling again on Mr. Bast.

BEAUTY IN THE BATH
Says she: "He bluntly told me I was infantile and recommended that I read several books. . . ."

> "As for myself, not only was he a beloved friend whose absence seems intolerable, but he was also a player through whom I was able to experience vicariously great portions of life which would have been, otherwise, totally lost to me. He was important first, because he was a living, breathing, feeling, thinking, erring human being, and, second, because he was simply a friend through whose guidance I was able to grow and through whose mistakes I was able to learn."

A sincere fan of Jimmy Dean,
Lynne Carter

in someone you've put high on a pedestal

18 Craze for speed proved fatal to Dean when he died in sports car crash. He's shown shortly before accident with trophies he won in auto races.

DID JIMMY DEAN LEAVE A SON?

A Persistent Story Coming Out of Hollywood Claims That the Teen Idol Fathered a Car-Hop's Baby Shortly Before he Died

By LARRY ASHENDEN

ONE of the most astounding stories yet to come from the Hollywood grapevine is the report that the late James Dean left a baby son. The rumor that Mary B.'s mysterious child could be none other than Dean's began making the rounds about three months after the sensitive, moody young actor died in the flaming crash of his Porsche sports car. Although there had been whispers touching on the subject before the fatal accident, the incredible report that Dean had left a son started moving with real intensity after his death.

It was an open secret that Pier Angeli, (who is not Mary B. of course) the slender, dark-haired graduate of New York's famed Actor's Studio, was Jimmy Dean's only true love. And Dean actually started down the road to self-destruction one Saturday night when he and Pier had their last date and she told him she had accepted Vic Damone's proposal on that very afternoon.

Friends say that was the greatest tragedy of Dean's life, and he began behaving like a pin-wheel gone berserk in an effort to forget what had happened. As most people close to Jimmy knew, glamorous starlets weren't the only girls in Hollywood he liked to take out for rides in his fancy sports cars. He also enjoyed rolling full blast into a drive-in restaurant for a chance to meet pretty car-hops who made themselves extra-available when Jimmy was on the lot.

And that was the way James Dean met Mary B. She was an exceptionally attractive car-hop at a drive-in on Sunset Boulevard, not too many miles from the Roosevelt hotel. After his heart-breaking good-bye to Pier Angeli, Dean came near the point

Jimmy with Pier Angeli, his one great love, who turned him down.

He tried to forget his heartbreak with film starlet Ursula Andress.

Terry Moore, always anxious for publicity, was another Dean date.

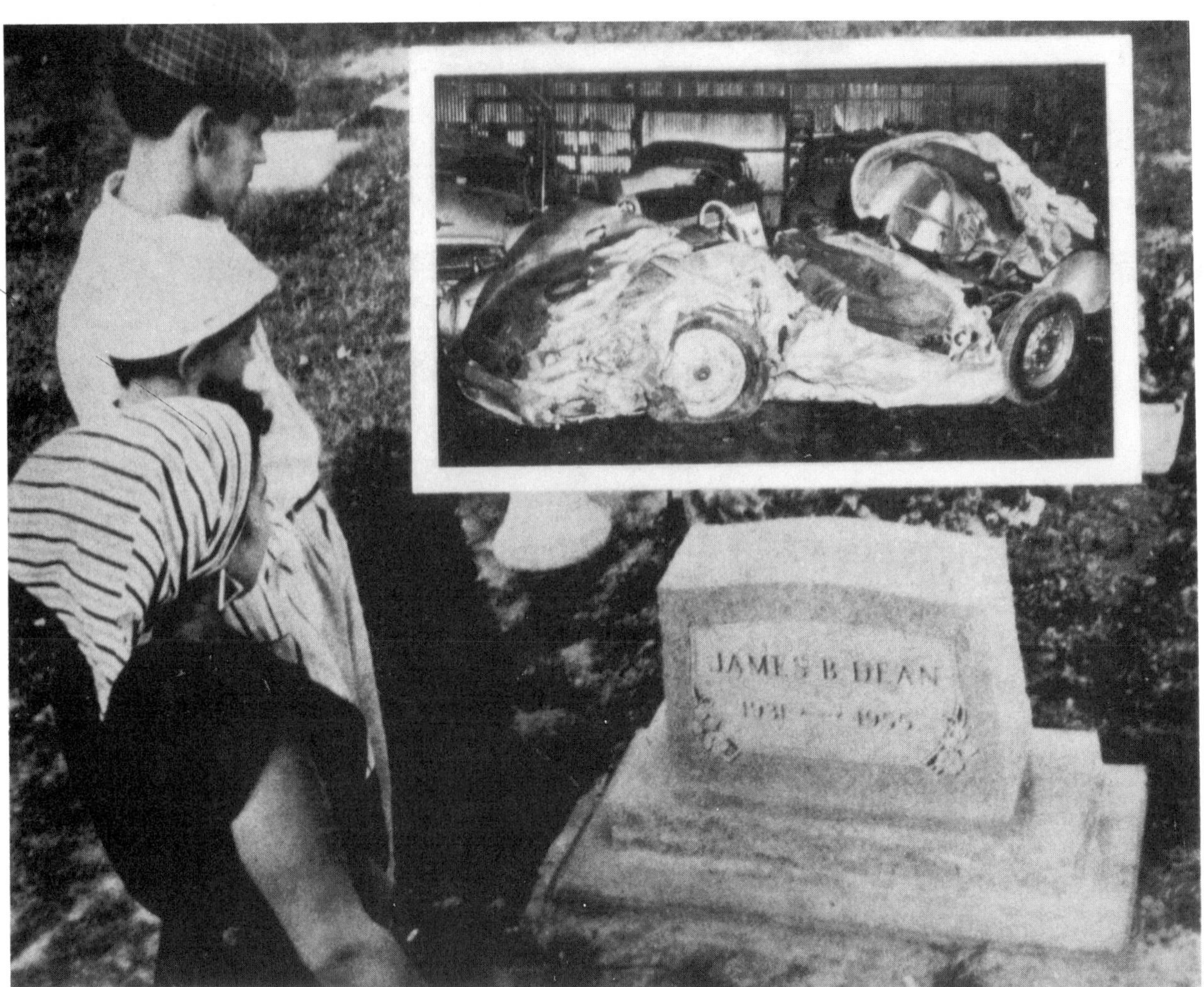

Thirty or 40 people travel to Fairmount, Ind., to visit Dean's grave every weekend. Inset: Ruins of the car in which he died in California.

DID JIMMY DEAN LEAVE A SON?

of completely turning his back on all actresses and showgirls. He turned more and more to working girls like Mary B. who somehow could give him more genuine sympathy and understanding than the glamorous starlets who were at his beck and call.

So "Mary B." whose actual name cannot be revealed, whirled to many a Pacific Coast pleasure spot with Jimmy during the months between November, 1954, when Pier Angeli married Vic Damone, and September, 1955, when Dean was killed. It was about the middle of the summer of 1955 when a well-known Hollywood news reporters picked up an intriguing bit of information about Mary B. The reporter learned that she had entered a hospital to have a baby boy out of wedlock, and that the child was later put into a foundling home and placed for adoption.

Who was the father? Although Mary B. would never say and behaved very much like a girl who was sworn to secrecy, many people around Hollywood who know the pretty car-hop say the father was none other than Jimmy Dean.

The crazy-quilt pattern of Jimmy's short but unhappy life points up at least the possibility of this bizarre outcome. Early in 1955, Dean went back to the little town of Fairmount, Indiana, where he was raised on a farm by an uncle and an aunt after the death of his mother. He brought a magazine photographer with him. One day Jimmy took the photographer to the town's mortuary. There he suddenly leaped into a casket, crossed his arms over his chest, and shouted "Shoot away!"

It seems that throughout his brief life, Dean was constantly concerned with a weird combination of love and death. His story began in the little town of Marion, Indiana, where he was born on February 8, 1931. Jimmy's (*Continued on page 65*)

DID JIMMY LEAVE A SON?

(Continued from page 20)

mother, Mildred, a slender, short, dark-haired farmer's daughter, met Winton, a tall, thin dental technician at a dance and married him a few months later.

After his mother's death, it was decided to send eight-year-old Jimmy to Fairmount to live with his grandmother. And it was Doctor James Deweerd, a Baptist minister in that little Indiana town, who first heard Jimmy pour out the haunting belief that he must be evil. Jimmy felt he was evil because his mother died and his father had sent him away.

Jimmy told the minister that he was afraid people would suspect how evil he was and not love him. The thought pursued Dean with such persistency that he began testing the people closest to him by giving them a hard time.

From that point on, Jimmy's behavior became neurotic almost to the point of being unbelievable. After graduation from high school in Indiana, he went to Los Angeles to live with his father. There he took a pre-law course at UCLA and was kicked out of a campus fraternity for busting a couple of fellow students on the nose. He changed his voice range from a middle range modulation, and alternated his speech between a mumble and a scream.

When he went to New York and entered Actor's Studio, his behavior led director Lee Strasberg to make a few predictions that turned out to be all too true. "I always had a strange feeling there was in Jimmy a sort of doomed quality," says Strasberg. "His behavior and personality seemed part of a pattern which inevitably had to lead to something destructive."

Getting along with people, particularly girls, always seemed a perpetual problem for Jimmy. One Hollywood actress recalls the first few weeks she knew him and how he would come up to her now and then and try to say something. But the words just wouldn't come out. "So do you know what he would do," says the actress. "He would hit me—hard too. Emotionally, I began to flinch when I saw him coming, and it was a long time before he was able to talk to me."

Dean quickly got a lot of attention on the Warner's lot. One coworker described him as always being "an uncooperative little tramp." In the studio cafeteria Jimmy would hum like a tramp, sing to himself, talk in a loud voice, and drum on the table with a spoon. At other times he would try to attract attention by slumping at a table, pulling his jacket or shirt up over his head and loudly slurping his soup. On the studio set, directors often had trouble finding him to do a scene. Then he would come running in at full speed, jumping and waving his arms before moving in front of the camera.

The glamorous names of Hollywood's beautiful girls zig-zagged back and forth across Jimmy's life with shooting star speed. In addition to Pier Angeli, his name was linked with Debbie Reynolds, Leslie Caron and Terry Moore. Others on his list of lissome beauties were Elizabeth Taylor, Natalie Wood and Ursula Andress, a blonde nineteen-year-old starlet who tried to make him forget Pier Angeli without success. But the weirdest of Dean's girl friends was Myla Nurmi, who made her name as Vampira of the television screen.

Vampira was eight years older than Jimmy, and she was believed to have some knowledge of mysticism and black magic. Friends say that she even predicted his death by blurting out at a party—"James Dean will die soon. I know because I am a witch." Not long before Jimmy's death, Vampira sent him a photo of herself beside an open grave with the message—"Darling, come join me."

But it was blue-eyed Ursula Andress who wept hysterically and tried to blame herself for his death. "I tried to help him out and to love him, but it just didn't work out," Ursula tearfully told her friends. "He needed help and was always asking for advice."

But until the mysterious Mary B. opens up and decides to talk, the truth of the most fascinating angle of Dean's brief love-life may never be known. If the report about a foundling son is true, then perhaps James Dean would live on—in the material form of another person—his own son. ■

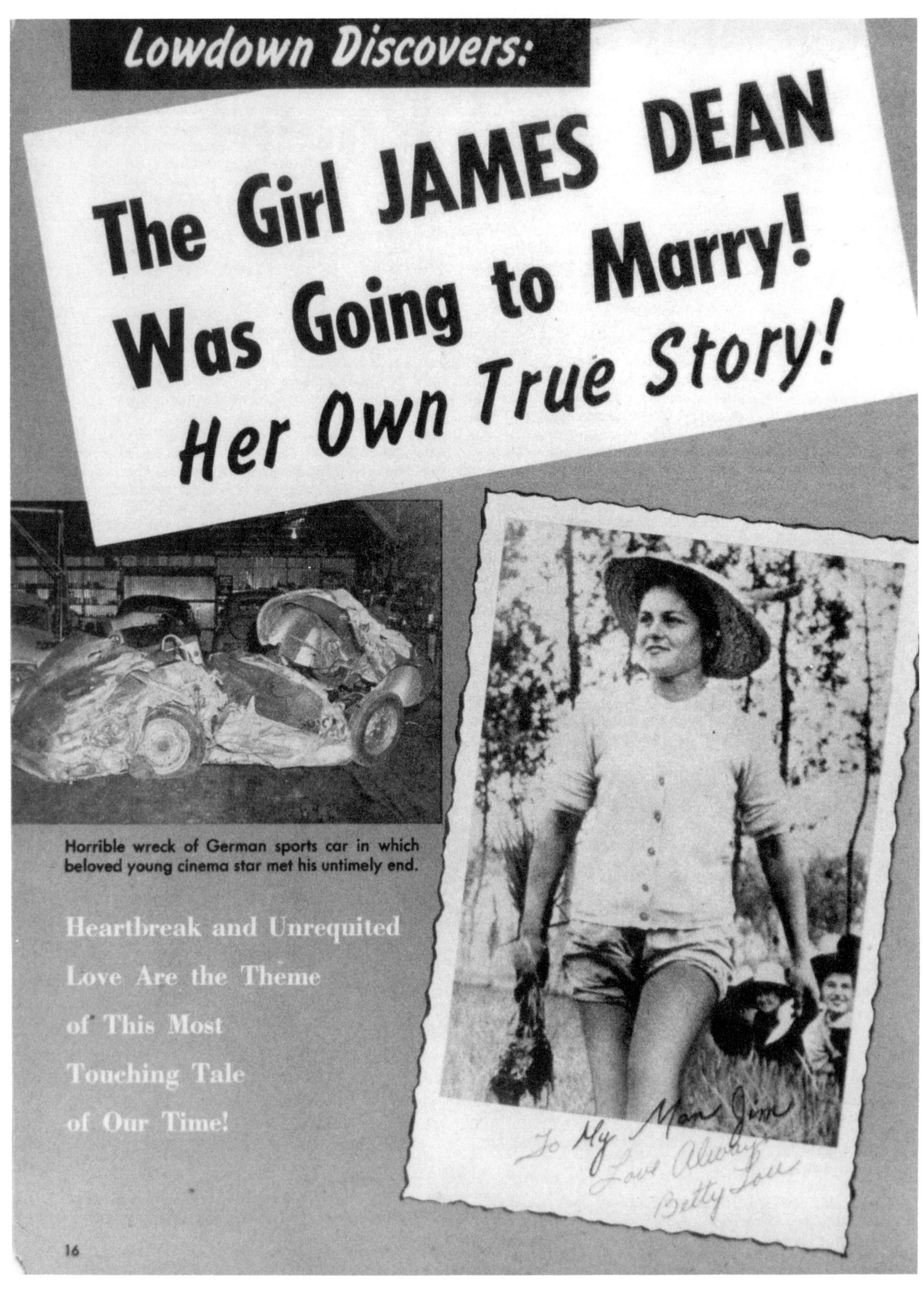
Lowdown Discovers:

The Girl JAMES DEAN Was Going to Marry! Her Own True Story!

Horrible wreck of German sports car in which beloved young cinema star met his untimely end.

Heartbreak and Unrequited Love Are the Theme of This Most Touching Tale of Our Time!

To My Man Jim
Love Always
Betty Lou

16

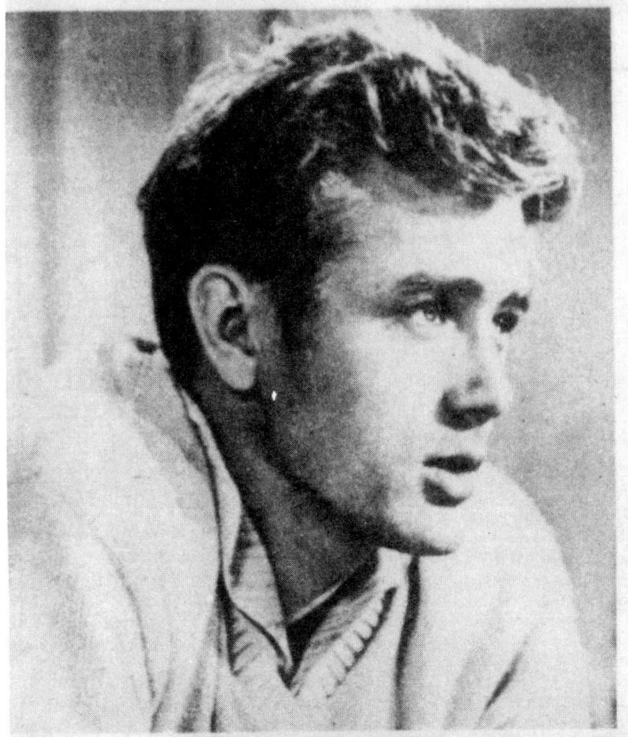

He postponed the wedding—until too late!

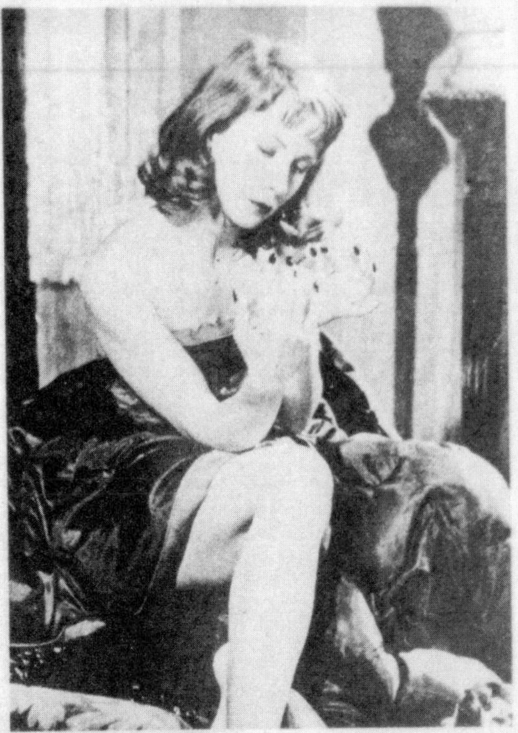

Julie Harris was rumored to have his heart.

By JOEL RALEIGH, Editor

(Editor's Note:—As is my custom, I personally investigate and write what I consider to be the most important story in each issue. It thus happened that I made five trips to Fairmount, Indiana, the tiny hamlet where James Dean was born—and where he was buried on October 8, 1955.

(The purpose of these trips was to settle once and for all the question of his death. It is a question alive in the hearts and minds of millions of American women of all ages who adore the memory of Jimmy.

(But while talking with people and running down the facts, I found myself obliged to frequently visit the cemetery. And it was there that I chanced upon one of the most disturbing stories ever to come to light.

(I met the girl James Dean was going to marry!

(He planned to marry her within a week of the date on which he lost his life.

(It happened this way. Often, I stood hard by his grave at the Fairmount burial grounds and observed the girls and women who came to weep, to pray. Many had come from thousands of miles away.

(But always, promptly at noon, I noticed a proud-faced girl arrive with a sprig of flowers. Tenderly she would kneel and place the sprig—simple daisies, the wild variety. Then she would catch her breath, rise and walk rapidly away.

(Observing her, I learned that daily she would return at six in the evening, and go through the very same ritual. She aroused my curiosity because she was beautiful, and also because her manner at the grave was somehow distinctive. She was not hysterical or weepy, just tender.

(I spoke with her and, to my surprise, she had a deep Southern accent. What was she doing in Indiana? Why did she come twice each day to pay homage at Jimmy's grave?

(She was alone in Fairmount. She was lonely. I managed to *(Continued on page 62)*

JIMMY DEAN

(Continued from page 17)

win her confidence. And finally, in response to my questioning, she presented indisputable evidence that she was Jimmy's girl, and he was her man.

(This evidence is presented to you in these sensational pages. They tell a tale that will rock the world of Jimmy Dean. It is a story I am proud to have uncovered. Read it and you will see why.)

•

Jimmy Dean died in his wrecked car right after he finished making "Giant," the current movie hit. He was expecting to marry Betty Lou Simmons just a few days after the picture was completed. It is as simple as that.

Betty Lou lives on a farm on the outskirts of Baton Rouge, Louisiana. She is today only nineteen, yet on her face are the sorrowful lines of the widow who was never truly married. This is the quintessence of her tragedy. For Betty Lou will never marry.

The tragic romance began on November 2, 1954. Jimmy was then on a short vacation which, as a rule, he took alone in a sports car, just knocking around here and there.

There hadn't been many girls in his life. For a while he ran about with Maila Nurmi, but she was too old for him and she also liked the "better" places. Jimmy was different. He preferred the simpler entertainment spots where a man could enjoy a beer in shirt-sleeves.

Another girl he took out occasionally, the beautiful starlet, Lili Kardell, liked him immensely and he liked her. But it was nothing more than a fleeting drug-store romance complete with one soda and two straws. That's about all. Maybe a good-night kiss, innocent as a child's caress.

Then, there was Julie Harris, the famed star with whom Dean did "East of Eden." Jimmy worshipped Julie and she tried to help him gain poise and presence. It was like a crush one has on a kind school teacher. That's about all the real romance Jimmy had off screen.

So here he was highballing along the road in his German Porsche sports car, seeking out back roads because he loved the lush overgrowth of Louisiana. He stopped off at Baton Rouge on some obscure business. Then he took a clay road leading to the north.

It was about two in the afternoon when he halted his car beneath a lichen hung weeping willow. He sat there drinking in the still, sylvan beauty. He was hot, dusty and perspired. He thought longingly of a shower or a dip in a stream. He consulted his road map. At that point his route was almost barren of towns. He was between Zachary, Louisiana and North Baton Rouge, an area which has the dreamlike quality of pre-Civil War days.

For a moment, he thought of driving into Zachary to see what he could find in the way of lodgings for the night.

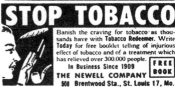

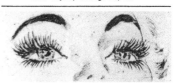

Any motel or tourist home with a shower would do. Suddenly he was attacked by a swarm of gnats. He tried to shoo them off with his road map but they just swirled about him.

"Try this," a melodious voice said. And there stood a girl, holding out a sheaf of rice leaves. Jimmy was startled. Then he smiled and looked at her again. She was wearing shorts and a halter. She was dark and lovely and his heart pounded within him.

Later on, he told her: "You know, in Hollywood I see the most glamorous girls in the world. Expensive faces and bodies. But you're wholesome and like a good piece of bread to a hungry man. You're like sweet well water to a thirsty man." That's the way he always spoke to Betty Lou.

Betty Lou invited him to get out his trunks, change at her house where she lived with a younger sister and her parents. Her father is a farmer who kneads out of the soil a bare living.

She got into the car with him and he drove slowly up the winding road to her humble abode. "Stranger here, Mom," she said. The mother, Mrs. Clara Simmons, smiled her greeting.

That's how it started. The two kids went swimming and Jimmy stayed for three days, insisting on paying for his room and board. It was the most idyllic experience of his life.

The kids held hands and then it was time for James Dean to go out of dreamland into reality. It was time for him to go back to Hollywood. He had his sports car shipped by freight and he flew. Before he left, he said: "Honey, I'll be back." She cried.

Oddly, she did not know that he was an actor. Living far from the cities, she was not in touch with the world, knew nothing of his fame and fortune. She accepted him for himself.

No, she did not know his importance, his stature. And if she did know, she would have been incapable of comprehending. For intrinsically, she is a simple farm girl with simple tastes.

When Jimmy got back to the Coast, he told his studio about his romance. A storm arose. "You're crazy, boy. You're on top of a career. You've got to have publicity when you get married. Your name has to be linked with the name of a big, big star. This is kid stuff."

They shouted at him, railed at him, told him he was a fool. But Jimmy insisted firmly: "My private life is my own."

They tried to tell him "for his own good" that he was throwing away his career. They also snickered, as Betty Lou recounts. "You don't have to marry that hillbilly if you want her so bad. You can have her without marrying her." Betty Lou has a letter from Jimmy that tells of this cynical and ugly attitude.

When a break came in Jimmy's schedule, he flew to Baton Rouge and hurried to the Simmons farmstead. He came bearing gifts and an offer of marriage.

He also came bearing clippings about himself and freely told the parents everything.

63

Ab Simmons, the father, was very grave. "Our girl is a nice girl. She knows nothing about the kind of life you lead. I will tell you frankly I wish you would go away and not come back."

Jimmy was stricken with pain and anguish. "I'm a small-town boy, born in a small town, with small-town ideas. That's how I want to live. I intend some day to retire and farm." He then blushed and apologized for his outburst.

The father looked at him quietly for a long while. "I believe you, boy. Be good to our Betty Lou." They shook hands and there it was; in effect, an engagement.

For a week, the kids had a fling. They went into Baton Rouge, danced, acted silly, petted; Betty Lou began to teach Jimmy how to talk with a Southern accent. A skilled actor, he took to it rapidly and this helped him a great deal when "Giant" was in the making. Mom and Pop Simmons laughed and laughed at the way he imitated their manner of speech.

Jimmy Dean made five flying trips to see Betty Lou. The wedding date was set for a week after the shooting schedule of "Giant" was to close. He planned to take Betty Lou on a sports car tour of the United States, make several more pictures and then move her parents and her kid sister to California where he intended to buy acreage in the Santa Clara Valley and raise prunes.

On March 6th, 1955, Jimmy sent Betty Lou a Western Union telegram that reads as follows:

BOUGHT YOU A DIAMOND RING AND HAVE PLACED ORDER FOR TEN COUNT THEM TEN CHILDREN STOP MISS YOU TERRIBLY AND PRAY FOR YOU EVERY NIGHT STOP PRAY FOR ME AND LOVE ME. JIMMY

Jimmy needed Betty Lou's prayers—for the following day he was killed.

There then broke the great weeping over America and Betty Lou's heart broke too, when she heard the news on the box radio set she had.

Betty Lou went to New Orleans and sold all the jewels Jimmy had bought for her. She got about $4,300 for them. Alone and wearing black, she entrained for the little town of Fairmount and the funeral. Her parents understood.

Betty Lou will soon go home again. She is just waiting for her money to run out, after which she will travel by bus to the little farmstead. She will walk the clay roads and sit beneath the great trees where once she sat with Jimmy.

She says she will never marry and this is to be believed. But she is wrong if she makes of her life a temple of mourning. Life must go on and the living must live.

It is good to know that Jimmy Dean had a soft island of peace and beauty, away from the hurly-burly of Hollywood, before he died.

And the press agents were dead wrong. For his marriage to the simple girl would have gotten for him more publicity than a romance with a gilded star. For all America loves a Cinderella, as indeed Betty Lou is. But for Betty Lou, midnight came too soon.

TALES FROM THE DARKSIDE

FROM SCANDAL AND OCCULT GENRES

Weary of all the unsubstantiated stories in circulation ("There was already too much information on the subject that was secondhand"), the author of "James Dean Speaks from the Grave" decides to go right to the source. "I wanted firsthand information for the readers of *True Strange,*" he explains. A medium, Mrs. Van Deusen, arranges a séance. There's just one thing they haven't counted on. The dead have rotten memories.

TRUE STRANGE: Ask him some of the details surrounding his birth.
MEDIUM: Born Marion, Ohio, in 1931.

Indiana, Jimmy—Marion, *Indiana*! How could you forget a thing like that? Well, we didn't come here for his curriculum vitae anyway. Dean is better on the "big questions."

"He believed he was put here to symbolize the confusion of young people," says the medium. This is getting serious; he's beginning to believe his press clippings.

"Dean had to die while still young because an older person cannot symbolize humanity's suffering," she continues, causing *True Strange* (and perhaps the reader) to conclude that "I must confess I was puzzled. But there's a lot of things we don't know about. How does the earth stay on a fixed course? What is electricity? Electronics? Radio waves? Television?" Nurse!

True Strange specialized in occult and supernatural stories, hence its tolerant attitude toward the spirit world. The scandalographers, on the other hand, prided themselves on maintaining the private eye's code of deduction and cool reason, even when dealing with a subject as elusive as black magic.

"After much checking and rechecking of the facts, after many talks with the persons involved, and after several days of taking exclusive on-the-spot photographs, the final decision was that the story should be told. . . ." So begins the Case of James Dean's Black Madonna. But confronted with voodoo vixen Vampira, the investigator's mind soon crumbles. "The rational mind revolts against anything to do with the evil arts—but sometimes one meets facts which are difficult to explain. Such as the fact that James Dean in the summer of 1955 became more and more moody. . . ."

No good would come of this, you can be sure. James Dean—victim of voodoo vendetta—is buried on October 8, 1955, "and on that very same day, as luck or something else would have it, Vampira's TV contract with the American Broadcasting Company was terminated." It's like electricity—there are some things you just can't explain.

The Mexican said: "That was Señor Dean in that car. He drives that road every night between sundown and sunrise. It is as though he is looking for something or someone. Or as if he is a lost spirit, looking for a place to rest."

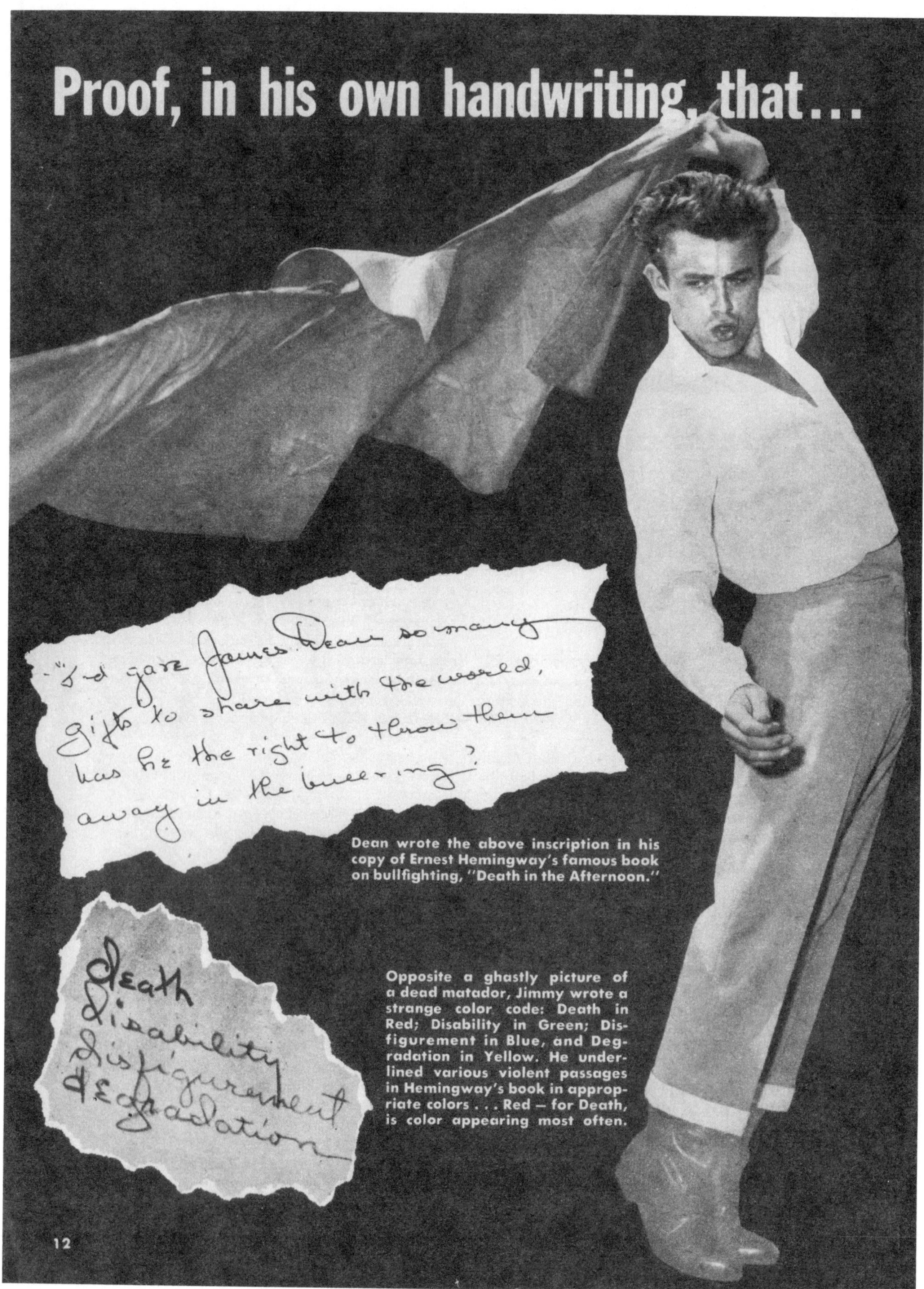

Proof, in his own handwriting, that...

"G-d gave James Dean so many gifts to share with the world, has he the right to throw them away in the bullring?

Dean wrote the above inscription in his copy of Ernest Hemingway's famous book on bullfighting, "Death in the Afternoon."

Death
Disability
Disfigurement
Degradation

Opposite a ghastly picture of a dead matador, Jimmy wrote a strange color code: Death in Red; Disability in Green; Disfigurement in Blue, and Degradation in Yellow. He underlined various violent passages in Hemingway's book in appropriate colors . . . Red — for Death, is color appearing most often.

12

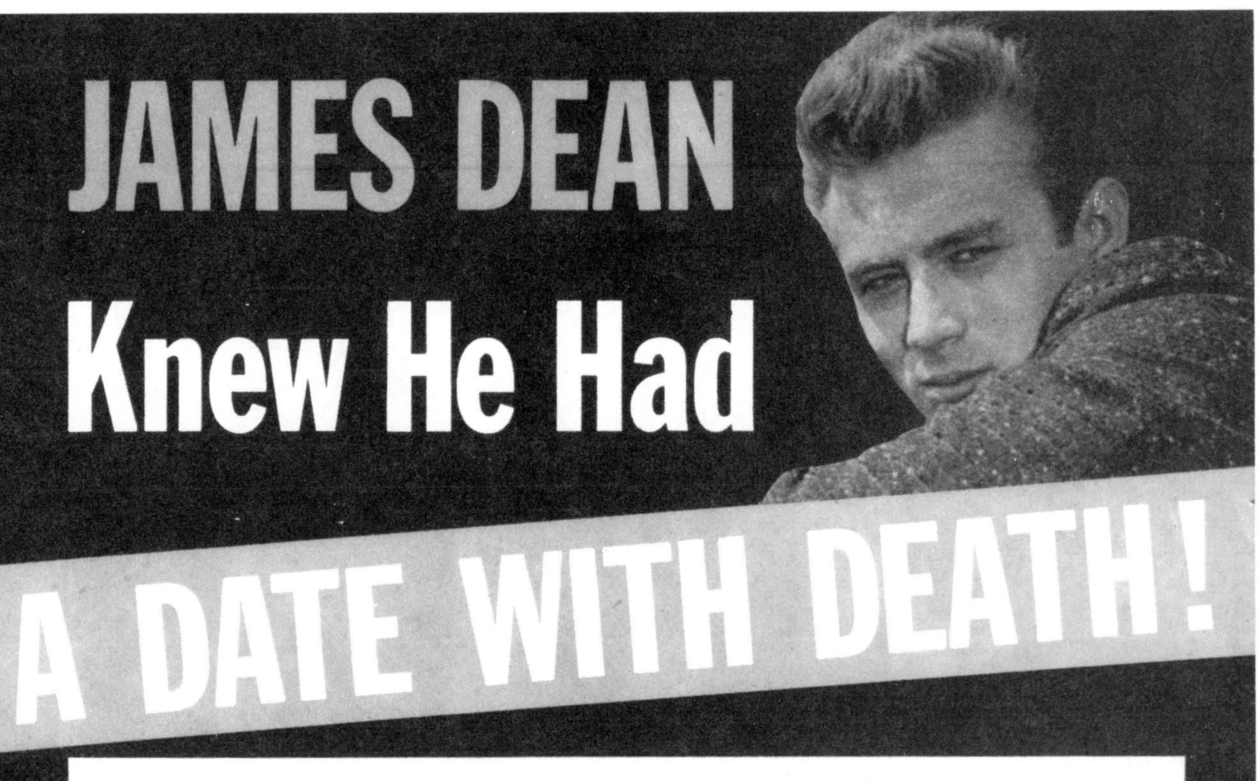

JAMES DEAN Knew He Had A DATE WITH DEATH!

Jimmy's fans thought they knew all about him, but they never knew—till now—that he had a premonition of a violent end . . .

By DAVID BROWNE

REAMS UPON REAMS of copy have been written about the intense life and untimely death of James Dean, brilliant young Hollywood film star whose meteoric career came to a violent end two years ago. Although his remains lie peacefully in a little shaded cemetery in Indiana, his fans refuse to let him die, and the silly rumor persists that he still lives in some secret seclusion because he was maimed beyond recognition.

The Facts Speak for Themselves

There have been rumors, too, that Dean knew he had a rendezvous with death and left cryptic messages with his friends that fatal day he drove off. None of these has ever turned up. But in the last month, solid, documentary evidence—the only concrete evidence of James Dean's preoccupation with death—has come to light.

This new evidence will probably send his fanatic followers into a whole new phase of analyzing Dean's premonitions and subconscious, but we will not attempt to offer any conclusions. The facts, written in James Dean's own hand, speak for themselves.

It was 5:59 in the afternoon in Bakersfield, California when Dean was crushed to death in the tangled steel of his racing car. Perhaps it was macabre coincidence, perhaps it was destiny that Dean's most cherished book was titled *Death in the Afternoon,* Ernest Hemingway's famous tome on bullfighting. The star had loaned the book to a close friend some weeks before the fatal accident.

Toyed with Idea of Becoming a Matador

Bullfighting, like auto racing, fascinated Dean, and it is no small coincidence that man seems to be extremely expendable in both of these sports.

The smell of death in the bull ring excited Dean and obviously he toyed with the idea of becoming a matador. He became a keen student of the sport and often practised passes at an imaginary bull in his apartment. The Hemingway epic became more than a book to him—it became Dean's conscience.

On page 348, opposite a photograph of the matador Joselito lying dead in the bull ring infirmary, is this inscription, written by Dean: *"God gave James Dean so many gifts to share with the world, has he the right to throw them away in the bull ring?"*

On page 368, opposite a photograph of the matador Granero who also lies dead *(Continued on page 46)*

JAMES DEAN *(Continued from page 13)*

He loved violence—and died violently

in the bull ring infirmary, Dean boldly inscribed four words, each in different colored crayon. The word "death" is written in red, "disability" in green, "disfigurement" in blue, and "degradation" in yellow. The colors are the key to the four violent categories in the book as Dean saw them.

On the second page of *Death in the Afternoon*, Hemingway observed that since the war had ended (World War I), the only place where violent death could be seen was in the bull ring. Dean underlined the words in red.

Yellow For Degradation

On page 60, where Hemingway writes of the disgrace that comes to a bullfighter who is gored because of a clumsy maneuver, the passage is underscored in yellow, for degradation.

On page 153, where the author writes of the horn wounds the bull fighter may suffer, the passage is underlined in green, Dean's color code for disability. And where Hemingway writes, on page 75, of an old matador's gnarled leg muscles, the passage is underlined in blue, for disfigurement.

Since this is a book which deals at length with violence, there are dozens of passages underscored by Dean in the four colors of his code, but the predominant color is red, for death.

The psychoanalyst could no doubt supply many reasons for Dean's preoccupation with death. But few will argue that to have this preoccupation he must also have had a strong premonition.

Dean Was Not Afraid

Granted that Dean was a rabid student of the bull ring, it would be reasonable to assume he would be interested in the styles and techniques that Hemingway so masterfully describes, but not one such passage is underlined. Dean's four categories were reserved only for violence.

James Dean was on cordial speaking terms with death. He was not afraid, because a man who constantly fears death does not press his fate by driving high-powered automobiles in speed races.

On page 348 of the book, in his own strong handwriting, Dean challenges his right to throw away his gifts in the bull ring. Perhaps death was a bigger challenge to him than life, but when death came to James Dean that autumn afternoon in Bakersfield, it was too late for him to learn that you don't have to press that old man with the scythe . . . He's got to get you, sooner or later. ▲▲▲

James Dean's Black Madonna

- The plea (at right) was scrawled on a copy of this photo of Vampira by an open grave.
- Vampira, West Coast TV star, is a practitioner of Black Magic.
- The photo carried Vampira's signature.
- It was sent to James Dean, her former lover.
- Shortly after he received the photo— and the plea—James Dean met sudden death.

By SAM SCHAEFFER

No actor ever rose to movie fame faster than James Dean. Blond, intense, he was at once compared with Marlon Brando.

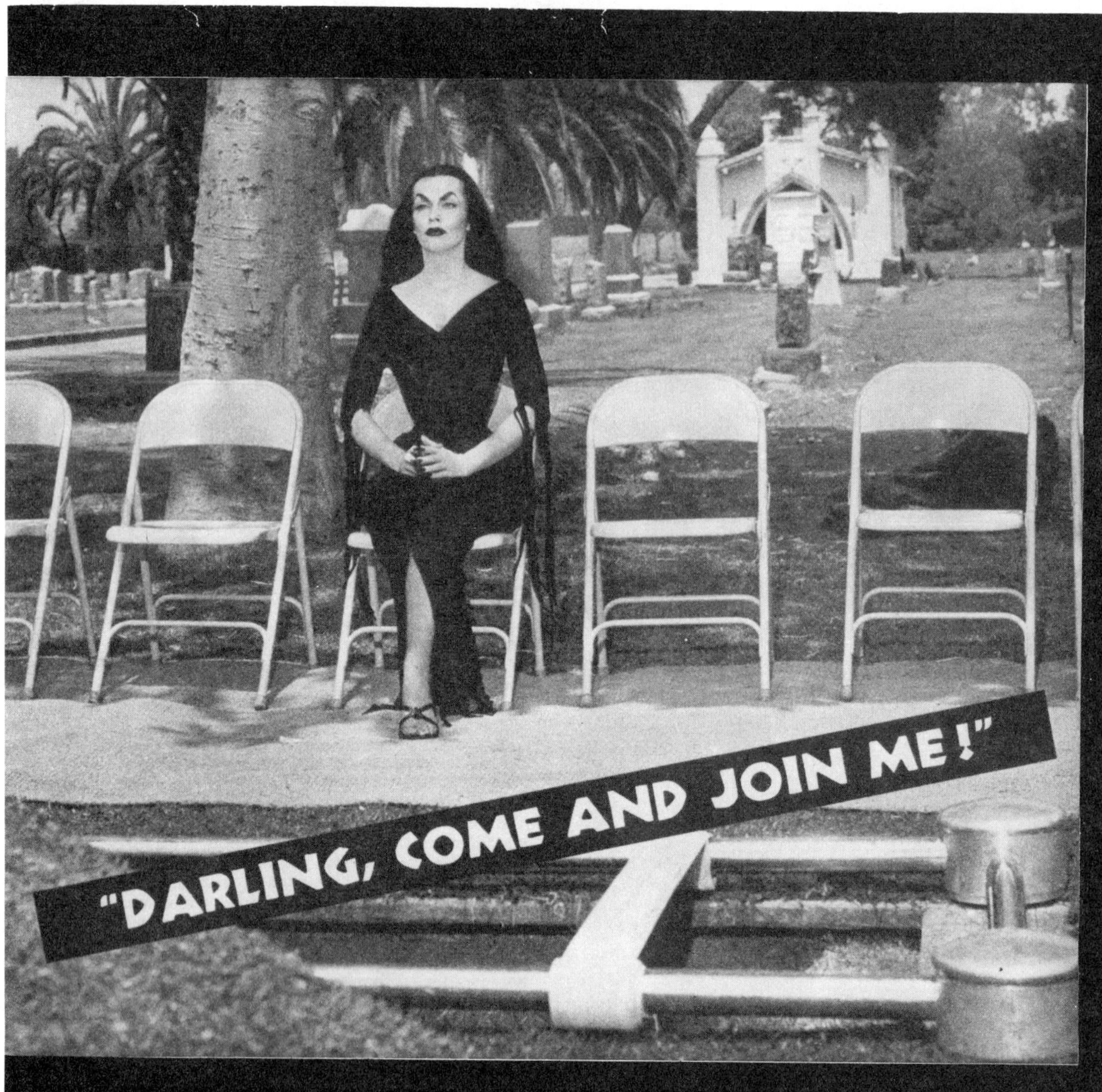
"DARLING, COME AND JOIN ME!"

ALL THE WORLD KNOWS how brilliant young actor James Dean met death on the evening of September 30, 1955 in a shattering sportscar crash near the small town of Cholane, California. But what the world does *not* know about that tragedy makes one of the most shocking stories ever to come out of Hollywood, U.S.A.

It's a story so chilling, so gruesome and macabre, that more than once in the course of tracking it down this reporter was tempted to drop it cold and run.

After much checking and rechecking of the facts, after many talks with the persons involved, and after several days of taking exclusive on-the-spot photographs, the final decision was that the story should and must be told. . . .

TURN THE PAGE

Following his affair with Vampira, Dean's eye turned to shapely starlet Ursula Andress. But his unstable temperament soon led to spats, and Ursula tossed Dean over for actor John Derek.

This is actual photo of black magic "altar" set up in Vampira's bathroom. Picture in center is Dean. At right is one of Vampira in a menacing pose. She had titled this one "Black Madonna."

James Dean *(Continued)*

As Dean sped north in his $7,000 Porsche speedster on the fatal night in September, traveling at better than 70 m.p.h. towards his rendezvous with eternity, a rather strange occurrence took place much farther to the south, in a dingy frame building on a certain Larrabee Street. This street is in prosaic West Hollywood—but if you'd looked thru the windows that night, you'd have thought you'd been suddenly transported to some witch-doctor's shack in the wilds of Haiti.

The interior of the house was bare of furniture and lit entirely by candlelight—except for a weird theatrical floodlight in the living room. On the walls and scattered about the floor were grotesque designs and objects of the kind associated with Black Magic.

Stuck on one wall, with a small golden dagger, were some sections cut out of a magazine photograph. The sections showed nothing more than the eyes and the ears of a young man.

Around 7 p.m. that evening the dagger suddenly fell to the floor.

The woman who lived in the house noticed this and left it where it lay.

The eyes and ears were from a photo of James Dean, who was then dying in a car-crash to the north.

The woman was Myla Nurmi, self-styled witch and necromancer, somewhat better known to West Coast TV audiences as Vampira.

It was the end of the strangest love story this writer has run across in a long career of movieland reporting.

How Dean Met Vampira

Shortly after he came to Hollywood, James Dean met Vampira at Googie's Restaurant, a prime hangout for the film city's hopeful young Bohemians. Vampira had by then acquired great local renown for her bizarre TV show, on which she appeared in ghoulish makeup, with a long, stringy wig and strange black robes. She had also acquired the very-good-palship of some of Hollywood's leading young oddballs—most notably Marlon Brando.

Altho Vampira was 32 years old, her eccentric charms made a strong impression on the moody, 24-year-old Dean. He became a frequent visitor at her weirdly-decorated house on Larrabee Street. Perhaps he was attracted by such unusual features as Vampira's black-painted bed with black sheets.

Just how it feels to act amorous against such a ghoulish decor—or why any sane person would prefer it—is a question we must leave to the psychiatrists. But just from the record, Dean was only one of several Hollywood Bohemians who could have answered that question from personal experience.

There's no telling how long the affair might have gone on if it hadn't been for that old Hollywood bugaboo—overnight success. James Dean made *East of Eden and* was acclaimed with superlatives previously reserved for his old friend and rival, Marlon Brando. Intoxicated by the heady stuff, Dean turned his romantic eye elsewhere.

He and Vampira remained friends of sorts. But like many another woman before her, the TV enchantress didn't take kindly to being demoted to platonic palship.

One night, in front of a group of friends, Dean gave Vampira a playful pinch and asked her if she remembered the days when their relationship had been definitely *un*platonic.

Vampira's reply, reduced to ladylike language, was that she remembered all right—and that, as a lover, his abilities left a great deal to be desired.

After Dean left the party, Vampira turned to the folks who remained and made a remark that is still in the minds of everyone who heard it:

"James Dean is going to die soon!" she said.

It was on that very same evening that the eyes and ears from one of Dean's photos went up on Vampira's wall—placed there, strangely enough, by Dean himself. On the way to the party, he and some friends had stopped by at Vampira's house and found the door open. For a prank Dean cut out the eyes and ears from a picture of himself in a fan magazine lying around, and stuck them to the wall with a little gold-handled knife from his pocket.

An Altar In The Bathroom

It's entirely possible he never did get to see the macabre "altar" which Vampira set up soon afterward on a cabinet in her bathroom—a photo of which is reproduced on these pages.

The central feature of this altar was a boyish picture of Dean, mounted on wood and autographed. To the right was a particularly macabre picture of Vampira herself, a photo she referred to as the "Black Madonna." To the left was a sign reading YE MUST BE BORN AGAIN, and in front were two tall candles in a small holder.

"How do you like my altar?" she casually asked a friend who wandered in on the gruesome setup.

"What do you mean, 'altar'?" the friend asked.

Vampira replied that she was using it for Black Magic against James Dean.

"But why?" the friend asked.

"Because I'm a witch," said Vampira.

It would be more reasonable to assume it was because Dean had left her for another girl, Swiss actress Ursula Andress, who later quarrelled with Dean and tossed him over for actor John Derek.

Another visitor to the Larrabee Street house told this reporter of seeing a voodoo doll, half black and half white, which Vampira said represented Dean.

James Dean himself was for a time interested in Black Magic. The rational mind revolts against anything to do with the evil arts—but sometimes one meets facts which are difficult to explain.

Preoccupied With Death

Such as the fact that James Dean, in the summer of 1955, became more and more moody, more and more positive that he did not have long to live.

And the even more gruesome fact that Vampira herself told of seeing a miniature noose suspended from Dean's own living room ceiling—a symbolic little horror contrived by his own hand.

On September 27, 1955, James Dean telephoned a friend and asked if she knew where he could get in touch with Vampira. The friend replied that she didn't know.

"Goodbye," Dean then said.

"Why?" the friend asked. "Where are you going?"

"From Salinas to the greatest to the grave," Dean answered cryptically, and hung up.

Salinas is the California town featured prominently in *East of Eden*, the film in which Dean was first hailed

Vampira hung upside down from a beam for this ghoulish picture, part of publicity build-up for her black magic TV program.

TURN THE PAGE

After Dean's death, these three ripped photos were found discarded on Vampira's front porch. The parts torn from each have ritual black magic significance.

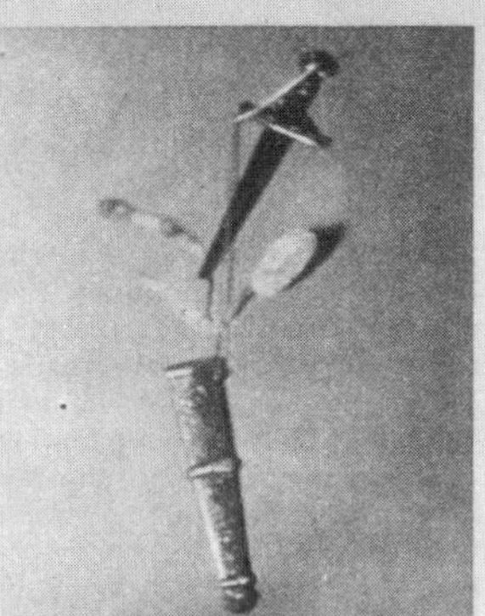

This picture, actually snapped in Vampira's living room, shows eyes and ears of James Dean, torn from a fan magazine, attached to wall with a golden dagger.

as great. Salinas is also the town Dean was heading for three days later, when sudden death cut short the trip.

Later in the afternoon of the 27th, the same friend of Dean's received a call from Vampira.

"Jim just called me," the necromancer said excitedly. "He asked if I'd light the candles at his funeral!"

Vampira then added one more piece to the fatal puzzle. She told of having just sent Dean a photo inscribed *Darling, come and join me. . . .*

That photo, also reproduced on these pages, was a particularly revolting publicity-still showing Vampira seated by an open grave.

Forty-eight hours later an auto driven by a college student turned left from Highway 466 onto Highway 41 and collided almost head-on with a speeding Porsche sportscar. James Dean was dragged dying from the twisted wreckage.

At around the same time, the golden dagger, pinning the actor's cut-up photo to a wall in Vampira's house fell to the floor.

From Salinas to the greatest to the grave. . . .

A coincidence that seems like something out of a weird tale of the supernatural?

Your reporter is only stating the facts.

There is one person, at least, who has been noticeably upset by the macabre aspects of the happenings.

That person is Vampira.

She told a friend that she thinks her Larrabee Street house is haunted by the late actor's ghost. She was so terrified after James Dean's death that she refused to sleep there any more. She spent nights at friends' places, returning to her own house of evil only to feed her seven cats.

The cats roam alone among the bizarre furnishings, rubbing their sides against such dainty items as a replica of a human skull with an ivory snake coiled thru one eye.

Vampira has removed all the photos and effigies she used in her Black Magic against James Dean. They and the voodoo doll were put out on the rickety front porch, in hope that some passerby would take them. In Black Magic, you see, it's considered bad luck to destroy any of the implements used. The ritual demands that they be taken away, or given to some unsuspecting stranger.

None of which is of much concern to James Dean any more.

His mortal remains were laid to earth on October 8, 1955, in his hometown in Indiana.

And on that very same day, as luck or something else would have it, Vampira's TV contract with the American Broadcasting Company was terminated. So she's not "Vampira" any more. She's just a 32-year-old ex-waitress named Myla Nurmi—with something to remember the rest of her life. ▲▲▲

THE END of the tragic tale was written on a dusky highway, when James Dean died in this twisted wreck.

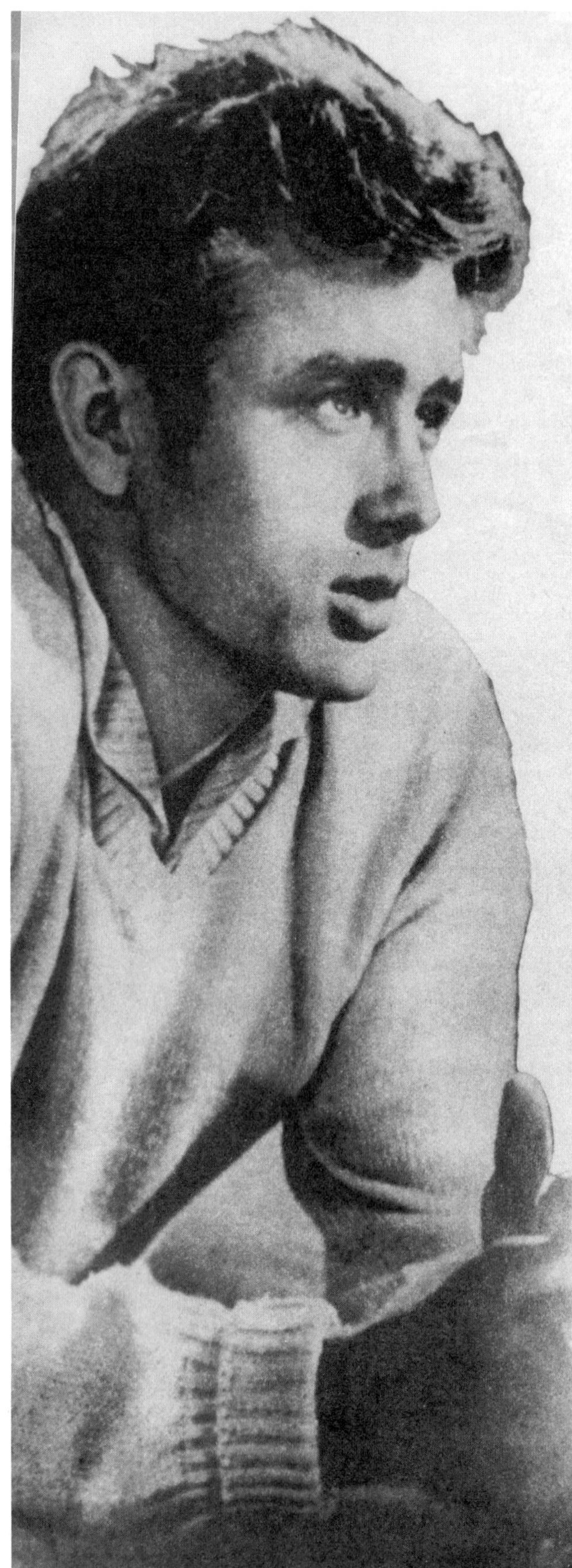

Here's a startling after-death revelation about a young Hollywood actor who died in a violent auto wreck. Lots of people are saying that fanatics and money-grabbers are keeping alive the name of James Dean. Here's a man who believes he may have talked with him; a man who wonders if . . .

JAMES DEAN SPEAKS FROM THE GRAVE

(Editor's Notes We are publishing this story just as it was received, and except for minor editing, nothing has been changed. With the current belief of "life after death" rising strongly, we're giving this one to our readers straight.)

BY ROBERT De KOLBE

LAST night I actually talked with Jimmy Dean. Though his voice was muffled and sounded as if from far off, I could understand him as clearly as if he were right next to me.

"And his message was not to me alone, but to all of his present-day mourners. 'Tell them,' he said, 'to stop mourning for me. I am very happy where I am. Here, there is no confusion, no unhappiness, no cold, no hunger.... And I have my mother with me, whom I lost when I was only seven years old....'"

The above dialogue I have written verbatim, the which I gathered at an interview with Anna M. Van Deusen. This woman, now 33 years old, was so "sensitive" during her college years, that she was one of the group selected to assist in the ESP investigations.

According to experts I questioned in the course of getting information for this story, Mrs. Van Deusen still retains the so-called "hyper-sensitivity." Just what it is, no one could explain satisfactorily. Roughly, as I gathered it, this sensitivity is necessary before anyone can practice telepathy, clairvoyance, or any sort of mediumship.

This reporter is just that—a reporter. While I am taking

Dean and Pier Angeli, whom he loved and lost. Her mommy objected to the actor's strange ways. Right, before getting the sports car, Dean burned up the roads on motorcycle.

These are the remains of James Dean's speedy German-built Porsche, which he cracked up on a California highway.

Artists and commercial distributors are today cleaning up selling life-like masks of Dean.

JAMES DEAN SPEAKS

no sides, pro or con, in this issue, I do want to point out that the "experts" I consulted about this woman were men whose names are big in the various sciences they represented. Three were top psychiatrists, three were philosophers; two were doctors of medicine, and three others were university professors, whose names, if I mentioned them, everyone would know instantly.

To further authenticate what Mrs. Van Deusen told me, I suggested a seance with just two of us composing it. She agreed to this readily. I explained to her that there was already too much information on this subject that was second-hand. I wanted first-hand information for the readers of True Strange.

On the night of the seance, just the two of us were locked in her studio. You can take my word that there were no tricks, no gimmicks, no sheeted characters standing behind drapes or secret doors, or anything like that. Mrs. Van Deusen is a college graduate and anything that smacked of phoney or fake would be an insult to her intelligence.

There were no mystic lights, no crystal balls and

Here he is with Ursula Andrews at Ciro's. The match didn't last long. "I never understood him," said Ursula.

Is this the end? Dean has become more famous in death than he ever was in life. Is his voice coming from here?

12

FROM THE GRAVE

no mysterious tables. Mrs. Van Deusen was not pale-faced, nor was she dresed in a long white flowing dress. Anna Van Deusen is a very pretty married woman. She dressed very simply in ordinary street clothes. In the center of the studio was a couch on which she reclined and alongside it a chair on which I sat.

The idea was that when she "went under" (into her trance, that is), I was to be close enough to ask questions. And I was to go very carefully on these so as not to suggest anything to her already over-sensitive mind.

I lowered the lights, while Mrs. Van Deusen made herself comfortable on the couch. Then, I sat down on the stool alongside her. For about five minutes she just laid there very quietly. At first, she looked to be in a deep sleep. Then a low moan came out of her. Then another. It sounded almost as if she were crying because of great suffering and confusion.

Van Deusen: "Wh-who was it you wanted again?"

De Kolbe: "James Dean."

Van Deusen: "Oh, yes. (*Continued on page* 68)

Natalie Wood, another good friend of Deans, accepts the "Audie" awarded to the late Dean, from Grace Kelley.

13

Flowers that are over three thousand years old, so frail and yet so eternal, make a strange impression upon one.

There was also found amid the bandages a small fruit-berry, the species of which it is difficult to determine. Perhaps it was a berry of the nepenthe, which brought oblivion. On a bit of stuff, carefully detached, was written within a cartouche the name of an unknown king belonging to a dynasty no less forgotten. This mummy fills up a vacant place in history and tells of a new Pharaoh.

The face was still hidden under it mask of linen and bitumen, which could not be easily detached, for it had been firmly fixed by an indefinite number of centuries. Under the pressure of the chisel a portion gave way, and two white eyes with great black pupils shone with fictitious life between brown eyelids. They were enameled eyes, such as it was customary to insert in carefully prepared mummies. The clear, fixed glance, gazing out of the dead face, produced a terrifying effect; the body seemed to behold with disdainful surprise the living beings that moved around it. The eyebrows showed quite plainly upon the orbit, hollowed by the sinking of the flesh. The nose, I must confess—and in this respect Nes Khons was less pretty than Tahoser—had been turned down to conceal the incision through which the brain had been drawn from the skull, and a leaf of gold had been placed on the mouth as the seal of eternal silence. The hair, exceeding fine, silky, and soft, dressed in light curls, did not fall below the tops of the ears, and was of that auburn tint so much prized by Venetian women. It looked like a child's hair dyed with henna, as one sees it in Algeria. I do not think that this color was the natural one. Nes Khons must have been dark like other Egyptians, and the brown tone was doubtless produced by the essences and perfumes of the embalmer.

Little by little the body began to show in its sad nudity. The reddish skin of the torso, as the air came in contact with it, assumed a bluish bloom, and there was visible on the side a cut through which had been drawn the entrails, and from which escaped, like the sawdust of a ripped-up doll, the sawdust of aromatic wood mixed with resin in grains that looked like colophony. The arms were stretched out, and the bony hands with their gilded nails imitated with sepulchral modesty the gesture of the Venus of Medici. The feet, slightly contracted by the drying up of the flesh and the muscles, seemed to have been shapely and small, and the nails were gilded like those of the hand.

What was she, after all, this Nes Khons, daughter of Horus and Rouaa, called Lady in her epitaph? Young or old, beautiful or ugly? It would be difficult to say. She is now not much more than a skin covering bones, and it is impossible to discover in the dry, sharp lines the graceful contours of Egyptian women, such as we see them depicted in temples, palaces, and tombs. But is it not a surprising thing, one that seems to belong to the realm of dreams, to see on a table, in still appreciable shape, a being which walked in the sunshine, which lived and loved five hundred years before Moses, two thousand years before Jesus Christ? For that is the age of the mummy which the caprice of fate drew from its caronnage in the midst of the Universal Exposition, amid all the machinery of our modern civilization.

● ● ●

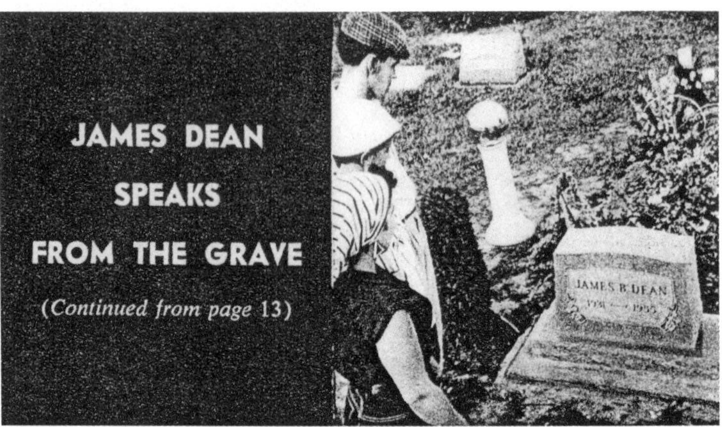

JAMES DEAN SPEAKS FROM THE GRAVE

(*Continued from page 13*)

Oh, they're so hard to find, I . . . Wait!. Energy. I'm coming upon great, massive amounts of energy. This will be it, but I'll have to search for him."

There was a long pause and more moaning from Mrs. Van Deusen's lips. Finally her hand was groping toward mine, found it and held it, tightly.

Van Deusen: "Let me hold it so that I have a link with the world of the living. I believe now I have contacted the one you seek."

De Kolbe: "Ask him some of the details surrounding his birth."

Van Deusen: "Born Marion, Ohio in 1931. Father and mother were named Winton and Mildred."

De Kolbe: "What emotional event happened while he was still a boy?"

Van Deusen: "Yes, yes. Was seven years old . . . his mother dies of cancer. He died a little, too. Never really got over it. Terrible shock. Had something to do with his own early death."

De Kolbe: "In what way?"

Van Deusen: "Idea of death was planted in his mind. These were the seeds of destruction, which he nursed all his short life. His thoughts were preoccupied with death. But death is nothing more than a cessation of a particular body, the energy lives on . . ."

De Kolbe: "Can he clarify that?"

Van Deusen: "Wherever he is, there is only energy. No bodies or human forms as we know them. When he died in that auto wreck, only his body was destroyed. The energy that had kept him alive simply returned to where it had come from originally."

(At this point I had a million different questions I would have liked to have asked. But if I had, they'd have been what is called "leading questions." Leading questions have the drawback of having suggestive connotations. That was Morey Bernstein's trouble in the Bridey Murphy affair. Experts accused him of having used leading questions and thereby suggesting what he wanted from his subject.)

De Kolbe: "Ask him, as far as he can tell, is there any reason or significance in life."

Van Deusen: "Each body that is born is an individual. Not the energy, just the body that is born. Certain cells and minute organisms in any one body are different from every other body. The pattern of a body's life is set even before it has been born by these cells and chromosomes. Not so the energy, however, this comes from a common universal fund . . . sort of like a bank. Whether a body turns out "good or bad" makes no difference. If a body turns out good, that was his or her reason for living. If a body turns out bad, that was his or her reason for living."

De Kolbe: "What was the body of James Dean's reason?"

Van Deusen: "He believes he was put here to symbolize the confusion of young people."

De Kolbe: "Why did he die so young?"

Van Deusen: "That's just it. If he had lived to be older, there would have been no symbol. He'd have lived in vain. An older person cannot symbolize humanity's suffering, then there might have never been any such thing as christianity. Dean had to die while still young."

De Kolbe: "But his acting—what of that?"

Van Deusen: "Just a device, whereby his confusion could be brought plainly into public eye."

De Kolbe: "Were there any notable events leading up to his death?"

Van Deusen: "Yes. Several. There were a few forces that tried to prevent him from dying."

De Kolbe: 'Such as?"

Van Deusen: "On the fatal day, someone suggested that Dean "ride" his racer to the track on a truck. More especially, there was the motorcycle cop who stopped him and gave him that ticket. These were actually energy forces trying to prevent him from dying. But Dean knew his time had come."

De Kolbe: "Did Dean have any preconceptions about so-called "life after death?"

Van Deusen: "Yes. A TV actress called Maila Nurmi, better known as Vampira, first suggested that there was some sort of life after death. With her, Dean did more than just dabble into the possibilities of the spirits' mysteries, re-incarnation, life after death and assorted ideas in black magic."

I knew now that something was actually happening. As I said before, I am neither pro nor con on this subject. I'd rather leave that to the experts. I am just reporting what I did, heard and saw. But I was sure of one thing: Mrs. Van Deusen, if she didn't have actual contact with the late Jimmy Dean, at least, sincerely thought she did. Whether or not she actually did have contact with some sort of universal energy, I do not know for certain. One other thing I do know is that there was absolutely no phoney or sham to Mrs. Van Deusen's trance. She was really "under."

Since James Dean's life and loves have been published heretofore and very widely at that, I did not go into those details here, I do not feel it was necessary. Most of us know the outline of his life and how he died.

I asked Mrs. Van Deusen one more question which I am saving till last because the answer was so startling.

It went like this:

De Kolbe: "What message does James Dean have for his fans, those people who loved him so—and apparently still do, since they are keeping his name alive?"

Van Deusen: "James Dean says, If possible, try to tell them not to despair for him or his untimely death. Tell them, if you can, that he'll be back. In some other shape or form, perhaps, but he shall be walking amongst them again real soon."

Mrs. Van Deusen began to stir rather uncomfortably. I asked no more questions. Probably the strain was beginning to tell on her. I simply sat quietly and let her come awake.

When she woke up she sat upright. "What did I say? anything helpful?"

I related the whole dialogue back to her. She was amazed, since she could recall nothing. Afterward, when she was fully awake and alert, she tried to explain it to me.

"If I actually did contact James Dean, and the words I spoke were actually his, *that* explains so much about life that we know nothing of. It answers the question of why we are here, where we go, where we came from."

I must confess I was puzzled. I'm puzzled because I don't know what to think. But there's a lot of things we don't know about. How does the earth stay on a fixed course? What is electricity? Electronics? Radio waves? Television? Try to get someone to explain these things to you in detail, logically and intelligently.

There are so many things we believe in, yet cannot actually see. Has anyone ever seen a radio wave? I could go on and on. But what's the use of it? I think it's time that our "experts" get on to the fact that here are some things that just cannot be explained. And they'll remain inexplicable until more and deeper research is done.

At night I often wonder if my indirect conversation with the late James Dean was real. To discover whether it was real or not, I am devoting myself to further research on this one subject. If James Dean does come back to this earth, I want to know why and I want to know how. And I am sure there are millions of people who feel the same as I do.

JIMMY DEAN'S ALIVE!

Never, in the history of movies, has there been such a mass uproar as has been happening since the "death" of James Dean. Jimmy has served as an inspiration, to millions of teenagers. Here, for the first time is THE TRUE STORY OF JIMMY DEAN.

IS THIS JIMMY?

36

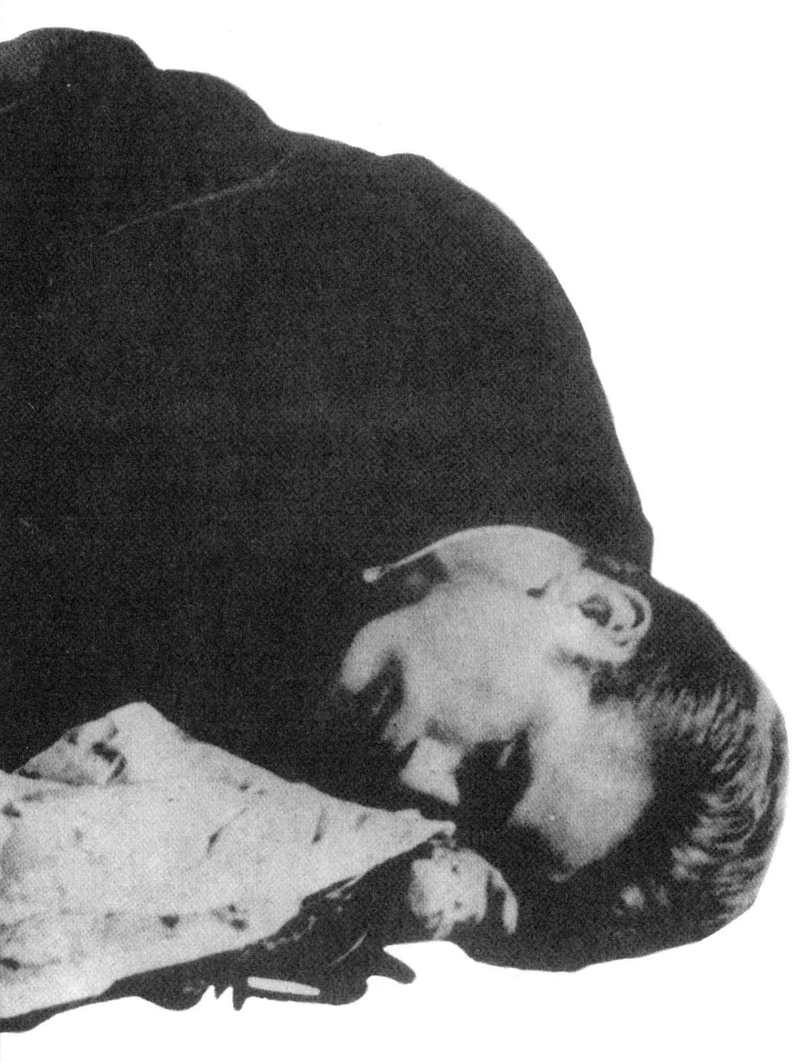

HE'S ALIVE!

DOES JIMMY ROAM THE STREETS OF NEW YORK?

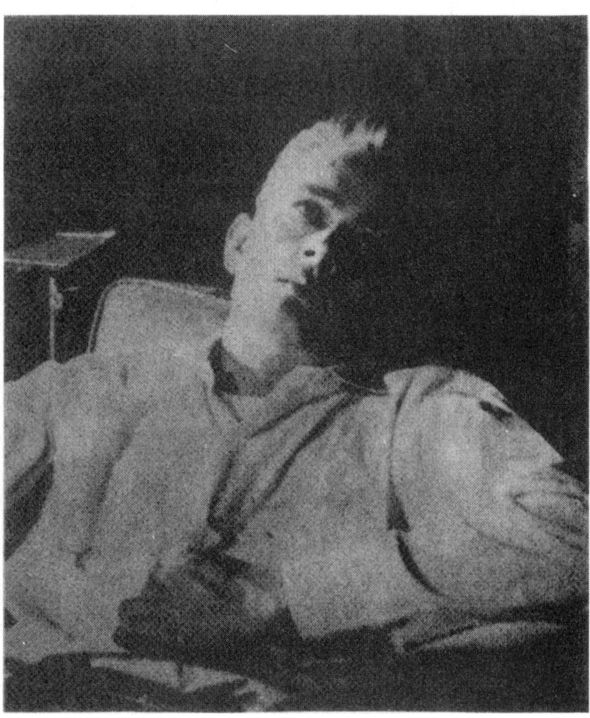

81

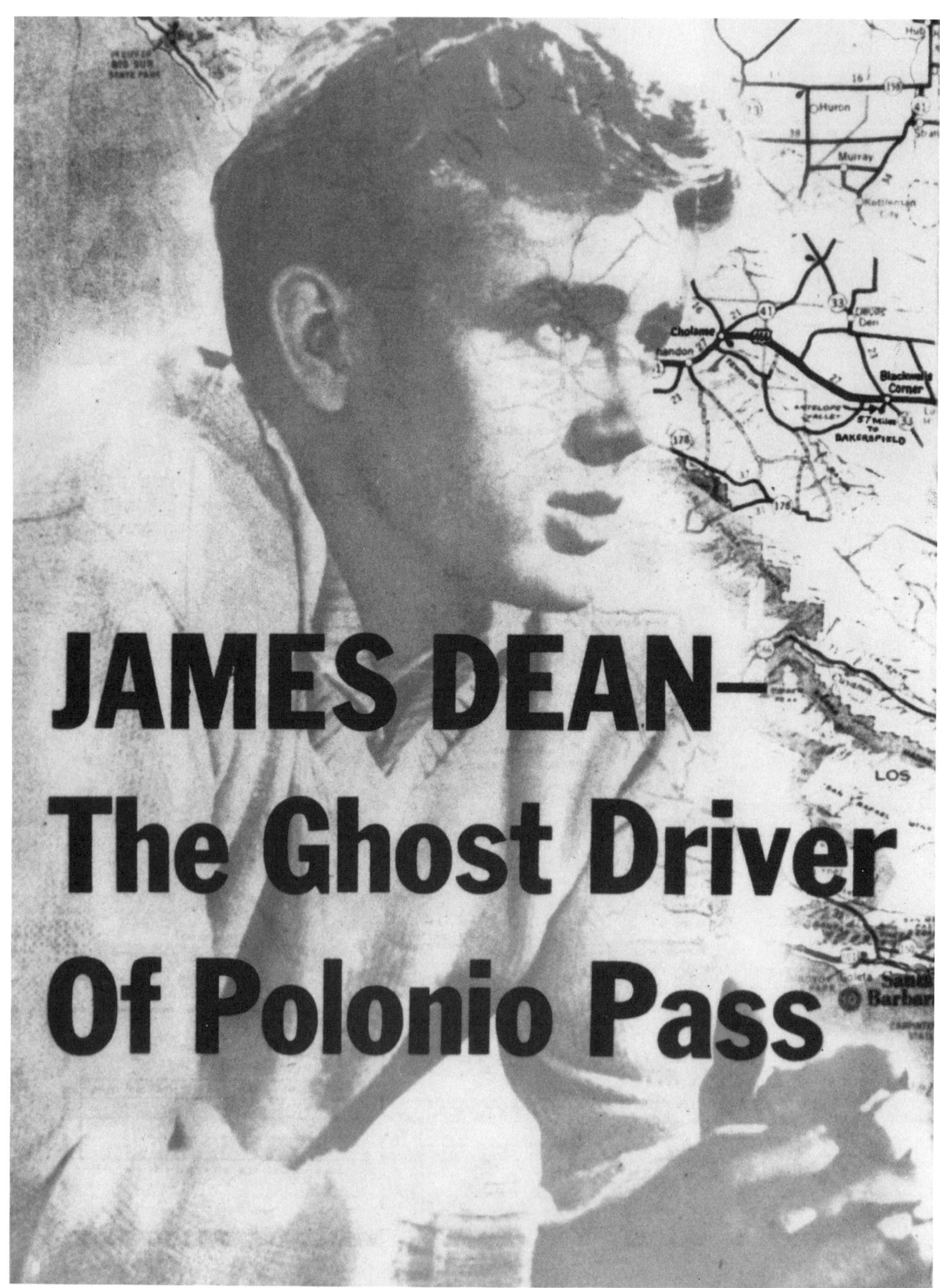

JAMES DEAN— The Ghost Driver Of Polonio Pass

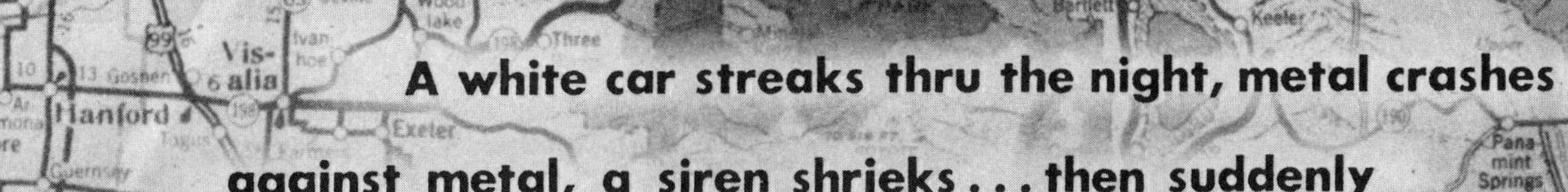

A white car streaks thru the night, metal crashes against metal, a siren shrieks . . . then suddenly there's nothing but quiet – there's nothing at all!

SAM SCHAEFFER

When one has left many things undone in life, sometimes it is not easy for the spirit to find rest.
— Mexican proverb

I THOUGHT A LOT about James Dean as I stood on a desolate stretch of highway just outside Cholame, California, a few weeks back. But mostly I thought about a magic night only a little over two years ago, when Jim and I were standing on Broadway together, the first time he ever saw his name up in lights on the Great White Way.

Manhattan was a city of a thousand-and-one kicks that night, a Bagdad-on-the-Subway for both of us . . .

And now, in mid-1957, I was thinking about that night again. Thinking about it because here, at the junction of Highways 41 and 466, I was looking upon another sort of marquee dedicated to James Dean.

But this was a macabre marquee, a shrine to a dead hero. And looking at it brought no kicks.

It brought a chill.

For it was on this spot that James Dean had met violent death in his speeding Porsche on the night of September 30, 1955.

Notes of Love

On the shoulder of the road there were flowers. Some were planted, others looked as if they'd been hurriedly tossed from passing cars, perhaps by teenage girls who still remembered the slouched, handsome figure of the boy who'd become loved all over the world as the *Rebel Without A Cause*.

Beyond the road's shoulder, on a small white fence, were thumbtacked some gilded crosses and small pieces of paper. The papers were notes written to James Dean, and I felt as though I were eavesdropping on another world as I read:

To Jimmy — now only in death shall we meet.

Jimmy, you'll always be remembered, you were the greatest, the absolute greatest.

Why did you leave us, Jimmy — why were you in such a hurry?

There were more—different words, different handwriting, but all just about the same. All tributes to a dead idol.

And as I stood there in that weird place of worship, I couldn't help remembering the satisfied grin that had crossed Jim's lips when he first saw his name up in lights.

And I wondered — what would he think of all this?

But it wasn't this eerie altar that had brought me all the way across the country to California. It was other things — whispers.

Whispers of unexplainable things — like a blurred, white sports car that raced thru the night; like the noise of screeching brakes and a shattering, ear-splitting collision where there were no cars; like a phantom ambulance that came careening out of nowhere and, siren screaming, disappeared back into nowhere.

Followed Same Route

I'd heard these whispers second-hand, in letters from Dean fans, or from the lips of people who had met other people who had told them they knew someone who had seen or heard these things.

So I decided to come to California myself.If a phantom Porsche could be seen racing thru the night on the road to Paso Robles, I wanted to see it myself. Or, failing that, I wanted to hear the stories first-hand from people who'd seen with their own eyes.

Then and only then could I come to some conclusion as to whether the whispers were fact or fiction — or something beyond either . . .

The best way to get at the truth, I decided when I arrived in Bakersfield — where James Dean had begun the last leg of his last journey on this earth — was to leave my rented car and hitchhike over the same route Jim had driven.

This way, I figured, I might meet some motorist who regularly made the trip and had heard or seen something of the "Ghost Driver of Polonio Pass" — as one letter-writer had called the apparition he claimed to have seen.

Polonio Pass is the section of Highway 466 just before it joins Highway 41. On the night of the fatal accident, Dean had been on his way from Bakersfield

TURN THE PAGE

James Dean *(continued)*

to Salinas, traveling at an estimated 90 miles an hour most of the time. Another car was coming up Highway 41, heading for Fresno.

The two cars smashed head on into one another at the junction of 466 and 41. Every bone in Dean's body was broken. He died in an ambulance a few minutes later.

Not far from this junction, about 18 miles due east to be more exact, is a supposedly haunted place called "The Devil's Den." Polonio Pass itself is in the Diablo (or "Devil's") Range of mountains, a section of the California Coast Range. Many of the valley towns in the neighborhood, I soon learned, are inhabited by people of strong Indian, Mexican and Filipino ancestry. Many of the native whites of the region have a touch of Indian blood in them, too.

The entire locale is a place replete with legends of old massacres, of lovers killed by thwarted suitors or vengeful relatives — of violent death and the restless dead.

So perhaps it's not strange that among such people one would hear whispers of a Ghost Driver of Polonio Pass. My job, however, was to separate superstition from fact. If possible, to see this Ghost Driver myself.

Evaded Direct Answers

I made the trip back and forth from Bakersfield to Paso Robles several times. If there was anything supernatural or ethereal riding this stretch of highway, I didn't meet up with it. Nor, apparently, had any of the good Samaritans who were kind enough to give me lifts.

We passed the unofficial shrine on every trip, of course, and even discussed things like Dean's premonition of death, his friendship with Vampira, and the hangman's noose he'd had hanging in his living-room. But that was all.

Nobody mentioned a single word about a Ghost Driver. And I didn't want to bring the subject up, because then I might be putting words into their mouths without meaning to.

It seemed I was chasing a story that just didn't exist. Then, as I was walking along the highway on what was about my seventh trip, a vintage model truck stopped and the driver asked if I wanted a lift.

I accepted. But as I'd made up my mind to "give up the ghost" and go home as soon as I got back to Bakersfield, I didn't even mention Dean until we approached the intersection of Highways 41 and 466.

There, purely from habit, I said, "I hear this is where James Dean was killed." Then, as if I hadn't already been here over a dozen times, I asked, "I wonder if you'd mind slowing down, I'd like to get a look at the spot."

The driver didn't mind. In fact, he came to a dead stop. He always stopped here, he said, to see if there were any new notes he hadn't read.

When we again got underway I questioned him about this morbid interest in Dean's death. He evaded any direct answers, but as I talked on and told him stories I'd heard, he probably figured me for a kindred soul — and finally loosened up.

The story the driver told me was as weird as any I've ever heard. It seems that on the night of December 30, 1955 — which was three months, to the day, after Dean's death — he was driving south on Route 41, headed for Paso Robles, when he began having engine trouble at the summit of Cottonwood Pass, about 10 miles from Route 466.

By coasting and babying the truck down the west side of the Pass, he rode out the 10 miles until he was within 100 feet of the intersection — when suddenly his headlights went dead and he was in total darkness.

Terrifying Sounds

Grabbing a flashlight, he climbed down and walked to the intersection to hail a passing truck for help. Hiking up 466 toward the east a way, so he wouldn't be right on the crossroads, he thought he heard a car coming from the direction of Bakersfield. He pointed the flashlight in that direction and waved it as a signal for the oncoming driver to stop.

He waved it only once — then stood frozen to the road. There was something about the high-pitched whirr of rubber tires and the low hum of the racing engine that told him the car was being driven at a terrific rate of speed.

The noise got louder and louder, the car coming closer and closer at a terrifying rate — seemingly coming right straight at him. He stood petrified, unable to move even though he felt certain the car was going to hit him dead on.

Then suddenly a blurred white streak whizzed by. A second later there was a screech of brakes, followed by the sickening crash of metal ripping metal and glass shattering into a million pieces. The sound was loud, the truck driver said, trying carefully to be precise, yet in a way it wasn't loud either. It was almost "like the echo of a sound."

Then, silence.

The crash brought him back to his senses. He hurried to the intersection, feeling sure that he would see a truly sickening sight.

He saw nothing.

No tire marks.

No wreakage.

No shattered glass . . .

Close To a Ghost

I was about to file this away as just one more interesting but uncorroborated story when my friend continued.

"I felt like an awful fool," he said. "Or I would have, if I didn't feel so damned scared at the same time. Don't ask me to explain it, but to this day I'll swear I saw that car streak by and heard that crash. I might have begun to doubt these things, though, if it weren't that, while I was standing there trying to figure out if I was awake or dreaming, I heard a truck coming toward me out of the darkness.

"This was a real solid truck all right, and it came to a stop right beside me. The driver, a Mexican, jumped out and without saying a word crossed himself and fell to his knees.

"He was more upset than even I was. When he finally got his voice and got up off his knees he said that about three miles back on the road a white car had passed him going like the wind. As he was on a down-grade and the truck was carrying a good load, he was able to keep the car in sight for most of the way — until he, too, came near the ill-fated intersection.

"Then he, too, had to stop *because his headlights went out.*

"After comparing notes with the Mexican," my friend continued, "believe me, I never felt so close to a ghost in all my life!"

I asked if either of them had noticed what time all this had happened. They hadn't checked their watches, he said, but it was probably around 6 o'clock in the evening.

James Dean's accident had occurred at 5:59.

"Working together," the driver continued, "we got the headlights fixed easily enough — a wire had jumped off in both cases. Maybe from a bump, I don't know. And my engine gave no trouble at all. Maybe it had been flooded and just standing idle awhile was all it needed. We decided not to lose sight of each other — it was one of those nights when it just didn't pay to be all by yourself. So we agreed to stick close all the way to Paso Robles.

A Lost Spirit

"Before getting back into his truck, the Mexican said to me, 'This is the place — this is the very place where that young Señor Dean was killed. It is a very bad place!' Then he crossed himself again and climbed into the cab.

"In Paso Robles we stopped at a one-arm diner for coffee. There were a couple of other Mexicans in the place, and my boy solemnly told them what we'd just gone thru. When he'd finished, don't you think one of those others didn't cross himself too. 'It is bad, very bad!' this other one said. 'That was Señor Dean in that car. He drives that road every night between sundown and sunrise. It is as though he is looking for something or someone'."

" 'Or as if he is a lost spirit, looking for a place to rest.' another said. They all looked significantly at each other at this remark, shook their heads as if agreeing, then crossed themselves — I guess to chase evil spirits away — again."

As we had now come to where the driver had to turn off and leave me, he ended his story and bade me good-night. But as I was getting out of the truck he added, "You know, I don't believe in ghosts and spirits that can't rest in peace. But ever since that night I always try to make that stretch of highway while the sun is still bright. No harm in being cautious, you know."

Before he went away, I asked for the name of the Mexican truck driver he'd been talking about. He said he never did know the name, but he gave me the address of the trucking company the fellow had been working for.

I found him easily, still working at the same place.

Weird Experience

Getting him to talk wasn't so easy, however. He guessed right away I was a reporter and, unlike the other fellow, he *did* believe in ghosts — and the less he had to do or say in regard to them the better.

I know some Spanish, however, and managed to convince him I'd never use his name if I wrote up the story. Once he was satisfied he was safe with me, he was almost eager to tell about his weird experience. And what he said backed up everything the other driver had said, detail by detail.

Furthermore, it came out that many natives of the region regard the junction of Highways 41 and 466 as a haunted place. They do all they can to avoid passing there after dark.

The Mexican told me of other strange events that had supposedly occurred there. And he gave me leads to some people involved.

One of these was a woman. *(Continued on page 56)*

James Dean *(Continued from page 11)*

She was English and, with her husband, had just come from Canada a few weeks after the fatal accident. She said she'd never even heard of James Dean until after the following incident.

One night, around mid-1956, she and her husband were driving from Wasco to their home in Paso Robles. They had passed thru Cholame and were well on their way to Paso Robles when they heard the scream of a siren coming toward them. A careful driver, the husband pulled to the side of the road to let the ambulance, fire engine or whatever it might be go by.

As they waited, the siren got louder and louder. Finally, like a banshee screaming in hell, the noise zoomed by.

But only the noise!

There was no fire engine or ambulance in sight . . .

I met several other people — practical, hard-working, church-going people — who also swore they'd heard this siren scream by them in the early evening darkness. Since no one remembered ever having this experience before the tragic accident, most agreed it must be the siren from the ambulance that raced Dean's body on to the city.

(There are some noises, the Mexicans say, like the scream of a young girl dying, or a mother being torn from her young, that are so piercingly intense with emotional energy that they leave their imprint on every tree, rock and grain of sand around them, to echo back for a long time to come.)

I don't know. I can only tell you what I heard from these people. And in all truth I have to admit that I rode thru Polonio Pass, back and forth, many times, both before, during and after sunset. I rode the path the ambulance took. I stood for hours at the tragic intersection.

And though I felt many strange things, and at times even broke out into a cold sweat of apprehension at the sound made by certain cars speeding down in my direction, I never once saw a white Porsche speed by or heard a siren or a crash.

And for every man or woman I talked to who had heard these things, or, like several, claimed they had almost wrecked their own cars when a speeding white sports car forced them over to the side of the road — for each of these there were others who used the road constantly and never heard a thing, and in fact pooh-poohed the whole business.

(But, as one old-timer told me, just as there are animals that can hear

sounds and seem to see things outside the range of humans, maybe there are some humans who are able to see and hear things beyond the ability of other humans.)

As I said before, I don't know. All I've tried to do here is set out the facts as I found them. If there is a Ghost Driver of Polonio Pass, I failed completely in my attempt to get personal evidence of that fact.

And, funny thing, now that I'm back East again, sometimes I think of the nights I spent hoping the "Ghost Driver" would turn up. And while I would have given anything to have it happen at the time — now I feel mighty glad it didn't.

Death Can't Change Him

I remember Jimmy as one of the most wholesome kids I've ever met. After he became a big star he began playing around with hangman's nooses and black magic articles — but I think that was just another act with him, like the time, I remember, when, for a couple of weeks straight, he pretended he was a famous bull-fighter.

Fundamentally he was one helluva wholesome guy. I don't think death changed him any — and that's the way I prefer to remember him.

That's also why, the next time I go to California, I'm going to keep clear of Polonio Pass even if it means going five hundred miles out of my way.

I'm a guy who doesn't believe in stretching his luck too far. ▲▲▲

A SCANDALOGRAPHY

1955 TO 1962

BY ALAN BETROCK AND H. GORDON SCHNEIDER

10/55	*Celebrity*	James Dean: Why He Spits in Hollywood's Face
12/55	*Private Lives*	Is James Dean a Dandy?
2/56	*Whisper*	James Dean's Black Madonna
4/56	*Whisper*	James Dean's Fans Speak Their Mind
5/56	*Rave*	Did James Dean Really Die?
5/56	*Inside*	Did James Dean Commit Suicide?
5/56	*Anything Goes*	Did Jimmy Dean Commit Suicide?
8/56	*Whisper*	The Girl James Dean Left Behind
9/56	*Exposed*	James Dean: God of a Morbid Cult
9/56	*Uncensored*	Those James Dean Whispers
11/56	*Rave*	James Dean Tells His Life Story in His Own Words
12/56	*Whisper*	James Dean Vs. Elvis Presley
1/57	*Behind The Scene*	The Other Man in Vic Damone-Pier Angeli's Life
1/57	*Lowdown*	Revealed! James Dean's Torrid Love Letters
1/57	*Hush-Hush*	Did James Dean Commit Suicide?
1/57	*Rave*	I Was a Friend of Jimmy Dean
2/57	*Inside Story*	The Amazing James Hoax!
2/57	*Whisper*	How James Dean Got an Oscar
3/57	*On The QT*	Was Jimmy Dean a Psycho?
3/57	*Uncensored*	The Romance James Dean Couldn't Kill
4/57	*Suppressed*	The Star That Elvis and Jimmy Made (Natalie Wood)
4/57	*Frauds*	Why They Made a Saint of James Dean
4/57	*Inside*	The Unvarnished Truth About James Dean
4/57	*Rave*	Why Jimmy Dean Didn't Win Any Oscars
4/57	*Rave*	I Learned About Love from Jimmy Dean
5/57	*Lowdown*	The Girl James Dean Was Supposed to Marry
6/57	*Suppressed*	Money From the Grave
6/57	*Private Lives*	Jimmy Dean's Alive! (plus other related Dean stories)
7/57	*On the QT*	Did Jimmy Dean Leave a Son?
7/57	*On The QT*	Letters to the Editor (especially about James Dean)
9/57	*Rave*	Why Jimmy Dean Is a Living Lie
12/57	*Whisper*	James Dean: Ghost of Polonio Pass
1/58	*Confidential*	James Dean Knew He Had a Date with Death—Proof in His Own Handwriting
3/58	*On The QT*	My Death Drive With James Dean
4/61	*Top Secret*	The Girls Who Worship the Corpse of James Dean
4/62	*Top Secret*	The Man Who Freed Pier Angeli of James Dean's Ghost

For information regarding publications about exploitation magazines, rock 'n' roll magazines, James Dean, tabloids, scandal mags, and cult movies write to *Shake Books*, 449 12th Street, #2R, Brooklyn, N.Y. 11215. *Shake* also provides a reprint service for all scandal magazine articles, 1952–66, on all personalities.